D8647640

Illuminations

Margaret Atwood

Elizabeth Bishop

Marie-Claire Blais

Ernest Buckler

Morley Callaghan

Roch Carrier

Mavis Gallant

Jack Hodgins

Margaret Laurence

Alistair MacLeod

Joyce Marshall

Fredelle Bruser Maynard

W.O. Mitchell

Alice Munro

Alden Nowlan

James Reaney

Mordecai Richler

Sinclair Ross

Gabrielle Roy

Guy Vanderhaeghe

Sheila Watson

Illuminations

THE DAYS OF OUR YOUTH

SELECTED BY

Andrew Garrod and David Staines

INTRODUCTIONS AND BIBLIOGRAPHIES BY
DAVID STAINES, UNIVERSITY OF OTTAWA
QUESTIONS FOR DISCUSSION AND WRITING BY
ANDREW GARROD, UNIVERSITY OF MANITOBA

gage PUBLISHING LIMITED
TORONTO ONTARIO CANADA

ISBN 0-7715-1470-0

DESIGN
Frank Newfeld

ILLUSTRATIONS
Mark Craig
Susan Hedley
Nancy Kettles

COVER
COMPUTER ART
Frank Newfeld
Jenniffer Julich

1 2 3 4 5 6 7 8 JD 91 90 89 88 87 86 85 84

Printed and bound in Canada
by John Deyell Company

Contents

Central

Western

QUESTIONS FOR DISCUSSION AND WRITING

Introduction

Illuminations presents twenty-one writers exploring various experiences of childhood and adolescence. There is a range of time periods from infancy through childhood and from pre- and early teens through later adolescence. Blais' Emmanuel is one day old; Carrier's little boy has just begun grade one. Buckler's David is eleven, Gallant's Linnet, eighteen.

Some of the authors choose third-person narrators to recount the story from a detached perspective. Some choose to narrate the material through the young person's eyes. Most of the writers in this collection choose first-person adult narrators who look back on their childhood experiences with an understanding that has come to them in later years. Whatever the choice of narrator, these pieces of short fiction illuminate events in childhood and adolescence. In some, the illumination eludes the young person during the experience and comes to the adult narrator only through the later understanding that often results from geographical and temporal distance. In others, the illumination comes during the experience itself.

It is tempting to assume automatically that author and narrator or protagonist are one and the same. Yet Margaret Atwood's experience at the publication of her third novel, *Lady Oracle*, offers a salutary warning against the error of confusing autobiography and fiction. Earlier, some reviewers of her novel *Surfacing* had mistakenly assumed that the narrator was Atwood herself and that she was writing down her own experiences. Therefore, to avoid a similar misunderstanding of *Lady Oracle*, Atwood gave her narrator flaming red hair and made her grossly overweight as a child. Atwood herself does not have red hair and has never been overweight. And yet, in the first interview about *Lady Oracle*, the interviewer eagerly wanted to know how Atwood had managed to lose so much weight.

Such a misreading is not uncommon. When writers turn to childhood events for their fiction they may borrow and transform material from their own upbringing–not surprising, since the childhood a writer knows most clearly is likely to be his or her own. At the same time, however, readers must be careful not to assume that there are always autobiographical connections between the fictional character and the author. *Illuminations* offers one example of pure autobiography, Fredelle Bruser Maynard's evocative reminiscence of her Jewish Christmas. The book also contains some examples of strongly autobiographical fiction, like Gabrielle Roy's "Wilhelm" and Margaret Laurence's "A Bird in the House," where the writers are consciously transforming episodes or aspects of their younger years into fiction. Other stories, as their introductions note, contain only a few autobiographical details.

The arrangement of the stories in four sections corresponding to geographical regions in Canada may seem at first to point up the importance of setting and environment to a writer's experience. Yet the geographical boundaries blur, in the end, because what is represented here is not division but unity. The stories develop similar themes, focus on similar problems, recount similar understandings–from coast to coast. The young actor of the Annapolis Valley shares the same youthful embarrassment and anxiety that plague the would-be concert pianist on Vancouver Island. Settings shape and inform the experiences of youth, to be sure, yet the experiences themselves transcend regional–even national–boundaries to speak of the fantasies and fears, joy and pain common to all human beings caught up in the sometimes humorous, sometimes agonizing process of growing up.

In the following stories you will discover moments of illumination that go beyond settings, familial environments, and sometimes even gender. And you will hear echoes of your own fantasies and fears, joy and pain in the experiences of the young protagonists.

Illuminations

Elizabeth Bishop

Though born in Worcester, Massachusetts (1911), Elizabeth Bishop considered herself a Canadian by familial upbringing, if not by birth. If home is where one starts from, her home was Great Village, Nova Scotia. At an early age her paternal grandfather left his birthplace of White Sands on the southeastern coast of Prince Edward Island for Rhode Island and, later, Massachusetts. His son John married Gertrude Bulmer, a girl of frail emotional health from the Acadian countryside of Nova Scotia. Eight months after the birth of their only child, Elizabeth, John Bishop died suddenly. Unable to withstand the shock of his death, his wife entered a sanatorium; she never did recover. Thus when she was less than a year old, Elizabeth Bishop lost both her parents. She was taken from Worcester to live with her mother's family in Great Village and saw her mother only one more time before her death in 1936.

The young Elizabeth Bishop experienced a variety of homes during her early years. Her first home, until she was six, was Great Village, near the head of the Bay of Fundy. Here was a world of family affection, simple dignity, and life close to the soil. After the age of six, she lived for a time with her father's parents in Worcester, Massachusetts, and later with her mother's married sister in Boston. Summers, the joyous times, she spent at a camp on Cape Cod or back in her first home of Great Village.

Throughout her life Bishop was passionately fond of travelling. After graduation from Vassar College in 1934, she moved to New York City and then, the following year, to Europe. France and Florida, Mexico and Brazil–these were her homes for extended periods. In 1970 she returned to the United States to settle in Boston. For her, as for so many Maritimers, Nova Scotia and New England were part of the same extended eastern coast.

One of the finest poets of the twentieth century, Bishop does not reveal in her writings any exhaustive philosophy or approach to life. Rather she shows the rich texture and variety of the world with all its joys and pains, injustices and confusions. Marie-Claire Blais

points out: "One cannot read a single line either of her poetry or prose without feeling that a real poet is speaking...whose eye is both an inner and outer eye. The outer eye sees with marvellous, objective precision, the vision is translated into quite simple language, and this language, with the illuminated sharpness of something under a microscope, works an optical magic, slipping in and out of imagery, so that everything seen contains the vibrations of meaning on meaning."

Shortly before Bishop died in 1979, Dalhousie University conferred on her an honorary Doctor of Laws. Hailing her as "a distinguished poet and friend of Nova Scotia," the citation proclaimed: "Because of her father's sudden death and her mother's illness, Miss Bishop spent her early years at the home of her maternal grandparents in Great Village. She has travelled much and lived for many years in Brazil, but the mark of her Nova Scotia years is discernible in the setting, the imagery, and the temper of her most memorable work. Elizabeth Bishop's poetry is notable for its clarity of perception, its sculptured finish, its quiet but searching wit, its compassion, and its capacity to reveal the extraordinary in what had seemed to be the ordinary stuff of daily life."

One of the few short stories Bishop wrote, "In the Village," first published in 1953, is an adult's recollections of her childhood in a Nova Scotia village. The details and images of the story reflect the Great Village world of the young Elizabeth Bishop.

In
the Village

A scream, the echo of a scream, hangs over that Nova Scotian village. No one hears it; it hangs there forever, a slight stain in those pure blue skies, skies that travellers compare to those of Switzerland, too dark, too blue, so that they seem to keep on darkening a little more around the horizon—or is it around the rims of the eyes?—the color of the cloud of bloom on the elm trees, the violet on the fields of oats; something darkening over the woods and waters as well as the sky. The scream hangs like that, unheard, in memory—in the past, in the present, and those years between. It was not even loud to begin with, perhaps. It just came there to live, forever—not loud, just alive forever. Its pitch would be the pitch of my village. Flick the lightning rod on top of the church steeple with your fingernail and you will hear it.

She stood in the large front bedroom with sloping walls on either side, papered in wide white and dim-gold stripes. Later, it was she who gave the scream.

The village dressmaker was fitting a new dress. It was her first in almost two years and she had decided to come out of black, so the dress was purple. She was very thin. She wasn't at all sure whether she was going to like the dress or not and she kept lifting the folds of the skirt, still unpinned and dragging on the floor around her, in her thin white hands, and looking down at the cloth.

"Is it a good shade for me? Is it too bright? I don't know. I haven't worn colors for so long now....How long? Should it be black? Do you think I should keep on wearing black?''

Drummers sometimes came around selling gilded red or green books, unlovely books, filled with bright new illustrations of the Bible stories. The people in the pictures wore clothes like the purple dress, or like the way it looked then.

It was a hot summer afternoon. Her mother and her two sisters were there. The older sister had brought her home, from Boston, not long before, and was staying on, to help. Because in Boston she had not got any better, in months and months—or had it been a year? In spite of the doctors, in spite of the frightening expenses, she had not got any better.

First, she had come home, with her child. Then she had gone away again, alone, and left the child. Then she had come home. Then she had gone away again, with her sister; and now she was home again.

Unaccustomed to having her back, the child stood now in the doorway, watching. The dressmaker was crawling around and around on her knees eating pins as Nebuchadnezzar had crawled eating grass. The wallpaper glinted and the elm trees outside hung heavy and green, and the straw matting smelled like the ghost of hay.

Clang.

Clang.

Oh, beautiful sounds, from the blacksmith's shop at the end of the garden! Its grey roof, with patches of moss, could be seen above the lilac bushes. Nate was there—Nate, wearing a long black leather apron over his trousers and bare chest, sweating hard, a black leather cap on top of dry, thick, black-and-grey curls, a black sooty face; iron filings, whiskers, and gold teeth, all together, and a smell of red-hot metal and horses' hoofs.

Clang.

The pure note: pure and angelic.

The dress was all wrong. She screamed.

The child vanishes.

Later they sit, the mother and the three sisters, in the shade on the back porch, sipping sour, diluted ruby: raspberry vinegar. The dressmaker refuses to join them and leaves, holding the dress to her heart. The child is visiting the blacksmith.

In the blacksmith's shop things hang up in the shadows and shadows hang up in the things, and there are black and glistening piles of dust in each corner. A tub of night-black water stands by the forge. The horseshoes sail through the dark like bloody little moons and follow each other like bloody little moons to drown in the black water, hissing, protesting.

Outside, along the matted eaves, painstakingly, sweetly, wasps go over and over a honeysuckle vine.

Inside, the bellows creak. Nate does wonders with both hands, with one hand. The attendant horse stamps his foot and nods his head as if agreeing to a peace treaty.

Nod.

And nod.

A Newfoundland dog looks up at him and they almost touch noses, but not quite, because at the last moment the horse decides against it and turns away.

Outside in the grass lie scattered big, pale granite discs, like millstones, for making wheelrims on. This afternoon they are too hot to touch.

Now it is settling down, the scream.

Now the dressmaker is at home, basting, but in tears. It is the most beautiful material she has worked on in years. It has been sent to the woman from Boston, a present from her mother-in-law, and heaven knows how much it cost.

Before my older aunt had brought her back, I had watched my grandmother and younger aunt unpacking her clothes, her "things." In trunks and barrels and boxes they had finally come, from Boston, where she and I had once lived. So many things in the village came from Boston, and even I had once come from there. But I remembered only being here, with my grandmother.

The clothes were black, or white, or black-and-white.

"Here's a mourning hat," says my grandmother, holding up something large, sheer, and black, with large black roses on it; at least I guess they are roses, even if black.

"There's that mourning coat she got the first winter," says my aunt.

But always I think they are saying "morning." Why, in the morning, did one put on black? How early in the morning did one begin? Before the sun came up?

"Oh, here are some house dresses!"

They are nicer. Clean and starched, stiffly folded. One with black polka dots. One of fine black-and-white stripes with black grosgrain bows. A third with a black velvet bow and on the bow a pin of pearls in a little wreath.

"Look. She forgot to take it off."

A white hat. A white embroidered parasol. Black shoes with buckles glistening like the dust in the blacksmith's shop. A silver mesh bag. A silver calling-card case on a little chain. Another bag of silver mesh, gathered to a tight, round neck of strips of silver that will open out, like the hatrack in the front hall. A silver-framed photograph, quickly turned over. Handkerchiefs with narrow black hems—"morning handkerchiefs." In bright sunlight, over breakfast tables, they flutter.

A bottle of perfume has leaked and made awful brown stains.

Oh, marvellous scent, from somewhere else! It doesn't smell like that here; but there, somewhere, it does, still.

A big bundle of postcards. The curdled elastic around them breaks. I gather them together on the floor.

Some people wrote with pale-blue ink, and some with brown, and some with black, but mostly blue. The stamps have been torn off many of them. Some are plain, or photographs, but some have lines of metallic crystals on them—how beautiful!—silver, gold, red, and green, or all four mixed together, crumbling off, sticking in the lines on my palms. All the cards like this I spread on the floor to study. The crystals outline the buildings on the cards in a way buildings never are outlined but should be—if there were a way of making the crystals stick. But probably not; they would fall to the ground, never to be seen again. Some cards, instead of lines around the buildings, have words written in their skies with the same stuff, crumbling, dazzling and crumbling, raining down a little on little people who sometimes stand about below: pictures of Pentecost? What are the messages? I cannot tell, but they are falling on those specks of hands, on the hats, on the toes of their shoes, in their paths—wherever it is they are.

Postcards come from another world, the world of the grandparents who send things, the world of sad brown perfume, and morning. (The grey postcards of the village for sale in the village store are so unilluminating that they scarcely count. After all, one steps outside and immediately sees the same thing: the village, where we live, full size, and in color.)

Two barrels of china. White with a gold band. Broken bits. A thick white teacup with a small red-and-blue butterfly on it, painfully desirable. A teacup with little pale-blue windows in it.

"See the grains of rice?" says my grandmother, showing me the cup against the light.

Could you poke the grains out? No, it seems they aren't really there any more. They were put there just for a while and then they left something or other behind. What odd things people do with grains of rice, so innocent and small! My aunt says that she has heard they write the Lord's Prayer on them. And make them make those little pale-blue lights.

More broken china. My grandmother says it breaks her heart.

"Why couldn't they have got it packed better? Heaven knows what it cost."

"Where'll we put it all? The china closet isn't nearly big enough."

"It'll just have to stay in the barrels."

"Mother, you might as well use it."

"*No*," says my grandmother.

"Where's the silver, Mother?"

"In the vault in Boston."

Vault. Awful word. I run the tip of my finger over the rough, jewelled lines on the postcards, over and over. They hold things up to each other and exclaim, and talk, and exclaim, over and over.

"There's that cake basket."

"Mrs. Miles..."

"Mrs. Miles' spongecake..."

"She was very fond of her."

Another photograph–"Oh, that *Negro* girl! That friend."

"She went to be a medical missionary. She had a letter from her, last winter. From Africa."

"They were great friends."

They show me the picture. She, too, is black-and-white, with glasses on a chain. A morning friend.

And the smell, the wonderful smell of the dark-brown stains. Is it roses?

A tablecloth.

"She did beautiful work," says my grandmother.

"But look–it isn't finished."

Two pale, smooth wooden hoops are pressed together in the linen. There is a case of little ivory embroidery tools.

I abscond with a little ivory stick with a sharp point. To keep it forever I bury it under the bleeding heart by the crab-apple tree, but it is never found again.

Nate sings and pumps the bellows with one hand. I try to help, but he really does it all, from behind me, and laughs when the coals blow red and wild.

"Make me a ring! Make me a ring, Nate!"

Instantly it is made; it is mine.

It is too big and still hot, and blue and shiny. The horseshoe nail has a flat oblong head, pressing hot against my knuckle.

Two men stand watching, chewing or spitting tobacco, matches, horseshoe nails– anything, apparently, but with such presence; they are perfectly at home. The horse is the real guest, however. His harness hangs loose like a man's suspenders; they say pleasant things to him; one of his legs is doubled up in an improbable, affectedly polite way, and the bottom of his hoof is laid bare, but he doesn't seem to mind. Manure piles up behind him, suddenly, neatly. He, too, is very much at home. He is enormous. His rump is like a brown, glossy globe of the whole brown world. His ears are secret entrances to the underworld. His nose is supposed to feel like velvet and does, with ink spots under milk all over its pink. Clear bright-green bits of stiffened froth, like glass, are stuck around his mouth. He wears medals on his chest, too, and one on his forehead, and simpler decorations– red and blue celluloid rings overlapping each other on leather straps. On each temple is a clear glass bulge, like an eyeball, but in them are the heads of two other little horses (his dreams?), brightly colored, real and raised, untouchable, alas, against backgrounds of silver blue. His trophies hang around him, and the cloud of his odor is a chariot in itself.

At the end, all four feet are brushed with tar, and shine, and he expresses his satisfaction, rolling it from his nostrils like noisy smoke, as he backs into the shafts of his wagon.

The purple dress is to be fitted again this afternoon but I take a note to Miss Gurley to say the fitting will have to be postponed. Miss Gurley seems upset.

"Oh dear. And how is–" And she breaks off.

Her house is littered with scraps of cloth and tissue-paper patterns, yellow, pinked, with holes in the shapes of A, B, C, and D in them, and numbers; and threads everywhere like a fine vegetation. She has a bosom full of needles with threads ready to pull out and make nests with. She sleeps in her thimble. A grey kitten once lay on the treadle of her sewing machine, where she rocked it as she sewed, like a baby in a cradle, but it got hanged on the belt. Or did she make that up? But another grey-and-white one lies now by the arm of the machine, in imminent danger of being sewn into a turban. There is a table covered with laces and braids, embroidery silks, and cards of buttons of all colors– big ones for winter coats, small pearls, little glass ones delicious to suck.

She has made the very dress I have on, "for twenty-five cents." My grandmother said my other grandmother would certainly be surprised at that.

The purple stuff lies on a table; long white threads hang all about it.

Oh, look away before it moves by itself, or makes a sound; before it echoes, echoes, what it has heard!

Mysteriously enough, poor Miss Gurley—I know she is poor—gives me a five-cent piece. She leans over and drops it in the pocket of the red-and-white dress that she has made herself. It is very tiny, very shiny. King George's beard is like a little silver flame. Because they look like herring- or maybe salmon-scales, five-cent pieces are called "fish-scales." One heard of people's rings being found inside fish, or their long-lost jackknives. What if one could scrape a salmon and find a little picture of King George on every scale?

I put my five-cent piece in my mouth for greater safety on the way home, and swallow it. Months later, as far as I know, it is still in me, transmuting all its precious metal into my growing teeth and hair.

Back home, I am not allowed to go upstairs. I hear my aunts running back and forth and something like a tin washbasin falls bump in the carpeted upstairs hall.

My grandmother is sitting in the kitchen stirring potato mash for tomorrow's bread and crying into it. She gives me a spoonful and it tastes wonderful but wrong. In it I think I taste my grandmother's tears; then I kiss her and taste them on her cheek.

She says it is time for her to get fixed up, and I say I want to help her brush her hair. So I do, standing swaying on the lower rung of the back of her rocking chair.

The rocking chair has been painted and repainted so many times that it is as smooth as cream—blue, white, and grey all showing through. My grandmother's hair is silver and in it she keeps a great many celluloid combs, at the back and sides, streaked grey and silver to match. The one at the back has longer teeth than the others and a row of sunken silver dots across the top, beneath a row of little balls. I pretend to play a tune on it; then I pretend to play a tune on each of the others before we stick them in, so my grandmother's hair is full of music. She laughs. I am so pleased with myself that I do not feel obliged to mention the five-cent piece. I drink a rusty, icy drink out of the biggest dipper; still, nothing much happens.

We are waiting for a scream. But it is not screamed again, and the red sun sets in silence.

Every morning I take the cow to the pasture we rent from Mr. Chisolm. She, Nelly, could probably go by herself just as well, but I like marching through the village with a big stick, directing her.

This morning it is brilliant and cool. My grandmother and I are alone again in the kitchen. We are talking. She says it is cool enough to keep the oven going, to bake the bread, to roast a leg of lamb.

"Will you remember to go down to the brook? Take Nelly around by the brook and pick me a big bunch of mint. I thought I'd make some mint sauce."

"For the leg of lamb?"

"You finish your porridge."

"I think I've had enough now..."

"Hurry up and finish that porridge."

There is talking on the stairs.

"No, now wait," my grandmother says to me. "Wait a minute."

My two aunts come into the kitchen. She is with them, wearing the white cotton dress with black polka dots and the flat black velvet bow at the neck. She comes and feeds me the rest of the porridge herself, smiling at me.

"Stand up now and let's see how tall you are," she tells me.

"Almost to your elbow," they say. "See how much she's grown."

"Almost."

"It's her hair."

Hands are on my head, pushing me down; I slide out from under them. Nelly is waiting for me in the yard, holding her nose just under in the watering trough. My stick waits against the door frame, clad in bark.

Nelly looks up at me, drooling glass strings. She starts off around the corner of the house without a flicker of expression.

Switch. Switch. How annoying she is!

But she is a Jersey and we think she is very pretty. "From in front," my aunts sometimes add.

She stops to snatch at the long, untrimmed grass around the gate-post.

"Nelly!"

Whack! I hit her hipbone.

On she goes without even looking around. Flop, flop, down over the dirt sidewalk into the road, across the village green in front of the Presbyterian church. The grass is grey with dew; the church is dazzling. It is high-shouldered and secretive; it leans backwards a little.

Ahead, the road is lined with dark, thin old elms; grass grows long and blue in the ditches. Behind the elms the meadows run along, peacefully, greenly.

We pass Mrs. Peppard's house. We pass Mrs. McNeil's house. We pass Mrs. Geddes' house. We pass Hills' store.

The store is high, and a faded grey-blue, with tall windows, built on a long, high stoop of grey-blue cement with an iron hitching rail along it. Today, in one window there are big cardboard easels, shaped like houses—complete houses and houses with the roofs lifted off to show glimpses of the rooms inside, all in different colors—with cans of paint in pyramids in the middle. But they are an old story. In the other window is something new: shoes, single shoes, summer shoes, each sitting on top of its own box with its mate beneath it, inside, in the dark. Surprisingly, some of them appear to be exactly the colors and texture of pink and blue blackboard chalks, but I can't stop to examine them now. In one door, great overalls hang high in the air on hangers. Miss Ruth Hill looks out the other door and waves. We pass Mrs. Captain Mahon's house.

Nelly tenses and starts walking faster, making over to the right. Every morning and evening we go through this. We are approaching Miss Spencer's house. Miss Spencer is the milliner the way Miss Gurley is the dressmaker. She has a very small white house with the doorstep right on the sidewalk. One front window has lace curtains with a pale-yellow window shade pulled all the way down, inside them; the other one has a shelf across it on which are displayed four summer hats. Out of the corner of my eye I can see that there is a yellow chip straw with little wads of flamingo-colored feathers around the crown, but again there is no time to examine anything.

On each side of Miss Spencer's door is a large old lilac bush. Every time we go by Nelly determines to brush off all her flies on these bushes—brush them off forever, in one fell swoop. Then Miss Spencer is apt to come to the door and stand there, shaking with anger, between the two bushes still shaking from Nelly's careening passage, and yell at me, sometimes waving a hat in my direction as well.

Nelly leaning to the right, breaks into a cow trot. I run up with my stick.

Whack!

"Nelly!"

Whack!

Just this once she gives in and we rush safely by.

Then begins a long, pleasant stretch beneath the elms. The Presbyterian manse has a black iron fence with openwork four-sided pillars, like tall, thin bird cages, bird cages for storks. Dr. Gillespie, the minister, appears just as we come along, and rides slowly toward us on his bicycle.

"Good day." He even tips his hat.

"Good day."

He wears the most interesting hat in the village: a man's regular stiff straw sailor, only it is black. Is there a possibility that he paints it at home, with something like stove polish? Because once I had seen one of my aunts painting a straw-colored hat navy blue.

Nelly, oblivious, makes cow flops. Smack. Smack. Smack. Smack.

It is fascinating. I cannot take my eyes off her. Then I step around them: fine dark-green and lacy and watery at the edges.

We pass the McLeans', whom I know very well. Mr. McLean is just coming out of his new barn with the tin hip roof and with him is Jock, their old shepherd dog, long-haired, black and white and yellow. He runs up barking deep, cracked, soft barks in the quiet morning. I hesitate.

Mr. McLean bellows, "Jock! You! Come back here! Are you trying to frighten her?"

To me he says, "He's twice as old as you are."

Finally I pat the big round warm head.

We talk a little. I ask the exact number of Jock's years but Mr. McLean has forgotten.

"He hasn't hardly a tooth in his head and he's got rheumatism. I hope we'll get him through next winter. He still wants to go to the woods with me and it's hard for him in the snow. We'll be lost without him."

Mr. McLean speaks to me behind one hand, not to hurt Jock's feelings: *"Deaf as a post."*

Like anybody deaf, Jock puts his head to one side.

"He used to be the best dog at finding cows for miles around. People used to come from away down the shore to borrow him to find their cows for them. And he'd always find them. The first year we had to leave him behind when we went up to the mountain to get the cows I thought it would kill him. Well, when his teeth started going he couldn't do much with the cows any more. Effie used to say, 'I don't know how we'd run the farm without him.' "

Loaded down with too much black and yellow and white fur, Jock smiles, showing how few teeth he has. He has yellow caterpillars for eyebrows.

Nelly has gone on ahead. She is almost up the hill to Chisolms' when I catch up with her. We turn in to their steep, long drive, through a steep, bare yard crowded with unhappy apple trees. From the top, through, from the Chisolms' back yard, one always stops to look at the view.

There are the tops of all the elm trees in the village and there, beyond them, the long green marshes, so fresh, so salt. Then the Minas Basin, with the tide halfway in or out, the wet red mud glazed with sky blue until it meets the creeping lavender-red water. In the middle of the view, like one hand of a clock pointing straight up, is the steeple of the

Presbyterian church. We are in the "Maritimes" but all that means is that we live by the sea.

Mrs. Chisolm's pale frantic face is watching me out the kitchen window as she washes the breakfast dishes. We wave, but I hurry by because she may come out and ask questions. But her questions are not as bad perhaps as those of her husband, Mr. Chisolm, who wears a beard. One evening he had met me in the pasture and asked me how my soul was. Then he held me firmly by both hands while he said a prayer, with his head bowed, Nelly right beside us chewing her cud all the time. I had felt a soul, heavy in my chest, all the way home.

I let Nelly through the set of bars to the pasture where the brook is, to get the mint. We both take drinks and I pick a big bunch of mint, eating a little, scratchy and powerful. Nelly looks over her shoulder and comes back to try it, thinking, as cows do, it might be something especially for her. Her face is close to mine and I hold her by one horn to admire her eyes again. Her nose is blue and as shiny as something in the rain. At such close quarters my feelings for her are mixed. She gives my bare arm a lick, scratchy and powerful, too, almost upsetting me into the brook; then she goes off to join a black-and-white friend she has here, mooing to her to wait until she catches up.

For a while I entertain the idea of not going home today at all, of staying safely here in the pasture all day, playing in the brook and climbing on the squishy, moss-covered hummocks in the swampy part. But an immense, sibilant, glistening loneliness suddenly faces me, and the cows are moving off to the shade of the fir trees, their bells chiming softly, individually.

On the way home there are the four hats in Miss Spencer's window to study, and the summer shoes in Hills'. There is the same shoe in white, in black patent leather, and in the chalky, sugary, unearthly pinks and blues. It has straps that button around the ankle and above, four of them, about an inch wide and an inch apart, reaching away up.

In those unlovely gilded red and green books, filled with illustrations of the Bible stories, the Roman centurions wear them, too, or something very like them.

Surely they are my size. Surely, this summer, pink or blue, my grandmother will buy me a pair!

Miss Ruth Hill gives me a Moirs' chocolate out of the glass case. She talks to me: "How is she? We've always been friends. We played together from the time we were babies. We sat together in school. Right from primer class on. After she went away, she always wrote to me—even after she got sick the first time."

Then she tells a funny story about when they were little.

That afternoon, Miss Gurley comes and we go upstairs to watch the purple dress being fitted again. My grandmother holds me against her knees. My younger aunt is helping Miss Gurley, handing her the scissors when she asks. Miss Gurley is cheerful and talkative today.

The dress is smaller now; there are narrow, even folds down the skirt; the sleeves fit tightly, with little wrinkles over the thin white hands. Everyone is very pleased with it; everyone talks and laughs.

"There. You see? It's so becoming."

"I've never seen you in anything more becoming."

"And it's so nice to see you in color for a change."

And the purple is real, like a flower against the gold-and-white wallpaper.

On the bureau is a present that has just come, from an uncle in Boston whom I do not remember. It is a gleaming little bundle of flat, triangular satin pillows–sachets, tied together with a white satin ribbon, with an imitation rosebud on top of the bow. Each is a different faint color; if you take them apart, each has a different faint scent. But tied together the way they came, they make one confused, powdery one.

The mirror has been lifted off the bureau and put on the floor against the wall.

She walks slowly up and down and looks at the skirt in it.

"I think that's about right," says Miss Gurley, down on her knees and looking into the mirror, too, but as if the skirt were miles and miles away.

But, twitching the purple skirt with her thin white hands, she says desperately, "I don't know what they're wearing any more. I have no *idea!*" It turns to a sort of wail.

"Now, now," soothes Miss Gurley. "I do think that's about right. Don't you?" She appeals to my grandmother and me.

Light, musical, constant sounds are coming from Nate's shop. It sounds as though he were making a wheel rim.

She sees me in the mirror and turns on me: "Stop sucking your thumb!"

Then in a moment she turns to me again and demands, "Do you know what I want?"

"No."

"I want some humbugs. I'm dying for some humbugs. I don't think I've had any humbugs for years and years and years. If I give you some pennies, will you go to Mealy's and buy me a bag?"

To be sent on an errand! Everything is all right.

Humbugs are a kind of candy, although not a kind I am particularly fond of. They are brown, like brook water, but hard, and shaped like little twisted pillows. They last a long time, but lack the spit-producing brilliance of cherry or strawberry.

Mealy runs a little shop where she sells candy and bananas and oranges and all kinds of things she crochets. At Christmas, she sells toys, but only at Christmas. Her real name is Amelia. She also takes care of the telephone switchboard for the village, in her dining room.

Somebody finds a black pocketbook in the bureau. She counts out five big pennies into my hand, in a column, then one more.

"That one's for you. So you won't eat up all my humbugs on the way home."

Further instructions:

"Don't run all the way."

"Don't stop on the bridge."

I do run, by Nate's shop, glimpsing him inside, pumping away with one hand. We wave. The beautiful, big Newfoundland dog is there again and comes out, bounding along with me a ways.

I do not stop on the bridge but slow down long enough to find out the years on the pennies. King George is much bigger than on a five-cent piece, brown as an Indian in copper, but he wears the same clothes; on a penny, one can make out the little ermine trimmings on his coat.

Mealy has a bell that rings when you go in so that she'll hear you if she's at the switchboard. The shop is a step down, dark, with a counter along one side. The ceiling is low and the floor has settled well over to the counter side. Mealy is broad and fat and it looks as though she and the counter and the showcase, stuffed dimly with things every which way, were settling down together out of sight.

Five pennies buys a great many humbugs. I must not take too long to decide what I want for myself. I must get back quickly, quickly, while Miss Gurley is there and everyone is upstairs and the dress is still on. Without taking time to think, quickly I point at the brightest thing. It is a ball, glistening solidly with crystals of pink and yellow sugar, hung, impractically, on an elastic, like a real elastic ball. I know I don't even care for the inside of it, which is soft, but I wind most of the elastic around my arm, to keep the ball off the ground, at least, and start hopefully back.

But one night, in the middle of the night, there is a fire. The church bell wakes me up. It is in the room with me; red flames are burning the wallpaper beside the bed. I suppose I shriek.

The door opens. My younger aunt comes in. There is a lamp lit in the hall and everyone is talking at once.

"Don't cry!" my aunt almost shouts at me. "It's just a fire. Way up the road. It isn't going to hurt you. Don't *cry!*"

"Will! Will!" My grandmother is calling my grandfather. "Do you have to go?"

"No, don't go, Dad!"

"It looks like McLean's place." My grandfather sounds muffled.

"Oh, not their new barn!" My grandmother.

"You can't tell from here." He must have his head out the window.

"*She's* calling for you, Mother." My older aunt. "I'll go."

"No. *I'll* go." My younger aunt.

"Light that other lamp, girl."

My older aunt comes to my door. "It's way off. It's nowhere near us. The men will take care of it. Now you go to sleep." But she leaves my door open.

"Leave her door open," calls my grandmother just then. "Oh, why do they have to ring the bell like that? It's enough to terrify anybody. Will, be *careful.*"

Sitting up in bed, I see my grandfather starting down the stairs, tucking his nightshirt into his trousers as he goes.

"Don't make so much noise!" My older aunt and my grandmother seem to be quarreling.

"Noise! I can't hear myself think, with that bell!"

"I bet Spurgeon's ringing it!" They both laugh.

"It must have been heat lightning," says my grandmother, now apparently in her bedroom, as if it were all over.

"*She's* all right, Mother." My younger aunt comes back. "I don't think she's scared. You can't see the glare so much on that side of the house."

Then my younger aunt comes into my room and gets in bed with me. She says to go to sleep, it's way up the road. The men have to go; my grandfather has gone. It's probably somebody's barn full of hay, from heat lightning. It's been such a hot summer there's been a lot of it. The church bell stops and her voice is suddenly loud in my ear over my shoulder. The last echo of the bell lasts for a long time.

Wagons rattle by.

"Now they're going down to the river to fill the barrels," my aunt is murmuring against my back.

The red flame dies down on the wall, then flares again.

Wagons rattle by in the dark. Men are swearing at the horses.

"Now they're coming back with the water. Go to sleep."

More wagons; men's voices. I suppose I go to sleep.

I wake up and it is the same night, the night of the fire. My aunt is getting out of bed, hurrying away. It is still dark and silent now, after the fire. No, not silent; my grandmother is crying somewhere, not in her room. It is getting grey. I hear one wagon, rumbling far off, perhaps crossing the bridge.

But now I am caught in a skein of voices, my aunts' and my grandmother's, saying the same things over and over, sometimes loudly, sometimes in whispers:

"Hurry. For heaven's sake, *shut the door!*"

"Sh!"

"Oh, we can't go on like this, we..."

"It's too dangerous. Remember that..."

"Sh! Don't let her..."

A door slams.

A door opens. The voices begin again.

I am struggling to free myself.

Wait. Wait. No one is going to scream.

Slowly, slowly it gets daylight. A different red reddens the wallpaper. Now the house is silent. I get up and dress by myself and go downstairs. My grandfather is in the kitchen alone, drinking his tea. He has made the oatmeal himself, too. He gives me some and tells me about the fire very cheerfully.

It had not been the McLeans' new barn after all, but someone else's barn, off the road. All the hay was lost but they had managed somehow to save part of the barn.

But neither of us is really listening to what he is saying; we are listening for sounds from upstairs. But everything is quiet.

On the way home from taking Nelly to the pasture I go to see where the barn was. There are people still standing around, some of them the men who got up in the night to go to the river. Everyone seems quite cheerful there, too, but the smell of burned hay is awful, sickening.

Now the front bedroom is empty. My older aunt has gone back to Boston and my other aunt is making plans to go there after a while, too.

There has been a new pig. He was very cute to begin with, and skidded across the kitchen linoleum while everyone laughed. He grew and grew. Perhaps it is all the same summer, because it is unusually hot and something unusual for a pig happens to him; he gets sunburned. He really gets sunburned, bright pink, but the strangest thing of all, the curled-up end of his tail gets so sunburned it is brown and scorched. My grandmother trims it with the scissors and it doesn't hurt him.

Sometime later this pig is butchered. My grandmother, my aunt, and I shut ourselves in the parlor. My aunt plays a piece on the piano called "Out in the Fields." She plays it and plays it; then she switches to Mendelssohn's "War March of the Priests."

The front room is empty. Nobody sleeps there. Clothes are hung there.

Every week my grandmother sends off a package. In it she puts cake and fruit, a jar of preserves, Moirs' chocolates.

Monday afternoon every week.

Fruit, cake, Jordan almonds, a handkerchief with a tatted edge.

Fruit. Cake. Wild-strawberry jam. A New Testament.

A little bottle of scent from Hills' store, with a purple silk tassel fastened to the stopper.

Fruit. Cake. "Selections from Tennyson."

A calendar, with a quotation from Longfellow for every day.

Fruit. Cake. Moirs' chocolates.

I watch her pack them in the pantry. Sometimes she sends me to the store to get things at the last minute.

The address of the sanitarium is in my grandmother's handwriting, in purple indelible pencil, on smoothed-out wrapping paper. It will never come off.

I take the package to the post office. Going by Nate's, I walk far out in the road and hold the package on the side away from him.

He calls to me. "Come here! I want to show you something."

But I pretend I don't hear him. But at any other time I still go there just the same.

The post office is very small. It sits on the side of the road like a package once delivered by the post office. The government has painted its clapboards tan, with a red trim. The earth in front of it is worn hard. Its face is scarred and scribbled on, carved with initials. In the evening, when the Canadian Pacific mail is due, a row of big boys leans against it, but in the daytime there is nothing to be afraid of. There is no one in front, and inside it is empty. There is no one except the postmaster, Mr. Johnson, to look at my grandmother's purple handwriting.

The post office tilts a little, like Mealy's shop, and inside it looks as chewed as a horse's manger. Mr. Johnson looks out through the little window in the middle of the bank of glass-fronted boxes, like an animal looking out over its manger. But he is dignified by the thick, bevelled-edged glass boxes with their solemn, upright gold-and-black-shaded numbers.

Ours is 21. Although there is nothing in it, Mr. Johnson automatically cocks his eye at it from behind when he sees me.

21.

"Well, well. Here we are again. Good day, good day," he says.

"Good day, Mr. Johnson."

I have to go outside again to hand him the package through the ordinary window, into his part of the post office, because it is too big for the little official one. He is very old, and nice. He has two fingers missing on his right hand where they were caught in a threshing machine. He wears a navy-blue cap with a black leather visor, like a ship's officer, and a shirt with feathery brown stripes, and a big gold collar button.

"Let me see. Let me see. Let me see. Hm," he says to himself, weighing the package on the scales, jiggling the bar with the two remaining fingers and thumb.

"Yes. Yes. Your grandmother is very faithful."

Every Monday afternoon I go past the blacksmith's shop with the package under my arm, hiding the address of the sanitarium with my arm and my other hand.

Going over the bridge, I stop and stare down into the river. All the little trout that have been too smart to get caught — for how long now? — are there, rushing in flank movements, foolish assaults and retreats, against and away from the old sunken fender of Malcolm McNeil's Ford. It has lain there for ages and is supposed to be a disgrace to us all. So are the tin cans that glint there, brown and gold.

From above, the trout look as transparent as the water, but if one did catch one, it would be opaque enough, with a little slick moonwhite belly with a pair of tiny, pleated, rose-pink fins on it. The leaning willows soak their narrow yellowed leaves.

Clang.

Clang.

Nate is shaping a horseshoe.

Oh, beautiful pure sound!

It turns everything else to silence.

But still, once in a while, the river gives an unexpected gurgle. "*Slp*," it says, out of glassy-ridged brown knots sliding along the surface.

Clang.

And everything except the river holds its breath.

Now there is no scream. Once there was one and it settled slowly down to earth one hot summer afternoon; or did it float up, into that dark, too dark, blue sky? But surely it has gone away, forever.

Clang.

It sounds like a bell buoy out at sea.

It is the elements speaking: earth, air, fire, water.

All those other things — clothes, crumbling postcards, broken china; things damaged and lost, sickened or destroyed; even the frail almost-lost scream — are they too frail for us to hear their voices long, too mortal?

Nate!

Oh, beautiful sound, strike again!

Works by Elizabeth Bishop

POETRY

North and South. Boston: Houghton
  Mifflin, 1946.
Poems: North and South – A Cold Spring.
  Boston: Houghton Mifflin, 1955.
Questions of Travel. New York: Farrar,
  Straus and Giroux, 1965.
The Ballad of the Burglar of Babylon. New
  York: Farrar, Straus and Giroux, 1968.
The Complete Poems. New York: Farrar,
  Straus and Giroux, 1969.
Geography III. New York: Farrar, Straus
  and Giroux, 1976.
The Complete Poems 1927-1979. New York:
  Farrar, Straus and Giroux, 1983.

Interviews with Elizabeth Bishop

Christian Science Monitor, 70 (March 23,
  1978), 24.
Vassar Quarterly, 75 (Winter, 1979), 4-9.

Alden Nowlan

Alden Nowlan was born in Stanley, Nova Scotia, in 1933. He dropped out of school at the age of twelve and worked at various jobs on farms and in lumber camps and sawmills. When he was nineteen he left Nova Scotia for Hartland, New Brunswick, where he found employment with the town newspaper. For nearly two decades he pursued various forms of newspaper work while writing poetry and fiction. In 1968 he became Writer-in-Residence at the

University of New Brunswick, a position he held until his death in 1983. A writer with many avenues of interest, he was equally proficient in poetry, fiction, drama, journalism, and history.

The settings of Nowlan's poetry and fiction are frequently rural New Brunswick or Nova Scotia, where some of the poor and isolated inhabitants can seem eccentric in their behavior. Nowlan's vision is a combination of compassion and blunt realism, and his writings give voice to the traditions, joys, and sufferings of a rural Maritime world crippled by infertile soil and a wretched economy. "It's true that most of the fiction I've published to date has dealt with the lives of poor, rural people," Nowlan once remarked, "but that's partly because my early life was spent among poor, rural people and I'm the kind of writer who has to let his experience ferment before he can bottle it in fiction, and partly because almost everyone else writes about the urban, middle classes."

In his only novel, *Various Persons Named Kevin O'Brien* (1973), Nowlan tries to find the pattern to a man's early life. Kevin O'Brien, nearing thirty, narrates his own "fictional memoir," as the novel is subtitled. This memoir consists of eleven moments of insight or illumination.

Like Nowlan, Kevin is an introspective observer of the passing scene. Like his creator, he is a journalist who has spent considerable time assembling his impressions of his youth. "During my adolescence," Nowlan recalled, "I kept diaries, I wrote pompous letters to the editor, I wrote essays, short stories, novelettes, filled exercise books with verses. All of this no better and (aside from its pretentiousness) no different from what any other kid in the village could have done. I wrote in the way that other lonely and imaginative children invent imaginary playmates."

Now, in the early 1960s, Kevin is visiting his hometown of Lockhartville, an isolated Maritime village. "Lockhartville is one of those villages (if a few houses that happen to be situated along a four-mile stretch of dirt road can be called a village) that are more isolated now than they were fifty years ago. The passenger trains have ceased to run through. The main highways have bypassed not only the village itself but the nearest towns. . . . The presence of television only serves to widen the gap between Lockhartville and the rest of the world, since little or nothing that appears on the screen has the remotest connection with what can be seen from the window."

For the returning journalist, Lockhartville "is not fixed in present time as other places are. What happens to him there is almost independent of calendars, so that there are frequent moments when it is as if he were a ghost returning into the past to spy upon one or another of his former selves." As the narrator admits at the opening of the novel, Lockhartville is also "a verbal convenience, a quick, easy, and perhaps lazy way of denoting a certain set of experiences that possess a unity more easily sensed than defined."

Over the years, Kevin has tried to find the meaning of various incidents in his life; he has attempted to give them form and pattern. As a consequence, on his trip home he carries a briefcase containing a number of manuscripts in which he explores his past. He has a store of memories that he has shaped into memoirs, "those that have been mixed with oils and pressed on to the canvas with a palette knife as compared with those that float about in the mind like watercolor on moist paper."

"There Was an Old Woman from Wexford" is the fourth memoir in the novel.

There Was
an Old Woman
from Wexford

Back in the motel in the early hours of the morning, still too tense to sleep, Kevin O'Brien (1) eats a lobster roll and a potato salad from cardboard containers, (2) drinks beer, (3) glances through the entertainment section of the Saturday edition of the *Montreal Star*, (4) smokes another cigarette, and (5) watches the late late show on television with Michael Landon, the Little Joe Cartwright of *Bonanza*, playing in *I Was a Teenaged Werewolf.* The best line in the film is spoken when Michael Landon is identified as the monster on the grounds that, "It must be him: it's wearing his jacket!"

Afterwards he makes an unsuccessful attempt to begin a diary, a journal of his jaunt, as Boswell would have called it. Almost from the time when he first learned to write he has made sporadic attempts to keep a diary. The problem is that he can't resist putting down what he regards at the moment as important, although he knows very well that the point of keeping a diary is to record trivia, ideally the kind of trivia that reconfirms the sympathetic reader as a member of that great communion, the human race.

He takes a notebook from his briefcase, opens it and writes in the date. How did the day begin? Interviewing a federal cabinet minister in Halifax. That was less than twelve hours ago according to his watch, but in terms of his present mood it could have happened in the previous decade. The cabinet minister and the newspaper article in which Kevin has recorded his remarks represent one reality, Lockhartville represents another. It is almost as if he had passed through one of those time warps of science fiction. The clock and the calendar and the map are such liars!

One day he would write something about that and add it to the contents of the briefcase.

Every child has a past, Kevin reflects, but when we begin to have a personal history, it must mean that our first youth is gone. If I had kept a diary all these years, as I so often resolved to do, by now parts of it would read like notes for an historical novel—and I'm not yet thirty years old!

Yes, and he remembers certain events from as long ago as the previous century, having learned of them by word of mouth before he was old enough to read, or even to know there existed such a thing as History. His grandfather's grandfather, also named Kevin O'Brien, had escaped from the Irish potato famine only to die of cholera on an island off the Nova Scotia coast. But that is not what he remembers; that is what he has learned. What he remembers is that the other Kevin O'Brien, and scores like him, died flopping about on the shores of that island like fish out of water. "That's exactly what they looked like," his grandfather told him. "Like trout dying on the riverbank, God rest their souls." And there is a stone in one of the Lockhartville cemeteries, a ghastly white stone, on which are carved the words: *Kevin Michael O'Brien, 1825-1849.* But no one is buried there. Whatever may be left of the body of Kevin O'Brien, born 1825, died 1849, lies in a mass grave on the island on which he perished. As a child our Kevin O'Brien was a little proud and a little afraid of that stone and that empty grave.

He knows now that he was right to stay in a motel rather than in the old house as on previous visits. The house contained too many ghosts. (As if one ghost weren't more than enough.) Then there were mice and the filthy bedclothes that oppressed his spirit even more than they offended his senses.

He tears up the paper containing his scribblings and drops the scraps in the wastebasket with the food containers, the newspaper and the beer bottle caps. Then he gets into bed, turns off the lights and shuts his eyes. But it is a long time before he falls asleep. He lies there in the darkness, remembering....

There was that absolute darkness that is possible only in places where human beings are few and live far apart, a darkness in which the only solids are those close enough to touch. So nothing was substantial except his own body and the bed on which he lay listening to the sound of his grandmother singing.

It was hot. Outside his window the nightjars were whistling. It was strange and a little disquieting to hear birds whistling in the darkness. He had kicked away the quilts and wiggled, more than half asleep, out of his clammy underwear, so that now he lay curled up in the salty smell of his naked body, the moist pubescent odor of himself.

Her singing had awakened him many times during the past month. Sometimes he almost wept; sometimes, although he tried not to admit it to himself, he wished that something, anything, even death, would shut her up, and sometimes he went back to sleep without thinking about it at all.

She had sung "I Come to the Garden Alone." He had heard her sing it often before her illness. "That's a Billy Sunday hymn," she always explained. Proudly. Her brother—one of her brothers, David, who was killed with the Sixth Mounted Rifles, or Joseph, who could drink a forty-ouncer of navy rum and shoulder a hogshead of flour without batting an eye—her brother had heard Billy Sunday preach in Boston or Bangor or Portland and afterwards they took up the collection in baskets and every basket was filled to overflowing with five, ten, twenty, fifty and one hundred dollar bills. She described the baskets of money as Mary or Martha might have described the miraculous loaves and fishes.

And she had sung "There Is a Fountain Filled with Blood," while sitting in her rocking chair, a hot brick wrapped in an old sweater or stuffed into an old wool sock pressed hard against her belly to ease the pain, other bricks warming on the back of the wood stove (Enterprise Foundry, Sackville, New Brunswick), the teapot brewing as it always was; she added leaves (Red Rose Orange Pekoe) whenever it became too weak for her taste, emptied them only when there was no room left for water, simply opened the kitchen door and dashed them out into the yard. And what she smelled of was burning wool and ginger cloves and a liniment called Oil of Wintergreen.

> *There is a fountain filled with blood*
> *Drawn from Emmanuel's veins,*
> *And sinners plunged beneath that flood*
> *Lose all their guilty stains.*

The window blinds shrugged like the wings of some enormous mystic bird, like the wings of the blue heron that fed in the swamp between the river and the railroad. He was afraid of the blue heron, had always been afraid of it, yet he would stand sometimes for as long as thirty minutes, spying on it. From the hill overlooking the swamp the bird looked bigger and vastly stronger than he; certainly its legs were longer than his, or so it seemed to him, and he could imagine it running after him—in his imagination it ran rather than flew—and beating him down with its great beak, legs and wings. The wonder that he felt, watching it, was close to worship.

"Mother," a voice said. "Please, Mother." That would be his Aunt
Lorna, who would be hugging together the flaps of a faded red wrapper,
and who would not have put on her glasses. Her eyes looked naked
without glasses—it was the kind of stark white adult nakedness that
made him shifty-eyed with embarrassment; and there were faint pur-
plish indentations on her temples. "Keep the Lower Lights A'Burning"
his grandmother sang now, her voice louder, much louder, derisive and
defiant.

In Aunt Lorna's voice a deep-throated adult sorrow gave way
reluctantly to a whine almost like that of a small girl screwing down the
lid on a sob. He rolled over in bed and raised his head slightly, listening,
but he could not distinguish sentences; only words jutting out like rocks
from a river of murmurs. It was as if between the words *mother* and *bed*
and *late* and *please*, each of them repeated many times, his aunt were
droning wordlessly through her nose with the tip of her tongue pushing
hard against her lower teeth.

The old woman wore a black wig shaped like a soup bowl and
boasted about her jet-black hair. "There's not many women my age that
has hair to compare with mine, with not so much as a wisp of grey in it."
She rouged herself with bits of crepe paper moistened with saliva and
bragged about the youthful redness of her cheeks. As a young woman,
after her husband went to Saskatchewan to harvest wheat and did not
return, she had gone into the woods alone, with a horse, an axe and a
bucksaw, and come out with wood enough to keep her five small
children from freezing although, despite the fire, it got so cold at night
that water froze in the kitchen pails.

> *She's only a bird in a gilded cage,*
> *A wonderful sight to see.*
> *Some think that she's happy and free from care,*
> *But she's not what she seems to be.*

Once, so his grandmother had told him, a cobbler had lived in Lockhartville, a man who made shoes and repaired them. He, Kevin, had never
seen a cobbler but could remember visiting a clockmaker with his father.
The clockmaker wore either a beard or a great drooping moustache,
Kevin could not recall which; his skin was the color of a plucked
chicken, and his hair and suit were the same pepper and salt shade of
grey. What he called his shop was only a corner of his living room, a roll
top desk and a board covered with purple velvet from which hung a
great many pocket watches, some without hands, a few without faces,
their inner workings exposed. The house in which he lived, unlike the
other houses in the village, was lighted with gas rather than kerosene.

Kevin had never seen such white artificial light and the wicks, shaped like the thumbs of mittens but made from transparent gauze, almost mesmerized him. Whenever his grandmother spoke of the cobbler, Kevin gave him the clockmaker's face and hair.

The cobbler's name was Tulley Greenough. Just as it seemed important to Kevin that the man had been a cobbler and not, say, a millhand like his father, so it seemed important that his name had been Tulley Greenough and not John Smith or William Jones. Tulley Greenough was a name to savor, like the names of Caleb, the son of Jephunneh the Kenizzite, and Joshua, the son of Nun, who wholly followed the Lord.

One day the cobbler learned there was a cancer in his body, a cancer being an enormous spider that fed on its victim's flesh. (They had taken a tapeworm three yards long from the stomach of her brother Joseph, the old woman said. She had seen it, preserved in a jar of alcohol. And there was the scarlet woman in Wolfville who gave birth to five grey puppies.) Knowing the cancer would eat away his vitals if he did not destroy it, Tulley Greenough cut himself open with a cobbler's knife – cut himself open, snatched out the great hairy black spider and hurled it into the open fire where, clacking and hissing, it died. Its body was as big as a man's two doubled fists.

Kevin got out of bed and groped his way to the window, knelt there with his arms and chin on the ledge, night insects twanging the screen like an out of tune mandolin, a warm breeze that smelled of fresh-cut grass causing his hair to tickle his ears and forehead.

> *There goes that Boston burglar,*
> *In strong chains he'll be bound;*
> *For some crime or another*
> *He's being sent to Charlestown.*

She had bought an autoharp from a salesman who wore a white linen suit and a straw hat and told her, as she never tired of repeating, that she was a contralto. A contralto. She could interpret dreams and pronounce curses. As a child she had known a witch who made tables dance. She had ridden on a street car in Boston. She could dance a clog, a jig or a hornpipe. She had seen the face of Jesus in the sky. She could make up rhymes. She could live on two dollars a week. And she was a contralto. With jet-black hair and cheeks as apple-red as any sixteen-year-old girl's.

Allister, Kevin's cousin, had despoiled the harp in attempting, with a spike and a pair of pliers, to turn it into a guitar. She entombed the mutilated instrument in a cedar chest, taking it out occasionally before her illness to sing with it cradled, forlorn and silent, in her arms.

As I was leaving old Ireland,
    All in that month of June,
The birds were singing merrily,
    All nature seemed in tune.

Sing me a song, Granner. I like songs that tell stories best. Tell me a story, Granner. But as he had grown older he had become increasingly ashamed of her. Walking beside her on the street in Windsor. Her with her shopping bag and little frilly pink hat she'd bought at a Pythian Sisters rummage sale. The sight of that hat made him want to die and be buried and lie in his grave for a thousand years before being restored to life. Sometimes he shut his eyes tight and clenched his teeth as though preparing for a merciful bullet through the head.

My name is Peter Wheeler,
    I'm from a foreign shore.
I left my native country,
    Never to see it more.

And when she insisted on taking him into Livingston's Restaurant for a treat! Maple walnut ice cream with maple syrup sauce. And a root beer. For herself, a pot of tea. The coins knotted up in a handkerchief inside a change purse, the change purse at the very bottom of a handbag, the clasp of the handbag reinforced with a safety pin. Because money was immeasurably valuable, almost sacred. She would never accept the copper-colored five-cent pieces that were being issued because of the war. And she believed that threads of gold were woven into the paper notes—because if they were paper and nothing more what good would they be? When he was much younger she had shown him the threads, holding up a dollar bill to the light. And he had seen them.

Two nickels for the ice cream. One of them bearing a likeness of King George V. Another nickel for the sauce. A dime for the root beer bearing a very faint likeness of King Edward VII. A nickel and one, two, three, four, five pennies for the tea. Each coin the centre of a separate, solemn transaction. And the waitress so reassured by such weakness, so strengthened by it that her eyes shone with power, like Hitler's.

Poor Mary she lay at the door
As the wind it blew cross the wild moor.

But the worst came when she brought out her lunch. A handful of crackers and a scrap of cheese wrapped in greasy brown paper. To be eaten there while the other three billion people in the world looked on and grinned.

Thinking now of the shame he'd felt, Kevin almost blubbered, not so much out of pity for her or guilt at his secret treason, although these were part of it, as from a sudden desolate awareness of how powerless he was, of how little effect his real wishes had on himself, let alone the world that surrounded him.

He went back to bed and covered himself with the quilts. It was still uncomfortably hot but perhaps if he covered himself he would be more likely to fall asleep.

Tell me a story, Granner. "There wasn't a man in the eighteen counties could hold a candle to Joe Casey." That's how one such story began. Joe Casey, her father and Kevin's great-grandfather, had lived in the time when a man produced everything his family used except sugar, tea, rum and tobacco. To obtain the money for sugar and tea (Joe neither smoked nor drank) he sold stove wood in Wolfville and always just before entering the town he reined in his horses, climbed down from his wagon and adjusted his load, propping it up here and there with crooked sticks, so that it would appear to be larger than it was. Joe Casey could fool a townsman into believing a cord was two cords and a half. His daughter was so impressed with his skill that she was still celebrating it more than forty years after his death.

It was in celebration of Joe Casey as much as from poverty or frugality that she carried a stick of chalk to the rummage sales, with which to alter prices—spitting on her fingers and rubbing out one number, using the chalk to substitute another, so that she bought a pair of shoes for fifteen cents rather than a quarter of a dollar. She could as readily have slipped the shoes into her shopping bag and paid nothing. But that would have been theft, and theft was a sin. Thou shalt not steal. But thou shalt be cunning as a serpent. Blessed are they who survive, saith the Lord.

> *Tell him since he went away*
> *How sad has been our lot:*
> *The landlord came one winter's day*
> *And turned us from our cot.*

And another candle was lit to the memory of Joe Casey when she scavenged at the Windsor dump, gathering pumpkins that had grown there and selling them from door to door. Grown right in the country, Missus, the way the good Lord intended, with no fertilizer except manure. Nothin' like that hothouse stuff they sell in the stores. Fresh country-grown pumpkins. Thou shalt not lie for thou art a Baptist who was put under the water in December after a hole had been chopped in the river ice. But thou shalt outwit the townsmen for thereby cometh glory, and it is good in mine eyes. And thou shalt strive always to survive.

"Mother," this time it was the voice of Kevin's father and Kevin could see him as clearly as with his eyes. Shoeless, grey wool socks darned with yarn of another color, Levis pulled on over long-sleeved flannel underwear, the underwear partially unbuttoned because of the heat, thick curly grey hair on his chest, a belt, and suspenders that bore the word "Police" on their clasps as though designed for small boys playing cops and robbers. Saying, "You can't sit here like this all night, Mother," although he knew well enough that she could, and would.

> *Oh, saddle up my blackest horse*
>   *My grey is not so speedy,*
> *And I'll ride all night and I'll ride all day*
>   *Till I overtake my lady.*

> *Tum-a-link-tum-tum-me-ah-lie,*
>   *Tum-a-link-tum-ty-tee,*
> *I'll ride all night and I'll ride all day*
>   *Till I overtake my lady.*

"Mother, Mother, Mother," said Judd O'Brien, who had said the same thing in almost exactly the same tone a year earlier when he discovered that, by swearing that her adult children were unable to support her, she had persuaded the parish overseer of the poor to pay her two dollars a week.

The two dollars came with Perry Sandford the mailman who drove a Ford except when there was so much snow or mud that he had to harness his roan mare to a buggy or sleigh; and on the day it arrived the old woman enacted several rituals to render herself invisible, putting on a coat and hat she did not wear at any other time–a short black cloth coat with a collar, cuffs and hem of artificial fur, and a sky-blue cloche (she could dance the fox-trot and Charleston and never dreamed there were changing fashions in either clothes or dances). She went out the front door that was otherwise used only by radio licence inspectors, Jehovah's Witnesses, Mormons, peddlers and strangers asking the way to Truro or Halifax. She walked down the road, no matter how deep the snow was, or the mud, head down, limping a little, and met Perry out of sight of her son's house. He drove her to a store in a neighboring village where she cashed the cheque and bought a little treat, a bag of peppermints or maple buds, a loaf of raisin bread that for some unknown reason she always called plum loaf, a bottle of ginger beer, a half-dozen hot cross buns or a jelly roll. (And, oh God, what a sacramental interchange it was, the offering and acceptance of a tumbler half-full of soft drink, a small slice of pastry spread with jellied strawberries. Kevin quailed at the memory of it like one who is suddenly aware that he has been paid an honor he neither earned nor desired yet is too cowardly to refuse.) What was left of the money went into the cedar chest. "I've got the money to bury me," she boasted defiantly.

> Oh western wind when wilt thou blow
>   That the small rain down may rain?
> Christ that my love were in my arms
>   And I in my bed again.

And before he died there was such a hole in Joe Casey's throat that the tea he drank ran out through it and down his collar. He went to the barn and back on all fours and his last words, spoken to his wife who had offered to fetch him water, were: "Nobody has to wait on Joe Casey. Joe Casey can look after himself."

Now Kevin's father and aunt were talking together on the stairs. "That look in her eyes, Judd, when I talked to her; I don't think she even knew who I was, I swear I don't; she'll be dead by mornin' if she keeps this up, you mark my words, she'll be dead by mornin'."

"There's nothin' on God's green earth we can do for her, Lorna, you know that as well as I do, you heard what the doctor said."

"But he could give her somethin' maybe, somethin' to make her sleep."

"I'll be damned if he could, not if she didn't want him to. I don't know how she's hung on as long as she has, so help me God, I don't."

"Well, there's somethin' to be thankful for, the kids are asleep."

> There was a wild colonial boy,
>   Jack Dugan was his name.
> He was born and bred in Ireland,
>   At a place called Castlemaine.

Kevin did not know how long he had been awake. Perhaps he had slept and reawakened. He had heard her sing many songs, that was certain. But perhaps there had been times when he had only dreamt that he heard her singing. He was almost as unsure of the duration and sequence of events as he had been years before when he was delirious with pneumonia.

Should he go to the kitchen and talk with her? He had considered doing so, but was held back by fear; he was always afraid of the sick and unlike many of his fears this one was not coupled with an irresistible fascination. He was terrified of high places, yet climbed the tallest trees and cliffs, almost choking with the exaltation of it. But the fear inspired by the sick only made him shrink back into himself like a rabbit.

He found himself sitting on the couch in the kitchen. He was wearing his brown suit, a white shirt and a necktie, but his feet were bare. As always, the wool pants made his legs itch, and he wondered why he had put them on, together with the jacket, especially when it was so hot.

A gas lamp hung from the ceiling, replacing the kerosene lamp that normally stood on the table by the window. His grandmother sat where she always sat, with her autoharp in her arms, but all its strings had been restored.

And there was a third person in the room.

He was a man whose picture Kevin had seen in a book.

It was a very old book and had long since disappeared. His mother had read to him from it before he could read. He remembered a poem with the refrain *curfew shall not ring tonight* and another that contained the lines:

> *Morgan, Morgan the raider,*
> *And Morgan's terrible men,*
> *With Bowie knives and pistols*
> *Come galloping down the glen.*

Those poems were among the visions he had experienced in the dream time of infancy. They were one with the orchid he had brought home from a forbidden visit to the swamp and the falling star he had seen explode like a Roman candle when, in broad daylight, it crashed into the backyard.

There were pictures with the poems. In fact the pictures were part of the poems. There was a girl in a long white dress, swinging from the tongue of a bell that hung in a tower so tall that the top of it must have pricked the sky. There was a boy who wore a sword and spurs, one hand grasping his horse's saddle, the other reaching out to a woman; she, too, wore a long white dress.

And there was a picture that, as far as he could recall, did not connect with anything else.

A man sat at a desk surrounded by books and manuscripts and test tubes. He wore a costume that Kevin had later seen again in pictures of Keats, Byron and Shelley. And he was staring at a skull. It was the skull that had fascinated Kevin. Often, while looking at it, he had pressed his fingers against his face so as to feel his own skull under its thin jacket of flesh. He had never looked so closely at the man, yet the picture might not have excited him so much if the man had not been there. And now the man was sitting not eight feet away from him.

Neither the man nor the old woman seemed to be aware of Kevin's presence. She was performing for this man, Kevin realized, as she had performed for that other man in the white suit and the straw hat.

> As I was going to Derby town
>   All on a market day,
> I met the biggest ram, sir,
>   That ever fed on hay.
>
> And didn't he ramble!
>   He rambled up and down,
> And all around the town,
>   He rambled till the butcher cut him down.

She laughed and, awakening again in his own bed, Kevin heard her laughing. Her laughter was so joyous that it tickled the nerves in Kevin's throat so that he also laughed.

> Now this ram he had two horns, sir,
>   Two horns made out of brass,
> And one came out of his head, sir,
>   The other came out of his arse.
>
> And didn't he ramble!
>   He rambled up and down,
> And all around the town,
>   He rambled till the butcher cut him down.

"And what do you say to that, you old bugger? Tell me straight out now, you old fart, what do you say to that?"

"Mother, please," Lorna said.

"Mother, for God's sake," said Judd.

"Here's another for you," said Kevin's grandmother, and she sang:

> There was an old woman from Wexford,
>   In Wexford she did dwell,
> Who loved her husband dearly,
>   But another man twice as well!

Next morning when Kevin got up she was lying down in her room upstairs but by then it no longer mattered; the doctor had been there and gone and that didn't matter either. But it mattered very much, not only then but ever afterwards, that his grandmother, an old peasant woman, had sat up all through the last night of her life, singing songs to entertain herself and Death.

Works by Alden Nowlan

FICTION

Miracle at Indian River. Toronto: Clarke, Irwin, 1968.
Various Persons Named Kevin O'Brien. Toronto: Clarke, Irwin, 1973.

POETRY

The Rose and the Puritan. Fredericton: University of New Brunswick, 1958.
A Darkness in the Earth. Eureka, Calif.: Hearse, 1959.
Under the Ice. Toronto: Ryerson, 1960.
Wind in a Rocky Country. Toronto: Emblem Books, 1960.
The Things Which Are. Toronto: Contact, 1962.
Bread, Wine and Salt. Toronto: Clarke, Irwin, 1967.
The Mysterious Naked Man. Toronto: Clarke, Irwin, 1969.
Playing the Jesus Game: Selected Poems. Trumansburg, N.Y.: New/Books, 1970.
Between Tears and Laughter. Toronto: Clarke, Irwin, 1971.
I'm a Stranger Here Myself. Toronto: Clarke, Irwin, 1974.
Smoked Glass. Toronto: Clarke, Irwin, 1977.
I Might Not Tell Everybody This. Toronto: Clarke, Irwin, 1982.

DRAMA

Frankenstein (with Walter Learning). Toronto: Clarke, Irwin, 1976.
The Incredible Murder of Cardinal Tosca. Fredericton: Learning Productions, 1978.

CRITICISM

Double Exposure. Toronto: Clarke, Irwin, 1978.

HISTORY

Campobello: The Outer Island. Toronto: Clarke, Irwin, 1975.

Interviews with Alden Nowlan

The Fiddlehead, 81 (August-September-October, 1969), 5-13.
Saturday Night, 88 (May, 1973), 29-32.
Canadian Literature, 67 (Winter, 1975), 8-17.

Ernest Buckler

In his first novel, *The Mountain and the Valley* (1952), and in all his fiction, Ernest Buckler depicts the Nova Scotian world of the Annapolis Valley where he and his fictional characters reside. He has never felt the need to move beyond small farming communities to find settings for his writings. "You don't have to wander all over the bloody world and explore every niche and cranny in it to find out how people behave. In a small community like this even, you have a representation of every kind of action, of every kind of psychological mode. The whole thing, the whole macrocosm, is here in microcosm. You don't have to know any more people than these to know what is going on in the human psyche. So this is why I haven't felt the exorbitant need to travel; I feel it's pretty well all here."

Born in Dalhousie West, Nova Scotia, in 1908, Buckler received his undergraduate degree from Dalhousie University and his master's degree from the University of Toronto. After spending five years with a Toronto insurance company, he returned to live in Nova Scotia in 1936, settling on a farm near Bridgetown.

For Alden Nowlan, *The Mountain and the Valley* "is not only the best novel yet written by a Canadian, but one of the great novels of the English language." It is the story, from early childhood until death, of David Canaan, introspective and gifted with the spirit and understanding of an artist. Nestled in the quiet farming village of Entremont in the Annapolis Valley, the Canaan home is on the highway that runs through the Valley. On the north side of the highway is the North Mountain, "solid blue in the afternoon light of December that was pale and sharp as starlight, except for the milky ways of choppings where traces of the first snow never quite disappeared." On the south side is the South Mountain, "solid blue too at the bottom where the dark spruces huddled close, but snow-grey higher up where the sudden steepness and the leafless hardwood began." Though the mountain slopes are less than two kilometres high at their topmost point, they shut in the valley completely. Initially, David regards his small community as the embodiment of warmth and comfort; later, he comes to feel himself restricted within this isolated and isolating world.

Like Buckler, the character David is quiet and sensitive. Yet Buckler cautions the reader, "This novel— though it did try to show the texture of life in a village not altogether unlike the one I do know—and love— best, was not literally *autobiographical.* Except as all writing is—between the lines— autobiographical."

David is the centre of the novel, and the people who surround him help to define him: his grandmother, Ellen; his father, Joseph; his mother, Martha; his twin sister, Anna; and his older brother, Chris. For Buckler, the focus of fiction must be on the characters. "I think people's insides are so much more important and intriguing than their outsides. I think that the most important constituents of life itself are 'phrases' of illumination, not the chattering verbs. In relentless busy novels, I always feel like saying, 'Oh, for the love of God, stand still a minute till we can see what you're made of!' "

The Mountain and the Valley is a portrait of an artist as a young man in Nova Scotia. The first section of the novel consists of childhood incidents that the older David recalls. In "The Play," the climactic and final episode of this section, eleven-year-old David is participating in the Christmas concert at his school. He is appearing with thirteen-year-old Effie, whose father has recently drowned. That tragic accident has drawn David close to Effie: "He felt an awful guilt, to be without suffering himself, to have his own father so wonderfully safe beside him." His affection and empathy for Effie contribute to his behavior on stage the night of the concert.

The Play

The next night was the night of the concert. David's head felt light. The words of the play kept up an uncontrollable chatter in his mind. Supper made a taste in his mouth like the taste after running.

"Why won't you let us *hear* your piece, Dave?" his mother said.

He couldn't tell her why not. She wouldn't understand about the curtain and the spell. He felt as if his refusing was betrayal–but he could only speak the lines aloud *there*, or when he was by himself. Or with Effie and Anna.

He was saying them to himself as he poked hay in to the cows. He didn't hear his father's footsteps behind him.

"That sounds all right," Joseph said.

But they sounded silly to David then. He stopped short. He tried to imitate his father's voice in the barn. "Git yer head *back* there, you damn..." he shouted at the black cow.

As the time came closer still, the words touched his mind with the chill of bedclothes touching his flesh times he'd had a fever. His arms were trembling so when his mother made last-minute alterations in the sleeve lengths of his new suit that he could hardly hold them straight at his sides. He almost wished he'd refused to take a piece at all, like Chris had. Chris never had to do anything but *listen*.

A wire was stretched across the platform of the schoolhouse. Bedsheets were looped over it for a curtain. Behind this curtain a small corner of the stage had been screened off for a dressing room. Here the teacher and the children were clotted.

The children whispered frenziedly. They fussed continuously with their costumes. They ran to the teacher with bright, terrible confidences: "Miss Speakman, Tim can't find his star!" "Miss Speakman, the oil's almost below the wick." "Miss Speakman, it looks like the curtain's caught–right there, see?"

Miss Speakman fixed the lamp and the curtain. She made Tim another tinsel star. She told Cora, through the pins in her mouth, for heaven's sake to keep her head still. She said, "Danny, don't you dare to laugh tonight and spoil *everything.*"

Some of the children got out the scribbler pages their pieces were written on. The pages were worn furry at the creases. They read them over desperately, as if to catch the words before they rushed off the lines. Some whispered them out loud in a solemn voice. Some moved their lips and said them over only in their heads. Some of them peeked through the curtain.

The audience had straggled up the road with their lanterns, in groups of two and four, talking around the edge of things as they always did when they went together to something after dark. Now they were cramped awkwardly into the desk seats.

Once they had sat there as children themselves. They had had the thought ahead of no more school shiver in them like a different breath. But now they waited, patiently, for their own children to come out and say their pieces. These children seemed younger than they had ever been. They seemed older than these children would ever be.

The children peeked and giggled.

"I saw Mother, but she didn't see *me.*"

"Old Herb Hennessey's there!"

"Miss Speakman? I gotta go out!"

("Oh Lord! Well, slip out the side door. Now don't get snow on that crepe paper.")

"Miss Speakman, what time is it?"

"What time is it, Miss Speakman?"

"How much longer?"

("Oh, please be quiet. Why can't you act like David there? He isn't making a sound.")

He couldn't. He was absolutely still inside. The moment when he must say the first lines of the play had started to move toward him.

There was no comfort in anyone near. It was worse than being sick. Then the other faces were outside your pain, but when they smiled at you the pain softened. Now he was absolutely alone. Even Anna's smile was the smile of a photograph, a smile of some other time. The people outside the curtain seemed to have a cruel strangeness about them. He felt as if nakedness had spread his face and body wide and unmanageable. The words of the play were frozen. They had no feeling at all.

He tried to think of tomorrow. Somehow, tomorrow must come.

"Shhhhhh..." The moment stopped moving. The curtain was pulled back.

"Ladies and gentlemen..."

David listened to Anna's opening recitation. She said her piece better than the others–almost as if it were something she'd thought up herself; only hesitant for trying to say it exactly the way he'd told her to.

(For some reason Martha felt a little catch in her throat when Anna bowed–the rosette on her shoulder wasn't quite straight. She wished she could adjust it. And Joseph felt a kind of incredulity that his own Anna had been carrying around all those heavy words, all that time, behind her small soft face.)

The others said their pieces doggedly, as if they were reading the words off their mind. The spring of their nervousness kept jerking the words out one by one until the spring finally ran down. They said the funny parts in the dialogue as they read the words in a lesson they weren't quite sure how to pronounce. David wondered why the audience laughed. You could see they weren't speaking to each *other*; it was just the lines of the book talking back and forth. When they came back to the dressing room their excitement was only because it was over; not because for a minute they had made themselves into someone else.

The tableau came next. The teacher had planned this as a stunning surprise. The children had been pledged not to breathe a word of it beforehand.

Anna and Charlotte stood on two chairs. Effie stood, between and above them, on a step ladder. Everything was swathed first in sheets, then in billows of cheesecloth. The three figures were supposed to come out of a cloud. Their hair was combed out loose about their shoulders: Anna's a soft brown; Charlotte's coal black; and Effie's a light thin gold. Each had a silver crown–of stiff cardboard covered with pressed-out tea lead. Each had across her breast a wide band of flour bag dyed scarlet; with cut-out lettering so that a legend showed in white from the cheesecloth beneath.

Anna's was FAITH; Charlotte's HOPE; and Effie's LOVE.

"Now don't move," the teacher whispered.

The audience was as immobile as the girls. It was like a spell. It was as if some beautiful flower that grew only in warm climates had suddenly sprung up in their own fields. They didn't see where the cheesecloth gaped behind the ladder, or the little cracks in Effie's crown where the tea lead was joined or the tiny trembling of Anna's hand or Charlotte's black shoes that she had seen before Christmas.

(Bess was so startled she almost cried out. It was like a vision. So much like the picture of Effie she'd had sometimes in thought. She prayed, "Don't move, oh, please don't move." No woman her own age was sitting near her—they had located where she was sitting their first glance through the door, then sat somewhere else. But she didn't care. Effie was the loveliest thing anyone had ever seen and she was hers. Even if no one said so to her, they needn't, it was true...if Effie could just hold it that way.)

The curtain closed. Martha leaned ahead and whispered to Bess, "Wasn't they beautiful? What in the world held Effie *up* there?"

The defiance wilted. She could scarcely answer for tears: Martha had spoken to her about their two children being beautiful in the same way; she had added a little joke.

"I don't know," Bess said, "but she never moved, did she?"

The teacher disentangled the cheesecloth both hastily and with caution not to tear it. It would be cut up and distributed for table throws. The older boys, Chris amongst them, came back to set up the castle for the play.

The castle was a cardboard front; crenelated at the top like a geography castle, and nailed to uprights of two-by-four.

David wished desperately that he was Chris. Whatever Chris had to do was always so simple. It was like lifting. The weight was there and the muscles were there. You just put them together.

Effie was a princess, so she kept on her crown. She had a ruby necklace of wild rosebush seed-sacs. She had a brooch of Ellen's at the neck of her silk dress (though it had a real diamond, it didn't shine near so brightly as the rhinestone brooch her mother had bought her in town), and she wore a beaded and tasseled sash that Martha had come across in the attic. Her slippers came from an old trunk of Ellen's. They were too large, but they had high heels and were made not of leather but of some brocaded material almost like dress stuff.

David wore only his plain corduroy suit at first. At the very end he'd step behind the castle and come out in the crimson cape, with a piece of snow-white rabbit fur sewn on the collar. They had copied it from a picture of the little Plantagenets in his history book.

"And now, ladies and gentlemen..."

"Come on, Dave," Anna said.

She took his hand, as if for a minute she were the older one because it was he who must go. She could go no farther with him than the edge of the curtain. David stepped out on the stage.

It was like the time they'd taken Anna to the doctor's office. When they were almost there everything had become hostile and unfamiliar with the thought of Anna going in; but they had walked up the street just the same, because there was no way to jump out of the relentless minute now.

A searching light seemed to come from every face in the audience and focus on him.

"I came to play with you." The words might have been pebbles lying in his mouth.

They dropped through the surface of the silence and disappeared. But when the silence closed over them again it had a different quality. When the chipyard was so awry you didn't know where to begin cleaning it up but picked up a random object anyway, as soon as you did, the total plan sprang up instantly. The next words came like the notes of a tune on the organ your fingers went to without watching, as if they were the only notes there. He couldn't remember *learning* them at all. Faster and faster he came to the princess and the castle, actually. In the routeless movement of light or thought.

"Do you *always* play alone?"

He commanded the silence now, surely, masterfully. Now they all listened as if to someone who had come home from glory in a far place—not in envy, but endowed with some of the glory themselves, because that one's knowledge of his own wonder before them had no pride in it.

He thought, not proudly, but with gratitude toward them: oh, I'm glad I'm not like the others now. He knew how they were looking at him. They'd looked at him that way the day he calculated a rafter's length down to the fraction of an inch, by right-angled triangles. They hadn't believed he could find that out with just a pencil, but they'd taken a chance on cutting it as he said and it fitted exactly.

"I play alone too."

Oh, it was perfect now. He was creating something out of nothing. He was creating exactly the person the words in the play were meant for. He had the whole world of make-believe to go to. They had only the actual, the one that *came* to them.

How much better this was than saying the words to himself had been! The kind of better you could never imagine, until you were into it. (You thought you'd rather sit in the corner and listen to the fiddle music, but they made you fill up the set even if you were small; and then when you polkaed out they all clapped, they all laughed so warmly because where did you ever learn to dance like that? And then, oh then, when you all joined hands in the Big Ring!)

This was better than the cosiness of doing anything alone. He'd never do anything alone again. He'd take them with him always, in their watching. Closer somehow *because* they followed. It would be like the burning loyalty to his father (somehow suddenly to his father's mended socks drying on the oven door), when he spelled the long hard words in the evening lesson exactly right. Oh, this was perfect. There was a bated wonder coming from their faces: to know that this was David, but a David with the shine on him (they'd never suspected!) of understanding and showing them how everything was.

The first scene was over, and the curtains were drawn together for a minute.

One time the whole family had tried a thousand dollar contest. The object was to total correctly the myriad numbers that made up the shape of a huge elephant. They had traced the numbers one by one with dye, and he had added as they went. They had checked and rechecked until they were tired out. But when the total was sealed in the envelope, ready to go, a shine went out over everything. They had a lunch, and whenever two would reach for the sugar at the same time they'd both laugh and say, "No, no, you go on." All the next day he'd think suddenly of someone: "She's pretty, ain't she!" or "He's awfully strong." If anyone made a joke he'd laughed right out loud it seemed so funny. If he read a story that was sad he'd almost cry, because he'd never noticed the sadness in it like that before. If he looked over any work he'd done in his scribblers it seemed as if he'd done it far better than he'd known at the time. If any man spoke to him on the road, after he'd gone by, he'd think: "Gee, he's about as good a man as there is *around* here."

A shine like that went out over everything now.

None of all this was consecutive and time-taking like thought. It was glimpsed instantaneously, like the figures of space. And orchestrated in the subliminal key of memory: cold water reaching to the roots of his tongue when thirst in the haymow was like meal in his mouth...the touch of the crisp dollar bill he had changed his dented pennies for at the bank in town...the light on the water curling white over the dam when his line first came alive with the dark, secret sweep of the trout...the cut clover breathing through his open window just before summer sleep... the sound of his father's sleighbells the night of the day he'd sent for the fountain pen...the date of the Battle of Flodden looked up tremblingly in the book and found to be exactly the same as the one he'd put down, uncertainly, in the examination...the doctor coming out of the room and saying that Anna would be all right...his own name in printed letters on the envelope from the city...the moment in the dream when he climbed to the top of the mountain and looked down...

The curtains parted again for the last scene.

"But I am a prince..."

(He *is* some kind of prince, Martha thought. And Joseph watched as if he were touching a garment he was proud to own, but which he could never wear, because its texture was so much finer than his skin's.)

"I am a prince..."

When all the stray scraps in the door yard had been gathered into one pile, the flame roared through them, melting and levelling them, gathering up all their separate piecefulness into one great uniform consummation.

He thought, I will be the greatest actor in the whole world.

He stepped through the door of the castle for his cloak. He thought: When I go out, I'll kiss her. That wasn't in the play, but that's how it would really be.

He kissed Effie so precipitately that she was startled. Her head went back. Her crown came off and rolled across the floor.

Jud Spinney was lounging in a group of young men at the back of the room. He shouted gleefully, "That's it, Dave. Slap em *to* her!"

Once a sudden blow of sickness had struck the pit of his stomach when he smoked a moss cigarette. It sheared away everything but the shape and movements of the other boys watching him turn grey. This moment now was shorn of all its dimensions as suddenly as that one. He saw the raw edges of the flimsy cardboard and the verdigris on the clasp weldings of Effie's rhinestone brooch. He saw the parched underskin of the rabbit's fur on his foolish damn cloak. They were like the flame of a lamp that has burned on into the daylight.

Once he'd been trying to imitate the smile of a Zane Grey hero in the mirror and he'd turned and Chris was standing in the door. He felt the shame of having spoken the foolish words in this damn foolish play as he'd felt shame then.

Shame struck first, then anger. His breath trembled. His lips puckered over his teeth. The anger gave him a rough physical shove. He threw the cape on the floor, as one smashes a mirror that reminds of some hateful scar. Tripping over it, he stumbled from the stage.

The teacher cried, "Dave..." She tried to close the curtain quickly. "Dave..." Anna cried. He paid no attention. He grabbed his coat and rubbers. His cap was buried in the pile of other caps. He ran out the side door in his bare head.

He ran toward home, not because home or any other place was a place of escape, but in the blind way he'd pulled on his rubbers outside the door because they'd happened to be in his hand. He didn't feel the cold on his head or, missing the path, the weight of the drifts he plunged into. The anger hummed inside him louder than any information of feeling.

The shameful anger at that damn foolish...that damn treacherous play. The furious hatred of himself, of everyone, of everything. One rubber came off in the drifts. His new suit became sodden. He didn't notice. He despised, as if it were another person, the foolish treacherous part of himself that listened to books. That was the only part of him anyone saw...they thought that's what he was *like*. It was like some damn fool that kept telling people he was your brother.

He *knew* who yelled at him, the ignorant know-nothin. Oh, he'd fix him, when he got older. He'd never forget. The damn thing would say something smart and wait for the rest to laugh and then he'd just stare at him until he felt that even his face was funny-looking, and then he wouldn't hit him—oh, no—he'd just take him by the collar and turn him around...and walk away.

He hated the others almost equally, as if their hearing the guffaw had made them accomplices. When he grew up they'd *see* what he was like. A great surge went through him to leap ahead into time, into the strength that was coming.

Oh, they'd be surprised when they found out what he'd been like all the time. They thought he wasn't like his father. They'd see. A surge of identification with his father flooded him stronger than the grinding twist of the anger: his father's toughness which was to the toughness of the others as blood to dye. If the bastards had sense enough to know that. *Them* laughing at *him*. Oh, when he grew up he wouldn't make any account of the logs being jammed or his feet being wet or his axe being dull. When they knocked the snow off the bushes ahead of them in the log road, he'd come along behind them and walk right through the bushes and say, "For God's sake, what'r'ye doin?" Caution, caution—they'd see what he thought of that, they'd feel pretty goddarn small.

He said over all the oaths he knew in a harsh grinding pride. They thought it was kind of smart when they swore themselves. But they were kind of scared too. They laughed when he swore. They didn't know how he could swear. They didn't know how to swear at all. He'd swear so it scared them.

He said over all the words of sex he knew. They teased him about girls. They fooled around girls, but when it got right down to hard, meaning stuff they were kind of scared about that too. They'd feel pretty small when he showed them.... They wouldn't tease him then. They'd look kind of sober and foolish because not one of them would dare to go *that* far.

He'd go 'way from this place so fast and make so much money...and when he come back he'd drive down the road in a big car and pick up Bess (yes, Bess was the only one...) and when he passed any of them he'd nod at them as if he couldn't *quite* place them. He'd have to speak to them as long as he was here, but he'd never laugh with them again. He'd never have anything to say to them when he or they were in any kind of doubt or trouble, not as long as he lived.

"Dave...Dave..." He heard his father's voice. It was loud and deep, but shaken with calling as he ran.

He heard his mother's voice too, fainter, yet with more asking, "Dave...David..."

But the anger (which always bit itself more bitterly inside him when someone else tried to save something for him which because it was imperfect in any part he had to destroy totally) glowed fresh again. If they say anything to me when I get home, if they just open their mouth to me...

The running was hot in his throat now. His hands curled inward, flopping at his sides. He forced himself to run faster still. You couldn't escape this minute, everywhere you ran it was there. But you had to get home as soon as possible.

Ellen was still up. She stared at him.

"David!" she exclaimed. "Where's your cap? You'll catch your death of cold. Where's...?"

"I don't care," he shouted. It was not an answer to her, but to his own tumbling thoughts. "I'm all right. I don't care what you say."

He ran upstairs and into his room. He closed the door and began to tear off his clothes. The orange he'd taken from the tree, to eat after the concert, was lying on the bureau. He didn't touch it. Its skin was beginning to shrivel.

He heard his mother and father, then Chris and Anna, come in. He heard the nervous jumble of their first words with Ellen.

Martha came to the bottom of the stairs and called, "Dave." She put her foot on the first step.

"Shut up!" he screamed. "Leave me alone!"

Martha hesitated. Then she went back toward the kitchen.

It was no use. When the other children hurt themselves or were sick, she'd hold them and look into their faces. Strangely enough then, despite the pity or the fear, she'd feel how awful it must be for people

who had no children at all. But with David, those were the only times
when she seemed to lose him.

She hung up his cap which she'd been carrying. And looking at it on
the nail, she felt the most hopeless kind of wretchedness. She didn't
know why, or just what it was; but there was something about David's
clothes when he wasn't inside them that made her think of all the times
when his feet might have been cold, or he might have been hungry
somewhere and not wanted to ask anyone for anything to eat, or he
might have been frightened, without knowing it, and no one else there.

Joseph said nothing. How could he? Even when David was *willing* to
talk he couldn't seem to find any words that fitted what he meant to say
back.

David lay with his eyes closed when Chris came into the room and
undressed.

Chris didn't speak; but after he was in bed a while he let one arm fall
across David's shoulder as if it might have been a movement in his sleep.
The only way of reaching out that Chris knew was touch. David was like
a stranger when something was wrong. But somehow when Dave was
in trouble like this he seemed more like his own brother than ever.

David twisted away from Chris's arm and moved over to the very
edge of the bed. He heard Anna come upstairs. She stopped a minute
outside his door. Then he heard her go into her own room.

It wasn't until the house was completely still that the anger began to
settle. It settled bit by bit, building up a sore quiet lump physically in his
heart. He thought of the way he had sworn and bla'guarded. He said
over his prayers in fear and pleading.

Then he thought of the door, closed tight. (Chris, who humored
David's wishes even when they puzzled him, had left it as he'd found it.)
He thought of Anna standing there outside the door, but not intruding as
much as a word. Of the time his mother had worked at the cost of a new
wallpaper all evening and after she'd gone to bed he'd come across her
clumsy figures and seen that the multiplication was wrong and she could
never afford the wallpaper now. Of the time in town his father had
bought him the expensive suit instead of the durable one, because
another boy in the store was trying on only the expensive ones. He
thought of all the times any of them had surprised him with something
they thought he'd always wanted, and then tried not to let him see that
they could see it wasn't what he'd wanted at all. Fiercely, and guiltily
now, he thought of all the times in town when they'd fallen back from
the counter as better-dressed people approached and he'd separated
himself from them a little. (Oh, if it could only happen again.)

He wished the door could blow open, but it wouldn't. He wished he could make out he wanted a drink and go downstairs and leave the door open when he came up again, but he couldn't. He wished he could put Chris's arm back over his shoulder, but he couldn't. He wished he could open the door and go in and say something to Anna—not about this, just anything—but he couldn't.

He pulled the quilts over his head. He began to sob. "Anna... Anna..."

The next morning he went to look for the rubber he'd lost. As he came near Jud's place he kept watching the house, as if it might suddenly move toward the road. He wasn't afraid, but he'd desperately not know what attitude to take if Jud himself came out. The anger was no longer there to instruct him.

The snow had drifted over his tracks. Chris found the rubber in the spring, but he said nothing about it.

Works by Ernest Buckler

FICTION

The Mountain and the Valley. Toronto:
Clarke, Irwin, 1952.
The Cruelest Month. Toronto: McClelland
and Stewart, 1963.
Ox Bells and Fireflies. Toronto: McClelland
and Stewart, 1968.
*The Rebellion of Young David and Other
Stories.* Toronto: McClelland and
Stewart, 1975.

ESSAYS (PROSE AND VERSE)

Nova Scotia: Window on the Sea. Toronto:
McClelland and Stewart, 1973.
Whirligig. Toronto: McClelland and
Stewart, 1977.

Interview with Ernest Buckler

Conversations with Canadian Novelists.
Edited by Donald Cameron. Toronto:
Macmillan, 1973. Vol. 1, pp. 3-11.

Alistair MacLeod

"From time to time there are writers who come riding out of the hinterlands of this country called Canada. And they are writing about a life that they really know down to its smallest detail. And it is a life that is fierce and hard and beautiful and close to the bone." Though Alistair MacLeod used these words to describe other contemporary fiction writers, his phrases apply equally well to his own short stories.

Born in North Battleford, Saskatchewan, in 1936, MacLeod grew up in the coal-mining areas of Alberta and in the farming areas of Dunvegan and Inverness on the west coast of Cape Breton. He pursued most of his education in the Maritimes, obtaining his teaching certificate at Nova Scotia Teachers College, his bachelor's degree at Saint Francis Xavier University, and his master's degree at the University of New Brunswick. He received his doctorate from Notre Dame University in Indiana. Though he has worked as milkman, logger, and miner, his main areas of interest are teaching and writing. Currently a member of the Department of English at the University of Windsor, he has published both fiction and poetry in numerous periodicals in Canada and the United States.

The settings of MacLeod's collection of short stories, *The Lost Salt Gift of Blood* (1976), are often the rugged and turbulent terrain of Cape Breton, where life is "fierce and hard and beautiful and close to the bone." With a range of authentic details and a variety of tones from mellow laughter to tender pathos, MacLeod captures the conflicts within the sturdy Scottish families of the area. Cape Bretoners see themselves as distinct from Nova Scotians; they are islanders, not mainlanders. (The Strait of Canso marks more than a metaphorical boundary, as Cape Breton was often politically separated from Nova Scotia, yet ultimately reunited to it in 1820.) MacLeod's Cape Bretoners tend to be rugged individualists who live by and usually off the sea and find strength and solace in their deep-rooted traditions. His stories follow a pattern of slow modernization and consequent erosion of the traditional rural Cape Breton communities, as the older generations find themselves confronted by dissatisfied offspring who leave for the mainland, abandoning their parents' world in search of employment or advanced education.

In "The Boat," which was originally published in 1968 and later included in *The Lost Salt Gift of Blood*, the narrator is a professor "at a great Midwestern university." He looks back on the winter when he was fifteen, recalling the harbor, the wharf, and the boat that evoke his memories of his family. Unlike his mother, whose horizons were "the very literal ones she scanned with her dark and fearless eyes," he had sought more distant and more challenging horizons. As the narrator recaptures his Cape Breton childhood, he comes to know and understand his feelings for his parents.

The Boat

There are times even now, when I awake at four o'clock in the morning with the terrible fear that I have overslept; when I imagine that my father is waiting for me in the room below the darkened stairs or that the shorebound men are tossing pebbles against my window while blowing their hands and stomping their feet impatiently on the frozen steadfast earth. There are times when I am half out of bed and fumbling for socks and mumbling for words before I realize that I am foolishly alone, that no one waits at the base of the stairs and no boat rides restlessly in the waters by the pier.

At such times only the grey corpses on the overflowing ashtray beside my bed bear witness to the extinction of the latest spark and silently await the crushing out of the most recent of their fellows. And then because I am afraid to be alone with death, I dress rapidly, make a great to-do about clearing my throat, turn on both faucets in the sink and proceed to make loud splashing ineffectual noises. Later I go out and walk the mile to the all night restaurant.

In the winter it is a very cold walk and there are often tears in my eyes when I arrive. The waitress usually gives a sympathetic little shiver and says, "Boy, it must be really cold out there; you got tears in your eyes."

"Yes," I say, "it sure is; it really is."

And then the three or four of us who are always in such places at such times make uninteresting little protective chit-chat until the dawn reluctantly arrives. Then I swallow the coffee, which is always bitter, and leave with a great busy rush because by that time I have to worry about being late and whether I have a clean shirt and whether my car will start and about all the other countless things one must worry about when he teaches at a great Midwestern university. And I know then that that day will go by as have all the days of the past ten years, for the call and the voices and the shapes and the boat were not really there in the early morning's darkness and I have all kinds of comforting reality to prove it. They are only shadows and echoes, the animals a child's hands make on the wall by lamplight, and the voices from the rain barrel; the cuttings from an old movie made in the black and white of long ago.

I first became conscious of the boat in the same way and at almost the same time that I became aware of the people it supported. My earliest recollection of my father is a view from the floor of gigantic rubber boots and then of being suddenly elevated and having my face pressed against the stubble of his cheek, and of how it tasted of salt and of how he smelled of salt from his red-soled rubber boots to the shaggy whiteness of his hair.

When I was very small, he took me for my first ride in the boat. I rode the half-mile from our house to the wharf on his shoulders and I remember the sound of his rubber boots galumphing along the gravel beach, the tune of the indecent little song he used to sing and the odor of the salt.

The floor of the boat was permeated with the same odor and in its constancy I was not aware of change. In the harbor we made our little circle and returned. He tied the boat by its painter, fastened the stern to its permanent anchor and lifted me high over his head to the solidity of the wharf. Then he climbed up the little iron ladder that led to the wharf's cap, placed me once more upon his shoulders and galumphed off again.

When we returned to the house everyone made a great fuss over my precocious excursion and asked, "How did you like the boat?" "Were you afraid in the boat?" "Did you cry in the boat?" They repeated "the boat" at the end of all their questions and I knew it must be very important to everyone.

My earliest recollection of my mother is of being alone with her in the mornings while my father was away in the boat. She seemed to be always repairing clothes that were "torn in the boat," preparing food "to be eaten in the boat" or looking for "the boat" through our kitchen window which faced upon the sea. When my father returned about noon, she would ask, "Well how did things go in the boat today?" It was the first question I remember asking, "Well how did things go in the boat today?" "Well how did things go in the boat today?"

The boat in our lives was registered at Port Hawkesbury. She was what Nova Scotians called a Cape Island boat and was designed for the small inshore fishermen who sought the lobsters of the spring and the mackerel of summer and later the cod and haddock and hake. She was thirty-two feet long and nine wide, and was powered by an engine from a Chevrolet truck. She had a marine clutch and a high speed reverse gear and was painted light green with the name *Jenny Lynn* stencilled in black letters on her bow and painted on an oblong plate across her stern. Jenny Lynn had been my mother's maiden name and the boat was called after her as another link in the chain of tradition. Most of the boats that berthed at the wharf bore the names of some female member of their owner's household.

I say this now as if I knew it all then. All at once, all about boat dimensions and engines, and as if on the day of my first childish voyage I noticed the difference between a stencilled name and a painted name. But of course it was not that way at all, for I learned it all very slowly and there was not time enough.

I learned first about our house which was one of about fifty which marched around the horseshoe of our harbor and the wharf which was its heart. Some of them were so close to the water that during a storm the sea spray splashed against their windows while others were built farther along the beach as was the case with ours. The houses and their people, like those of the neighboring towns and villages, were the result of Ireland's discontent and Scotland's Highland Clearances and America's War of Independence. Impulsive emotional Catholic Celts who could not bear to live with England and shrewd determined Protestant Puritans who, in the years after 1776, could not bear to live without.

The most important room in our house was one of those oblong old-fashioned kitchens heated by a wood and coal burning stove. Behind the stove was a box of kindlings and beside it a coal scuttle. A heavy wooden table with leaves that expanded or reduced its dimensions stood in the middle of the floor. There were five wooden homemade chairs which had been chipped and hacked by a variety of knives. Against the east wall, opposite the stove, there was a couch which sagged in the middle and had a cushion for a pillow, and above it a shelf which contained matches, tobacco, pencils, odd fish hooks, bits of twine, and a tin can filled with bills and receipts. The south wall was dominated by a window which faced the sea and on the north there was a five-foot board which bore a variety of clothes hooks and the burdens of each. Beneath the board there was a jumble of odd footwear, mostly of rubber. There was also, on this wall, a barometer, a map of the marine area and a shelf which held a tiny radio. The kitchen was shared by all of us and was a buffer zone between the immaculate order of ten other rooms and the disruptive chaos of the single room that was my father's.

My mother ran her house as her brothers ran their boats. Everything was clean and spotless and in order. She was tall and dark and powerfully energetic. In later years she reminded me of the women of Thomas Hardy, particularly Eustacia Vye, in a physical way. She fed and clothed a family of seven children, making all of the meals and most of the clothes. She grew miraculous gardens and magnificent flowers and raised broods of hens and ducks. She would walk miles on berry-picking expeditions and hoist her skirts to dig for clams when the tide was low. She was fourteen years younger than my father whom she had married when she was twenty-six, and had been a local beauty for a period of ten years. My mother was of the sea as were all of her people, and her horizons were the very literal one she scanned with her dark and fearless eyes.

Between the kitchen clothes rack and barometer a door opened into my father's bedroom. It was a room of disorder and disarray. It was as if the wind which so often clamored about the house succeeded in entering this single room and after whipping it into turmoil stole quietly away to renew its knowing laughter from without.

My father's bed was against the south wall. It always looked rumpled and unmade because he lay on top of it more than he slept within any folds it might have had. Beside it, there was a little brown table. An archaic goose-necked reading light, a battered table radio, a mound of wooden matches, one or two packages of tobacco, a deck of cigarette papers and an overflowing ashtray cluttered its surface. The brown larvae of tobacco shreds and the grey flecks of ash covered both the table and the floor beneath it. The once-varnished surface of the table was disfigured by numerous black scars and gashes inflicted by the neglected burning cigarettes of many years. They had tumbled from the ashtray unnoticed and branded their statements permanently and quietly into the wood until the odor of their burning caused the snuffing out of their lives. At the bed's foot there was a single window which looked upon the sea.

Against the adjacent wall there was a battered bureau and beside it there was a closet which held his single ill-fitting serge suit, the two or three white shirts that strangled him and the square black shoes that pinched. When he took off his more friendly clothes, the heavy woollen sweaters, mitts and socks which my mother knitted for him and the woollen and doeskin shirts, he dumped them unceremoniously on a single chair. If a visitor entered the room while he was lying on the bed, he would be told to throw the clothes on the floor and take their place upon the chair.

Magazines and books covered the bureau and competed with the clothes for domination of the chair. They further overburdened the heroic little table and lay on top of the radio. They filled a baffling and unknowable cave beneath the bed, and in the corner by the bureau they spilled from the walls and grew up from the floor.

The magazines were the most conventional: *Time*, *Newsweek*, *Life*, *Maclean's*, *The Family Herald*, *The Reader's Digest*. They were the result of various cut-rate subscriptions or of the gift subscriptions associated with Christmas, "the two whole years for only $3.50."

The books were more varied. There were a few hard-cover magnificents and bygone Book of the Month wonders and some were Christmas or birthday gifts. The majority of them, however, were used paperbacks which came from those second-hand bookstores which advertise in the backs of magazines: "Miscellaneous Used Paperbacks 10¢ Each." At first he sent for them himself, although my mother resented the expense, but in later years they came more and more often from my sisters who had moved to the cities. Especially at first they were very weird and varied. Mickey Spillane and Ernest Haycox vied with Dostoyevsky and Faulkner, and the Penguin Poets' edition of Gerard Manley Hopkins arrived in the same box as a little book on sex technique called *Getting the Most Out of Love*. The former had been assiduously annotated by a very fine hand using a very blue-inked fountain pen while the latter had been studied by someone with very large thumbs, the prints of which were still visible in the margins. At the slightest provocation it would open almost automatically to particularly graphic and well-smudged pages.

When he was not in the boat, my father spent most of his time lying on the bed in his socks, the top two buttons of his trousers undone, his discarded shirt on the everready chair and the sleeves of the woollen Stanfield underwear, which he wore both summer and winter, drawn half way up to his elbows. The pillows propped up the whiteness of his head and the goose-necked lamp illuminated the pages in his hands. The cigarettes smoked and smouldered on the ashtray and on the table and the radio played constantly, sometimes low and sometimes loud. At midnight and at one, two, three and four, one could sometimes hear the radio, his occasional cough, the rustling thud of a completed book being tossed to the corner heap, or the movement necessitated by his sitting on the edge of the bed to roll the thousandth cigarette. He seemed never to sleep, only to doze and the light shone constantly from his window to the sea.

My mother despised the room and all it stood for and she had stopped sleeping in it after I was born. She despised disorder in rooms and in houses and in hours and in lives, and she had not read a book since high school. There she had read *Ivanhoe* and considered it a colossal waste of time. Still the room remained, like a solid rock of opposition in the sparkling waters of a clear deep harbor, opening off the kitchen where we really lived our lives, with its door always open and its contents visible to all.

The daughters of the room and of the house were very beautiful. They were tall and willowy like my mother and had her fine facial features set off by the reddish copper-colored hair that had apparently once been my father's before it turned to white. All of them were very clever in school and helped my mother a great deal about the house. When they were young they sang and were very happy and very nice to me because I was the youngest and the family's only boy.

My father never approved of their playing about the wharf like the other children, and they went there only when my mother sent them on an errand. At such times they almost always overstayed, playing screaming games of tag or hide-and-seek in and about the fishing shanties, the piled traps and tubs of trawl, shouting down to the perch that swam languidly about the wharf's algae-covered piles, or jumping in and out of the boats that tugged gently at their lines. My mother was never uneasy about them at such times, and when her husband criticized her she would say, "Nothing will happen to them there," or "They could be doing worse things in worse places."

By about the ninth or tenth grade my sisters one by one discovered my father's bedroom and then the change would begin. Each would go into the room one morning when he was out. She would go with the ideal hope of imposing order or with the more practical objective of emptying the ashtray, and later she would be found spellbound by the volume in her hand. My mother's reaction was always abrupt, bordering on the angry. "Take your nose out of that trash and come and do your work," she would say, and once I saw her slap my youngest sister so hard that the print of her hand was scarletly emblazoned upon her daughter's cheek while the broken-spined paperback fluttered uselessly to the floor.

Thereafter my mother would launch a campaign against what she had discovered but could not understand. At times although she was not overly religious she would bring in God to bolster her arguments saying, "In the next world God will see to those who waste their lives reading useless books when they should be about their work." Or without theological aid, "I would like to know how books help anyone to live a life." If my father were in, she would repeat the remarks louder than necessary, and her voice would carry into his room where he lay upon his bed. His usual reaction was to turn up the volume of the radio, although that action in itself betrayed the success of the initial thrust.

Shortly after my sisters began to read the books, they grew restless and lost interest in darning socks and baking bread, and all of them eventually went to work as summer waitresses in the Sea Food Restaurant. The restaurant was run by a big American concern from Boston and catered to the tourists that flooded the area during July and August. My mother despised the whole operation. She said the restaurant was not run by "our people," and "our people" did not eat there, and that it was run by outsiders for outsiders.

"Who are these people anyway?" she would ask, tossing back her dark hair, "and what do they, though they go about with their cameras for a hundred years, know about the way it is here, and what do they care about me and mine, and why should I care about them?"

She was angry that my sisters should even conceive of working in such a place and more angry when my father made no move to prevent it, and she was worried about herself and about her family and about her life. Sometimes she would say softly to her sisters, "I don't know what's the matter with my girls. It seems none of them are interested in any of the right things." And sometimes there would be bitter savage arguments. One afternoon I was coming in with three mackerel I'd been given at the wharf when I heard her say, "Well I hope you'll be satisfied when they come home knocked up and you'll have had your way."

It was the most savage thing I'd ever heard my mother say. Not just the words but the way she said them, and I stood there in the porch afraid to breathe for what seemed like the years from ten to fifteen, feeling the damp moist mackerel with their silver glassy eyes growing clammy against my leg.

Through the angle in the screen door I saw my father who had been walking into his room wheel around on one of his rubber-booted heels and look at her with his blue eyes flashing like clearest ice beneath the snow that was his hair. His usually ruddy face was drawn and grey, reflecting the exhaustion of a man of sixty-five who had been working in those rubber boots for eleven hours on an August day, and for a fleeting moment I wondered what I would do if he killed my mother while I stood there in the porch with those three foolish mackerel in my hand. Then he turned and went into his room and the radio blared forth the next day's weather forecast and I retreated under the noise and returned again, stamping my feet and slamming the door too loudly to signal my approach. My mother was busy at the stove when I came in, and did not raise her head when I threw the mackerel in a pan. As I looked into my father's room, I said, "Well how did things go in the boat today?" and he replied, "Oh not too badly, all things considered." He was lying on his back and lighting the first cigarette and the radio was talking about the Virginia coast.

All of my sisters made good money on tips. They bought my father an electric razor which he tried to use for awhile and they took out even more magazine subscriptions. They bought my mother a great many clothes of the type she was very fond of, the wide-brimmed hats and the brocaded dresses, but she locked them all in trunks and refused to wear any of them.

On one August day my sisters prevailed upon my father to take some of their restaurant customers for an afternoon ride in the boat. The tourists with their expensive clothes and cameras and sun glasses awkwardly backed down the iron ladder at the wharf's side to where my father waited below, holding the rocking *Jenny Lynn* in snug against the wharf with one hand on the iron ladder and steadying his descending passengers with the other. They tried to look both prim and wind-blown like the girls in the Pepsi-Cola ads and did the best they could, sitting on the thwarts where the newspapers were spread to cover the splattered blood and fish entrails, crowding to one side so that they were in danger of capsizing the boat, taking the inevitable pictures or merely trailing their fingers through the water of their dreams.

All of them liked my father very much and, after he'd brought them back from their circles in the harbor, they invited him to their rented cabins which were located high on a hill overlooking the village to which they were so alien. He proceeded to get very drunk up there with the beautiful view and the strange company and the abundant liquor, and late in the afternoon he began to sing.

I was just approaching the wharf to deliver my mother's summons when he began, and the familiar yet unfamiliar voice that rolled down from the cabins made me feel as I had never felt before in my young life or perhaps as I had always felt without really knowing it, and I was ashamed yet proud, young yet old and saved yet forever lost, and there was nothing I could do to control my legs which trembled nor my eyes which wept for what they could not tell.

The tourists were equipped with tape recorders and my father sang for more than three hours. His voice boomed down the hill and bounced off the surface of the harbor, which was an unearthly blue on that hot August day, and was then reflected to the wharf and the fishing shanties where it was absorbed amidst the men who were baiting their lines for the next day's haul.

He sang all the old sea chanties which had come across from the old world and by which men like him had pulled ropes for generations, and he sang the East Coast sea songs which celebrated the sealing vessels of

Northumberland Strait and the long liners of the Grand Banks, and of Anticosti, Sable Island, Grand Manan, Boston Harbor, Nantucket and Block Island. Gradually he shifted to the seemingly unending Gaelic drinking songs with their twenty or more verses and inevitable refrains, and the men in the shanties smiled at the coarseness of some of the verses and at the thought that the singer's immediate audience did not know what they were applauding nor recording to take back to staid old Boston. Later as the sun was setting he switched to the laments and the wild and haunting Gaelic war songs of those spattered Highland ancestors he had never seen, and when his voice ceased, the savage melancholy of three hundred years seemed to hang over the peaceful harbor and the quiet boats and the men leaning in the doorways of their shanties with their cigarettes glowing in the dusk and the women looking to the sea from their open windows with their children in their arms.

When he came home he threw the money he had earned on the kitchen table as he did with all his earnings but my mother refused to touch it and the next day he went with the rest of the men to bait his trawl in the shanties. The tourists came to the door that evening and my mother met them there and told them that her husband was not in although he was lying on the bed only a few feet away with the radio playing and the cigarette upon his lips. She stood in the doorway until they reluctantly went away.

In the winter they sent him a picture which had been taken on the day of the singing. On the back it said, "To Our Ernest Hemingway" and the "Our" was underlined. There was also an accompanying letter telling how much they had enjoyed themselves, how popular the tape was proving and explaining who Ernest Hemingway was. In a way it almost did look like one of those unshaven, taken in Cuba pictures of Hemingway. He looked both massive and incongruous in the setting. His bulky fisherman's clothes were too big for the green and white lawn chair in which he sat, and his rubber boots seemed to take up all of the well-clipped grass square. The beach umbrella jarred with his sunburned face and because he had already been singing for some time, his lips which chapped in the winds of spring and burned in the water glare of summer had already cracked in several places producing tiny flecks of blood at their corners and on the whiteness of his teeth. The bracelets of brass chain which he wore to protect his wrists from chafing seemed abnormally large and his broad leather belt had been slackened and his heavy shirt and underwear were open at the throat revealing an uncultivated wilderness of white chest hair bordering on the semicontrolled stubble of his neck and chin. His blue eyes had looked directly into the camera and his hair was whiter than the two tiny clouds which hung over his left shoulder. The sea was behind him and its immense blue flatness stretched out to touch the arching blueness of the sky. It seemed very far away from him or else he was so much in the foreground that he seemed too big for it.

Each year another of my sisters would read the books and work in the restaurant. Sometimes they would stay out quite late on the hot summer nights and when they came up the stairs my mother would ask them many long and involved questions which they resented and tried to avoid. Before ascending the stairs they would go into my father's room and those of us who waited above could hear them throwing his clothes off the chair before sitting on it or the squeak of the bed as they sat on its edge. Sometimes they would talk to him a long time, the murmur of their voices blending with the music of the radio into a mysterious vapor-like sound which floated softly up the stairs.

I say this again as if it all happened at once and as if all of my sisters were of identical ages and like so many lemmings going into another sea and, again, it was of course not that way at all. Yet go they did, to Boston, to Montreal, to New York with the young men they met during the summers and later married in those far away cities. The young men were very articulate and handsome and wore fine clothes and drove expensive cars and my sisters, as I said, were very tall and beautiful with their copper-colored hair and were tired of darning socks and baking bread.

One by one they went. My mother had each of her daughters for fifteen years, then lost them for two and finally forever. None married a fisherman. My mother never accepted any of the young men, for in her eyes they seemed always a combination of the lazy, the effeminate, the dishonest and the unknown. They never seemed to do any physical work and she could not comprehend their luxurious vacations and she did not know from whence they came nor who they were. And in the end she did not really care, for they were not of her people and they were not of her sea.

I say this now with a sense of wonder at my own stupidity in thinking I was somehow free and would go on doing well in school and playing and helping in the boat and passing into my early teens while streaks of grey began to appear in my mother's dark hair and my father's rubber boots dragged sometimes on the pebbles of the beach as he trudged home from the wharf. And there were but three of us in the house that had at one time been so loud.

Then during the winter that I was fifteen he seemed to grow old and ill at once. Most of January he lay upon the bed, smoking and reading and listening to the radio while the wind howled about the house and the needle-like snow blistered off the ice-covered harbor and the doors flew out of people's hands if they did not cling to them like death.

In February when the men began overhauling their lobster traps he still did not move, and my mother and I began to knit lobster trap headings in the evenings. The twine was as always very sharp and harsh, and blisters formed upon our thumbs and little paths of blood snaked quietly down between our fingers while the seals that had drifted down from distant Labrador wept and moaned like human children on the ice-floes of the Gulf.

In the daytime my mother's brother who had been my father's partner as long as I could remember also came to work upon the gear. He was a year older than my mother and was tall and dark and the father of twelve children.

By March we were very far behind and although I began to work very hard in the evenings I knew it was not hard enough and that there were but eight weeks left before the opening of the season on May first. And I knew that my mother worried and my uncle was uneasy and that all of our very lives depended on the boat being ready with her gear and two men, by the date of May the first. And I knew then that *David Copperfield* and *The Tempest* and all of those friends I had dearly come to love must really go forever. So I bade them all good-bye.

The night after my first full day at home and after my mother had gone upstairs he called me into his room where I sat upon the chair beside his bed. "You will go back tomorrow," he said simply.

I refused then, saying I had made my decision and was satisfied.

"That is no way to make a decision," he said, "and if you are satisfied I am not. It is best that you go back." I was almost angry then and told him as all children do that I wished he would leave me alone and stop telling me what to do.

He looked at me a long time then, lying there on the same bed on which he had fathered me those sixteen years before, fathered me his only son, out of who knew what emotions when he was already fifty-six and his hair had turned to snow. Then he swung his legs over the edge of the squeaking bed and sat facing me and looked into my own dark eyes with his of crystal blue and placed his hand upon my knee. "I am not telling you to do anything," he said softly, "only asking you."

The next morning I returned to school. As I left, my mother followed me to the porch and said, "I never thought a son of mine would choose useless books over the parents that gave him life."

In the weeks that followed he got up rather miraculously and the gear was ready and the *Jenny Lynn* was freshly painted by the last two weeks of April when the ice began to break up and the lonely screaming gulls returned to haunt the silver herring as they flashed within the sea.

On the first day of May the boats raced out as they had always done, laden down almost to the gunwales with their heavy cargoes of traps. They were almost like living things as they plunged through the waters of the spring and manoeuvred between the still floating icebergs of crystal-white and emerald green on their way to the traditional grounds that they sought out every May. And those of us who sat that day in the High School on the hill, discussing the water imagery of Tennyson, watched them as they passed back and forth beneath us until by afternoon the piles of traps which had been stacked upon the wharf were no longer visible but were spread about the bottoms of the sea. And the *Jenny Lynn* went too, all day, with my uncle tall and dark, like a latter-day Tashtego standing at the tiller with his legs wide apart and guiding her deftly between the floating pans of ice and my father in the stern standing in the same way with his hands upon the ropes that lashed the cargo to the deck. And at night my mother asked, "Well, how did things go in the boat today?"

And the spring wore on and the summer came and school ended in the third week of June and the lobster season on July first and I wished that the two things I loved so dearly did not exclude each other in a manner that was so blunt and too clear.

At the conclusion of the lobster season my uncle said he had been offered a berth on a deep sea dragger and had decided to accept. We all knew that he was leaving the *Jenny Lynn* forever and that before the next lobster season he would buy a boat of his own. He was expecting another child and would be supporting fifteen people by the next spring and could not chance my father against the family that he loved.

I joined my father then for the trawling season, and he made no protest and my mother was quite happy. Through the summer we baited the tubs of trawl in the afternoon and set them at sunset and revisited them in the darkness of the early morning. The men would come tramping by our house at 4:00 a.m. and we would join them and walk with them to the wharf and be on our way before the sun rose out of the ocean where it seemed to spend the night. If I was not up they would toss pebbles to my window and I would by very embarrassed and tumble downstairs to where my father lay fully clothed atop his bed, reading his book and listening to his radio and smoking his cigarette. When I appeared he would swing off his bed and put on his boots and be instantly ready and then we would take the lunches my mother had prepared the night before and walk off towards the sea. He would make no attempt to wake me himself.

It was in many ways a good summer. There were few storms and we were out almost every day and we lost a minimum of gear and seemed to land a maximum of fish and I tanned dark and brown after the manner of my uncles.

My father did not tan–he never tanned–because of his reddish complexion, and the salt water irritated his skin as it had for sixty years. He burned and reburned over and over again and his lips still cracked so that they bled when he smiled, and his arms, especially the left, still broke out into the oozing salt-water boils as they had ever since as a child I had first watched him soaking and bathing them in a variety of ineffectual solutions. The chafe-preventing bracelets of brass linked chain that all the men wore about their wrists in early spring were his the full season and he shaved but painfully and only once a week.

And I saw then, that summer, many things that I had seen all my life as if for the first time and I thought that perhaps my father had never been intended for a fisherman either physically or mentally. At least not in the manner of my uncles; he had never really loved it. And I remembered that, one evening in his room when we were talking about *David Copperfield*, he had said that he had always wanted to go to the university and I had dismissed it then in the way one dismisses his father's saying he would like to be a tight-rope walker, and we had gone on to talk about the Peggotys and how they loved the sea.

And I thought then to myself that there were many things wrong with all of us and all our lives and I wondered why my father, who was himself an only son, had not married before he was forty and then I wondered why he had. I even thought that perhaps he had had to marry my mother and checked the dates on the flyleaf of the Bible where I learned that my oldest sister had been born a prosaic eleven months after the marriage, and I felt myself then very dirty and debased for my lack of faith and for what I had thought and done.

And then there came into my heart a very great love for my father and I thought it was very much braver to spend a life doing what you really do not want rather than selfishly following forever your own dreams and inclinations. And I knew then that I could never leave him alone to suffer the iron-tipped harpoons which my mother would forever hurl into his soul because he was a failure as a husband and a father who had retained none of his own. And I felt that I had been very small in a little secret place within me and that even the completion of high school was for me a silly shallow selfish dream.

So I told him one night very resolutely and very powerfully that I would remain with him as long as he lived and we would fish the sea together. And he made no protest but only smiled through the cigarette smoke that wreathed his bed and replied, "I hope you will remember what you've said."

The room was now so filled with books as to be almost Dickensian, but he would not allow my mother to move or change them and he continued to read them, sometimes two or three a night. They came with great regularity now, and there were more hard covers, sent by my sisters who had gone so long ago and now seemed so distant and so prosperous, and sent also pictures of small red-haired grandchildren with baseball bats and dolls, which he placed upon his bureau and which my mother gazed at wistfully when she thought no one would see. Red-haired grandchildren with baseball bats and dolls who would never know the sea in hatred or in love.

And so we fished through the heat of August and into the cooler days of September when the water was so clear we could almost see the bottom and the white mists rose like delicate ghosts in the early morning dawn. And one day my mother said to me, "You have given added years to his life."

And we fished on into October when it began to roughen and we could no longer risk night sets but took our gear out each morning and returned at the first sign of the squalls; and on into November when we lost three tubs of trawl and the clear blue water turned to a sullen grey and the trochoidal waves rolled rough and high and washed across our bows and decks as we ran within their troughs. We wore heavy sweaters now and the awkward rubber slickers and the heavy woollen mitts which soaked and froze into masses of ice that hung from our wrists like the limbs of gigantic monsters until we thawed them against the exhaust pipe's heat. And almost every day we would leave for home before noon, driven by the blasts of the northwest wind, coating our eyebrows with ice and freezing our eyelids closed as we leaned into a visibility that was hardly there, charting our course from the compass and the sea, running with the waves and between them but never confronting their towering might.

And I stood at the tiller now, on these homeward lunges, stood in the place and in the manner of my uncle, turning to look at my father, and to shout over the roar of the engine and the slop of the sea to where he stood in the stern, drenched and dripping with the snow and the salt and the spray and his bushy eyebrows caked in ice. But on November twenty-first, when it seemed we might be making the final run of the season, I turned and he was not there and I knew even in that instant that he would never be again.

On November twenty-first the waves of the grey Atlantic are very very high and the waters are very cold and there are no signposts on the surface of the sea. You cannot tell where you have been five minutes before and in the squalls of snow you cannot see. And it takes longer than you would believe to check a boat that has been running before a gale and turn her ever so carefully in a wide and stupid circle, with timbers creaking and straining, back into the face of storm. And you know that it is useless and that your voice does not carry the length of the boat and that even if you knew the original spot, the relentless waves would carry such a burden perhaps a mile or so by the time you could return. And you know also, the final irony, that your father like your uncles and all the men that form your past, cannot swim a stroke.

The lobster beds off the Cape Breton coast are still very rich and now, from May to July, their offerings are packed in crates of ice, and thundered by the gigantic transport trucks, day and night, through New Glasgow, Amherst, St. John and Bangor and Portland and into Boston where they are tossed still living into boiling pots of water, their final home.

And though the prices are higher and the competition tighter, the grounds to which the *Jenny Lynn* once went remain untouched and unfished as they have for the last ten years. For if there are no signposts on the sea in storm there are certain ones in calm and the lobster bottoms were distributed in calm before any of us can remember and the grounds my father fished were those his father fished before him and there were others before and before and before. Twice the big boats have come from forty and fifty miles, lured by the promise of the grounds, and strewn the bottom with their traps and twice they have returned to find their buoys cut adrift and their gear lost and destroyed. Twice the Fisheries Officer and the Mounted Police have come and asked many long and involved questions and twice they have received no answers from the men leaning in the doors of their shanties and the women standing at their windows with their children in their arms. Twice they have gone away saying: "There are no legal boundaries in the Marine area"; "No one can own the sea"; "Those grounds don't wait for anyone."

But the men and the women, with my mother dark among them, do not care for what they say, for to them the grounds are sacred and they think they wait for me.

It is not an easy thing to know that your mother lives alone on an inadequate insurance policy and that she is too proud to accept any other aid. And that she looks through her lonely window onto the ice of winter and the hot flat calm of summer and the rolling waves of fall. And that she lies awake in the early morning's darkness when the rubber boots of the men scrunch upon the gravel as they pass beside her house on their way down to the wharf. And she knows that the footsteps never stop, because no man goes from her house, and she alone of all the Lynns has neither son nor son-in-law that walks toward the boat that will take him to the sea. And it is not an easy thing to know that your mother looks upon the sea with love and on you with bitterness because the one has been so constant and the other so untrue.

But neither is it easy to know that your father was found on November twenty-eighth, ten miles to the north and wedged between two boulders at the base of the rock-strewn cliffs where he had been hurled and slammed so many many times. His hands were shredded ribbons as were his feet which had lost their boots to the suction of the sea, and his shoulders came apart in our hands when we tried to move him from the rocks. And the fish had eaten his testicles and the gulls had pecked out his eyes and the white-green stubble of his whiskers had continued to grow in death, like the grass on graves, upon the purple, bloated mass that was his face. There was not much left of my father, physically, as he lay there with the brass chains on his wrists and the seaweed in his hair.

Work by Alistair MacLeod

FICTION

The Lost Salt Gift of Blood. Toronto: McClelland and Stewart, 1976.

Marie-Claire Blais

Novelist, poet, and dramatist, Marie-Claire Blais burst onto the Quebec literary scene with her first novel, *La belle bête*, written when she was only eighteen. The eldest of five children, she was born in a working-class district of Quebec City in 1939. After eleven years in a convent school, she left without graduating and worked as a secretary. She moved from home when she was eighteen to live in a rented furnished room, devoting herself to writing, and taking a few courses in literature and philosophy at Laval University.

In her novels Blais presents a bleak portrait of men and women trapped in hostile environments that diminish and debase their human dignity. The human condition is not, for Blais, a cause for rejoicing. "After all there is no one anywhere who faces himself, nobody is able to admit what kind of person he is. So there is sadness. A lot of people do not see when they are bad, when they are guilty. This is a side of truth, of reality. It is hard to admit, but we are not very good." For Margaret Atwood, Blais' fictional universe is "characterized by brutality, suffering and repression, symbolized by... those hulking, child-beating farmers and the tubercular urban poor that haunt her books. This was, at least in part, the Quebec of her own... childhood."

Blais constructs her novels as poems. "It is a kind of writing I love, novels which are written like poems, because within the construction of the poem...there is a *totalité*. I try to make my books like symbolic visions. There is a symbolic way to say things and my books are the way I see life and what I see I want to say by symbols–...there is the total meaning of life for me. But anyway, it is all a picture, it is all art while life goes on, it is a picture of the emotions of love or fear."

Une saison dans la vie d'Emmanuel (1965) presents the first winter in the life of Emmanuel, the sixteenth child in his family. In the following selection, the remarkable opening chapter of the novel, it is the day of Emmanuel's birth. Members of his family are perceived through the eyes and ears of this new-born infant: Grand-mère Antoinette, who presides over the household with her authoritarian presence; Emmanuel's father, a man not even named, whose ignorance makes him despise education; Emmanuel's mother, another un-named figure, who has already returned to work in the fields; and two of Emmanuel's brothers, Jean-LeMaigre and Number Seven. Emmanuel is the frame of the novel, and Grand-mère Antoinette is the centre, for all the action revolves around her.

The only clue to the setting of the novel is the severe winter and the characters' names. Quebec is not named, even though the novel is in fact grounded in rural Quebec society. The book is a criticism of that society, though not designed primarily as social criticism. For the real subject of Blais' novel is not a society but the human condition. "When I write...I see only the individual human problem. In *Saison* there are things that could happen in other places than Quebec....It is a true fable."

In her later novels Blais is less bleak than in her earlier fiction. Looking back at *Une saison dans la vie d'Emmanuel*, she remarks, "Artistically it was something of a breakthrough for me. It was the first time that I could combine humor and tragedy in my work."

A Season
in the Life of
Emmanuel

G rand-mère Antoinette's feet dominated the room.
They lay there like two quiet, watchful animals, scarcely twitching at all
inside their black boots, always ready to spring into action; two feet
bruised by long years of work in the fields (opening his eyes for the first
time in the dusty morning light, he couldn't see them yet, was not yet
aware of the hidden wound in the leg, beneath the woolen stocking, of
the ankles swollen within their prisons of leather and laces...), two
noble and pious feet (did they not make the journey to church once
every morning, even in winter?), two feet brimming with life, and
etching forever in the memories of those who saw them, even only
once, their sombre image of authority and patience.

Born without fuss, this winter morning, Emmanuel was listening to
his grandmother's voice. Immense and all-powerful, she seemed to be
ruling the whole world from her armchair. (Don't cry, what have you
got to cry about? Your mother has gone back to work on the farm. Just
you keep quiet till she gets home. Ah, you're already so selfish, already
so wicked. Already in a temper!) He called for his mother. (You've
picked a bad time to be born, we've never been so poor, it's a hard winter
for everyone, the war, the food shortage, and you the sixteenth too...)
She sat complaining to herself in a low voice, telling the beads of a grey
rosary hanging from her waist. (I've got my rheumatism too, but no one
ever mentions it. I have my troubles too. And besides I hate newborn
babies; insects they are, crawling around in the dust! You'll behave just
like the others, you'll be ignorant and cruel and bitter.... You didn't give

79

a thought to all the worries you were bringing me, I have to think of everything, what name to give you, the christening...)

It was cold inside the house. There were faces all around him; figures kept appearing. He looked at them but didn't recognize them yet. Grand-mère Antoinette was so huge that he couldn't see all of her. He was afraid. He shrank into himself, closing up like a shell. (Enough of that, said the old woman, look around you, open your eyes, I'm here, I give the orders here! Look at me, properly, I am the only one here who is worthy of this house. I am the one who sleeps in the scented room, I store the soap under my bed...) "We shall have plenty of time," Grand-mère Antoinette said, "there is no hurry for today..."

(His grandmother had a vast bosom, he couldn't see her legs under the heavy skirts, dry sticks, cruel knees, such strange garments swaddling her body as it shivered in the cold.) He tried to hook his delicate fists onto her knees, to bury himself in the cave of her lap (for he was discovering that she was so thin beneath those mountains of cloth, those rough skirts, that for the first time he was not afraid of her). But those woolen clothes still kept him at a distance from the icy bosom, from the breasts she was crushing into herself with one hand in a gesture of alarm or self-defense; for whenever you approached that body, stifled inside its austere dress, you felt that you were approaching some sleeping freshness within her, an ancient and proud desire that none had ever fulfilled–you wanted to go to sleep in her, as in some warm river, to lie and rest upon her heart. But she kept Emmanuel at a distance with that same gesture of the hand that had once rejected love, and punished man's desires.

"Oh Lord, another boy, what is to become of us?" But she quickly regained her confidence: "I am strong, child. You can give your life into my keeping. Put your trust in me."

He listened to her. Her voice rocked him with a monotonous, defeated chant. She wrapped him in her shawl, not fondling him but rather plunging him into the folds of cloth and into the smells of them as though into a bath. He held his breath. Sometimes, without meaning to, she scratched him slightly with her bent fingers; she held him aloft and shook him, and once more he called for his mother. (Bad boy, she said impatiently.) He dreamed of his mother's breast coming to appease his thirst and quiet his rebellious cries.

"Your mother is out working, as usual," Grand-mère Antoinette said. "Today is just a day like any other. You think only of yourself. I've got work to do too. Newborn babies are dirty. They disgust me. But you see,

I'm good to you, I wash you, I take care of you, and you will be the first to be glad when I die..."

But Grand-mère Antoinette believed herself to be immortal. And her whole triumphant being was immortal for Emmanuel too, as he lay gazing up at her in astonishment. "Ah, my child, no one is listening to you, there is no use in crying. You will soon learn that you're alone in this world!

"You too will be afraid..."

The beams of the sun shone in through the window. In the distance, the landscape was confused, unapproachable. Emmanuel could hear voices, steps all around him. (He trembled with cold as his grandmother washed him, or rather drowned him several times in icy water...) "There," she said, "it's all over. There's nothing to be afraid of. I'm here. One gets used to everything, you'll see."

She smiled. He felt the desire to respect her silence; he no longer dared to complain, for it seemed to him suddenly that he had already been familiar for a long while with cold, with hunger, and perhaps even with despair. In the cold sheets, in the cold room, he had suddenly been filled with a strange patience. The knowledge had come to him that all this misery would never end; but he had consented to live. Standing at the window, Grand-mère cried out, almost with joy:

"Here they are. I can feel them coming up the stairs, listen to their voices. Here they all are, the grandchildren, the children, the cousins, the nieces, and the nephews; you think they've been buried under the snow on their way to school, or else dead years ago, but they are always there, under the tables, under the beds, spying on me with their eyes shining in the dark. They are waiting for me to hand out lumps of sugar to them. There are always one or two around my armchair, or my rocking chair when I rock myself of an evening...

"They snigger, they play with my shoelaces. They run after me the whole time with that stupid sniggering of theirs, with that begging, hypocritical look in their eyes. I chase them away like flies, but they come back, they fasten themselves on me like a bunch of vermin, they gnaw at me..."

Grand-mère Antoinette was admirable as she tamed the tide of children roaring around her feet. (Where did they come from? Did they rise up out of the darkness, out of the black night? They smelled of the night, they spoke with the voice of the night, they crawled around the bed, and they had the familiar smell of poverty...)

"Ah, that's enough!" Grand-mère Antoinette said. "I don't want to hear another sound from any of you, out of my way all of you, go back to your beds...Vanish, I don't want to see any more of you, ah! heavens, what a smell!"

But then, accompanying the distribution with a few blows of her cane, she handed out the lumps of sugar they were waiting for with open mouths, panting with impatience and hunger, the sugar, the crumbs of chocolate, all the grimy treasures she had accumulated and now emptied out again from her skirts and from her strait-laced bodice. "Get away, get away," she cried.

She drove them off with an all-powerful hand (later, he was to see her walking in the same way through a host of chickens, and rabbits, and cows, sowing curses broadcast as she went, to recover some tearful baby that had fallen in the mud), she beat them back toward the staircase, still throwing them the lumps of sugar, which they scrabbled for as best they might, this flood of children, of animals, that later, once again, would emerge from their mysterious lair and come back, scratching at the door anew, to beg from their grandmother.

His mother came in. He recognized her. She didn't come over to him, not at first. He was ready to believe she had deserted him. He recognized her sad face, her drooping shoulders. She didn't seem to remember having brought him into the world that very morning. She was cold. He saw her hands clenching around the brimming milk pail. (He's over there, Grand-mère Antoinette said, he's hungry, he's been crying all day.) His mother was silent. She would always be silent. Some of his brothers were coming back from school and knocking the snow off their boots against the door. (Come here, Grand-mère said, but she hit out at them lightly with the tip of her cane when they passed under the lamp.) In the distance the sun was still red on the hill.

"And Number Seven, what have you done with Number Seven? As long as I live, you'll continue to go to school..."

His mother's waist was gently bellying out: she was bending over as she set down the second pail of milk.

"To think they've gone and lost Number Seven in the snow again," Grand-mère Antoinette said.

The bucket ran over. Little drops of milk rolled across the floor in the lamplight. Grand-mère was scolding, reprimanding, sometimes slapping a chapped cheek as it passed within her reach.

"You ought to thank me, ah! if I weren't here you'd never get to school, would you, eh?"

"Grand-mère," a man's voice said from the depths of the kitchen, "school isn't necessary."

The man's voice was merely a murmur. It faded, it disappeared. Standing leaning against the wall, her head tilted slightly onto one shoulder, his mother listened in silence. Perhaps she was asleep. Her dress was open, showing her pale, drooping breasts. Her sons looked at her in silence, and they too were waiting, waiting for night to fall on the hill.

"A hard winter," the man said, rubbing his hands together over the stove. "But perhaps it will be a good spring..."

He removed his snow-soaked clothes. He put them to dry on a chair near the fire. He took off his thick boots, then his socks. The smell of wet clothing spread through the house.

(He had taken everything from his mother's heart, he had drunk all her milk with an avid mouth, and now he pretended to be asleep...)

"There are orphanages too," the man's voice said.

"I prefer the Noviciat," Grand-mère Antoinette replied. "It doesn't cost anything, and they teach them how to behave."

"But I don't understand what they need all this schooling for," the father muttered into his beard.

"Ah! Men don't understand about these things," Grand-mère Antoinette said with a sigh. "But Grand-mère," the man's voice continued in the depths of the kitchen, while the flames flickered slowly up from the stove (and a little girl at the window looked out with boredom at the setting sun, hands clasped behind her back), "Grand-mère, I know more about life than you do, I know what my children are destined for!"

"For God!" Grand-mère Antoinette replied.

His mother took him in her arms. She was protecting him now with her fragile body, supporting his head so that he could feed and drink in peace; but Grand-mère's long silhouette was still keeping watch, very close, driven by some strange duty to find out what was happening in the hidden parts of his being, sometimes interrupting the insipid meal he was absorbing in a dream. (He was draining his mother, he was drinking up everything inside her!) She, his mother, said nothing, no longer answering, calm, deep, deserted perhaps. He was there, but she had forgotten him. He was producing no echo in her, either of joy or of desire. He slipped into her and lay there without hope.

"That child sees everything," Grand-mère Antoinette said, "you can't hide anything from him." (What shall we call him? David? Joseph? There have been too many Josephs in recent generations. They were weak men! The Emmanuels have all been strong, they took good care of their land.)

"Let us call him Emmanuel."

His mother listened solemnly. Sometimes she lifted her head in surprise, her lip trembled, and she seemed to want to say something, but she said nothing. They heard her sigh, then go to sleep.

"We must settle when he is to be baptized," Grand-mère said.

The father spoke of waiting until spring. "Spring is a good time for baptisms," he said.

"Next Sunday," Grand-mère Antoinette said. "And I'll take him down to be baptized myself."

The mother bowed her head.

"My wife thinks Sunday will do very well too," the man said.

She sat there in her armchair, majestic and contented, and the dark spread little by little over the hill, veiling the white forest and the silent fields. (You should thank me for taking these decisions out of your hands, Grand-mère Antoinette thought in her armchair.)

The man yawned beside the fire. Grand-mère Antoinette was throwing him fleeting, sidelong glances. No, I shall not lift a finger to serve that man, she thought to herself. He thinks I shall do as my daughter does; but I won't bring him his bowl of warm water, or his clean clothes. No, no, I won't budge from my armchair. He is expecting a woman to come and wait on him. But I won't get up.

But something moved beneath the pointed toe of her boot, something shapeless that she tried to push away. Lord! a mouse, a squirrel, there's something under my dress...

"Go back to the school and bring back Number Seven, I'll teach him to dawdle about on the roads. Put on your boots, go on, you. You're not to go out, Jean-Le Maigre, you're coughing too much! Where were you just then? Were you reading under the table again?"

"I'll burn your book for you," the father's voice said. "I've told you, Grand-mère, we don't want books in this house."

"Jean-Le Maigre is talented; Monsieur le Curé said so," Grand-mère Antoinette replied.

"He's consumptive," the man said, "what good can it possibly do him to learn anything? I can't think what that Curé thinks he's about— there's nothing to be done with Jean-Le Maigre. He's got one lung rotting away!"

His mother listened. Tomorrow, at the same hour, they would say the same words all over again, and she would make that same slight movement of the head, that sign of silent protest in Jean-Le Maigre's defense, but, like today, she would merely listen, say nothing, perhaps feel astonishment that life should repeat itself with such precision, and she would think again: "How long the night's going to be." A strand of hair fell across her brow; she had already closed her eyes, and now she bent over her latest child, her face still gloomy and half asleep.

Standing on one leg, book in hand, Jean-Le Maigre gazed searchingly at the newborn infant with a moist gaze. "Who's he?" he asked, without interest. Without waiting for the reply, he coughed, sneezed, and disappeared again behind his book.

"I can see you, Jean-Le Maigre," Grand-mère said. "You think you're safe, but I can see you."

"You can't see me. No one can see me when I'm reading," Jean-Le Maigre answered.

"Watch out then; I'm going to make you drink your syrup soon," Grand-mère said.

"I'm not here," Jean-Le Maigre replied. "I'm dead."

"Perhaps you are," was Grand-mère's reply, "but I'm alive, and as long as I'm alive you'll drink your syrup."

"But what good can it possibly do?" the man's voice asked. The old woman thought of pronouncing one of the curses that the man beside the stove was calmly expecting; he was shrugging his shoulders, already feeling the pleasurable blow of her insult. But Grand-mère Antoinette, disdainfully smiling in her armchair, chose to remain silent—no, this time she would not say that word, she would remain proud and unapproachable. "Well," the man said, turning toward the stove, with its now dying fire, "you're right, Grand-mère, it's just as well they should get used to going to school in winter..."

Grand-mère Antoinette, speaking in a clipped, contemptuous tone, replied that she had known harder winters than any of them, and the man, dressing himself clumsily in the shadows, suddenly felt the familiar, daily sense of shame that only the presence of this woman could inspire in him. "Winters as black as death," Grand-mère Antoinette went on, with contempt for the man's body, watching him out of the corner of one eye. "Oh! It's not the first I've seen...."

"Yes, it's a gloomy evening," the man commented in weary tones. With his dirt-blackened nails, Jean-Le Maigre was gracefully turning the pages of his book. As happy as a prince in his tattered clothes, he was in a hurry to read it.

"Oh heavens, how funny it is," he exclaimed through a wild burst of laughter.

"I wouldn't laugh if I were you," the father said. "I might take that book of yours away from you."

Jean-Le Maigre shook his head, revealing the pale brow beneath his hair. "It's too late, I've read every page. You can't burn the pages I've read. They're all written here!"

For the first time, the man raised his eyes in a sombre gaze toward the mother and child. Then he forgot them again immediately. He looked at the bowl of dirty water on the stove. He was beginning to feel more and more constricted in his waistcoat.

"It's stifling in here," he said.

The button suddenly burst off his shirt collar. "It's not going to be me who sews that button on," Grand-mère Antoinette said. "You know it'll be you," the man replied, "it is always you, Grand-mère!"

"Jean-Le Maigre," Grand-mère said, raising a triumphant head to look at her grandson, "listen, the Noviciat.... There are infirmaries, warm dormitories....You'd like it there..."

"Oh, Grand-mère," Jean-Le Maigre replied from behind his book, "let me read in peace and cough in peace, since I enjoy it."

Jean-Le Maigre coughed again. Oh Lord, it felt so good! He sneezed, he laughed, he wiped his nose on his dirty shirt.

"Grand-mère," he said, "I know this book by heart now."

"I'm going to give him a hiding, that Jean-Le Maigre of yours," the father's voice said.

"Come over by me," Grand-mère Antoinette said to Jean-Le Maigre. "No one can hurt you when you're near me."

Jean-Le Maigre scratched his nose, then his ears. "What is it now?" Grand-mère Antoinette asked. "Nothing," Jean-Le Maigre replied. She pulled the ragged child against her, brushed the thin fringe of hair back from his forehead, and made a discovery that astounded no one.

"My God, his head is full of lice again!"

Works by Marie-Claire Blais

FICTION

La belle bête. Quebec: Institut Littéraire, 1959. [*Mad Shadows.* Trans. Merloyd Lawrence. Toronto: McClelland and Stewart, 1960.]

Tête Blanche. Quebec: Institut Littéraire, 1960. [*Tête Blanche.* Trans. Charles Fullman. Toronto: McClelland and Stewart, 1961.]

Le jour est noir. Montreal: Editions du Jour, 1962. [*The Day Is Dark.* Trans. Derek Coltman. New York: Farrar, Straus and Giroux, 1967.]

"Les voyageurs sacrés." *Ecrits du Canada Français*, 14 (1962), 193-257. [*Three Travelers.* Trans. Derek Coltman. New York: Farrar, Straus and Giroux, 1967.]

Une saison dans la vie d'Emmanuel. Montreal: Editions du Jour, 1965. [*A Season in the Life of Emmanuel.* Trans. Derek Coltman. New York: Farrar, Straus and Giroux, 1966.]

L'insoumise. Montreal: Editions du Jour, 1966. [*The Fugitive.* Trans. David Lobdell. Ottawa: Oberon Press, 1978.]

David Sterne. Montreal: Editions du Jour, 1967. [*David Sterne.* Trans. David Lobdell. Toronto: McClelland and Stewart, 1973.]

Les manuscrits de Pauline Archange. Montreal: Editions du Jour, 1968. [*The Manuscripts of Pauline Archange.* Trans. Derek Coltman. New York: Farrar, Straus and Giroux, 1969.]

Vivre! Vivre! Montreal: Editions du Jour, 1969. [*The Manuscripts of Pauline Archange, Part II.* Trans. Derek Coltman. New York: Farrar, Straus and Giroux, 1969.]

Les apparences. Montreal: Editions du Jour, 1970. [*Dürer's Angel.* Trans. David Lobdell. Vancouver: Talonbooks, 1976.]

Le loup. Montreal: Editions du Jour, 1972. [*The Wolf.* Trans. Sheila Fischman. Toronto: McClelland and Stewart, 1974.]

Un Joualonais sa Joualonie. Montreal: Editions du Jour, 1973. [*St. Lawrence Blues.* Trans. Ralph Manheim. New York: Farrar, Straus and Giroux, 1974.]

Une liaison Parisienne. Montreal: Stanké/Quinze, 1975. [*A Literary Affair.* Trans. Sheila Fischman. Toronto: McClelland and Stewart, 1979.]

Les nuits de l'Underground. Montreal: Stanké, 1978. [*Nights in the Underground.* Trans. Ray Ellenwood. Don Mills: General Publishing, 1979.]

Le sourd dans la ville. Montreal: Stanké, 1979. [*Deaf to the City.* Trans. Carol Dunlop. Toronto: Lester and Orpen Denys, 1981.]

Visions d'Anna. Montreal: Stanké, 1982.

POETRY

Pays voilés. Quebec: Editions Garneau, 1963.

Existences. Quebec: Editions Garneau, 1964.

DRAMA

L'exécution. Montreal: Editions du Jour, 1968. [*The Execution.* Trans. David Lobdell. Vancouver: Talonbooks, 1976.]

Fièvre et autres textes dramatiques. Montreal: Editions du Jour, 1974.

L'Océan. Montreal: Quinze, 1977.

Interviews with Marie-Claire Blais

Tamarack Review, 37 (Autumn, 1965), 29-34.

Châtelaine, August, 1966, 21-3;51-4. Reprinted in *Quebec 67*, vol. 4, no. 9 (February, 1967), 22-32.

Roch Carrier

A small Quebec town is the setting for "The Nun Who Returned to Ireland" and all the other stories in Roch Carrier's *Les enfants du bonhomme dans la lune.* Like this collection, many of his writings attempt to unfold Quebec's past and present through realistic portraits of village life. "I told myself that maybe by writing I could really live what people had lived before, some years before," he states. "...a little village, which is a microcosm, would be a good place for me to let live all those forces which were in the French Canadian. I did not want to understand the situation in an intellectual way, because when you are intellectual you always go in a system, and I did not want to have any system." Carrier's little Quebec village is a microcosm of Quebec; the behavior and attitudes of the villagers can be seen as reflecting important dimensions of the Quebec people; the innocence of the children is the innocence of all children.

Carrier was born in the Quebec village of Sainte-Justine-de-Dorchester in 1937. After classical college and a master's degree from the Université de Montreal, he taught Greek culture for two years at Collège St. Louis in Edmundston, New Brunswick, before continuing literary studies and obtaining his doctorate from the Université de Paris. He returned to Canada from France in 1964 and taught for several years at the Université de Montreal. Then he set aside his academic career to become resident dramatist with the Théâtre du Nouveau Monde in Montreal, where he dramatized some of his own novels. At present he lives in Montreal and devotes his full attention to writing.

Carrier's fiction explores Quebec's past and its relationship to the present. Refusing to see contemporary Quebec in a void, Carrier tries to understand the present by examining the political, religious, and social forces that determined the past and by which the present was shaped. By returning to his childhood world and re-creating it in art, Carrier believes that he and other Quebec writers are creating the foundations of Quebec literature. "Here and now in Quebec the young writers have the feeling that we are building the French-Canadian Québécois literature. It's an important time to do it. In doing it, we have the feeling of saving things from the past, and we have also the feeling of preparing what is coming."

In "The Nun Who Returned to Ireland," as in all his fiction, Carrier does not explain or describe his characters in detail; instead he allows them to define themselves in brief and telling dramatic moments.

The Nun
Who Returned
to Ireland

After my first day of school I ran back to the house, holding out my reader.

"Mama, I learned how to read!" I announced.

"This is an important day," she replied; "I want your father to be here to see."

We waited for him. I waited as I'd never waited before. And as soon as his step rang out on the floor of the gallery, my first reader was open on my knees and my finger was pointing to the first letter in a short sentence.

"Your son learned to read today," my mother declared through the screen door. She was as excited as I.

"Well, well!" said my father. "Things happen fast nowadays. Pretty soon, son, you'll be able to do like me–read the newspaper upside down in your sleep!"

"Listen to me!" I said.

And I read the sentence I'd learned in school that day, from Sister Brigitte. But instead of picking me up and lifting me in his arms, my father looked at my mother and my mother didn't come and kiss her little boy who'd learned to read so quickly.

"What's going on here?" my father asked.

"I'd say it sounds like English," said my mother. "Show me your book." (She read the sentence I'd learned to decipher.) "I'd say you're reading as if you were English. Start again."

I reread the short sentence.

"You're reading with an English accent!" my mother exclaimed.

"I'm reading the way Sister Brigitte taught me."

"Don't tell me he's learning his own mother tongue in English," my father protested.

I had noticed that Sister Brigitte didn't speak the way we did, but that was quite natural because we all knew that nuns don't do anything the way other people do: they didn't dress like everybody else, they didn't get married, they didn't have children and they always lived in hiding. But as far as knowing whether Sister Brigitte had an English accent, how could I? I'd never heard a single word of English.

Over the next few days I learned that she hadn't been born in our village; it seemed very strange that someone could live in the village without being born there, because everyone else in the village had been born in the village.

Our parents weren't very pleased that their children were learning to read their mother tongue with an English accent. In whispers, they started to say that Sister Brigitte was Irish—that she hadn't even been born in Canada. Monsieur Cassidy, the undertaker, was Irish too, but he'd been born in the village, while Sister Brigitte had come from Ireland.

"Where's Ireland?" I asked my mother.

"It's a very small, very green little country in the ocean, far, far away."

As our reading lessons proceeded I took pains to pronounce the vowels as Sister Brigitte did, to emphasize the same syllables as she; I was so impatient to read the books my uncles brought back from their far-off colleges. Suddenly it was important for me to know.

"Sister Brigitte, where's Ireland?"

She put down her book.

"Ireland is the country where my parents were born, and my grandparents and my great-grandparents. And I was born in Ireland too. I was a little girl in Ireland. When I was a child like you I lived in Ireland. We had horses and sheep. Then the Lord asked me to become his servant..."

"What does that mean?"

"The Lord asked me if I wanted to become a nun. I said yes. So then I left my family and I forgot Ireland and my village."

"Forgot your village?"

I could see in her eyes that she didn't want to answer my question.

"Ever since, I've been teaching young children. Some of the children who were your age when I taught them are grandparents now, old grandparents."

Sister Brigitte's face, surrounded by her starched coif, had no age; I learned that she was old, very old, because she had been a teacher to grandparents.

"Have you ever gone back to Ireland?"

"God didn't want to send me back."

"You must miss your country."

"God asked me to teach little children to read and write so every child could read the great book of life."

"Sister Brigitte, you're older than our grandparents! Will you go back to Ireland before you die?"

The old nun must have known from my expression that death was so remote for me I could speak of it quite innocently, as I would speak of the grass or the sky. She said simply:

"Let's go on with our reading. School children in Ireland aren't so disorderly as you."

All that autumn we applied ourselves to our reading; by December we could read the brief texts Sister Brigitte wrote on the blackboard herself, in a pious script we tried awkwardly to imitate; in every text the word Ireland always appeared. It was by writing the word Ireland that I learned to form a capital I.

After Christmas holidays Sister Brigitte wasn't at the classroom door to greet us; she was sick. From our parents' whispers we learned that Sister Brigitte had lost her memory. We weren't surprised. We knew that old people always lose their memories and Sister Brigitte was an old person because she had been a teacher to grandparents.

Late in January, the nuns in the convent discovered that Sister Brigitte had left her room. They looked everywhere for her, in all the rooms and all the classrooms. Outside, a storm was blowing gusts of snow and wind; you couldn't see Heaven or earth, as they said. Sister Brigitte, who had spent the last few weeks in her bed, had fled into the storm. Some men from the village spotted her black form in the blizzard: beneath her vast mantle she was barefoot. When the men asked her where she was going, Sister Brigitte replied in English that she was going home, to Ireland.

Works by Roch Carrier

FICTION

Jolis deuils. Montreal: Editions du Jour, 1964.

La guerre, yes sir! Montreal: Editions du Jour, 1968. [*La Guerre, Yes Sir!* Trans. Sheila Fischman. Toronto: Anansi, 1970.]

Contes pour mille oreilles. Montreal: Ecrits du Canada français, 1969.

Floralie, où es-tu? Montreal: Editions du Jour, 1969. [*Floralie, where are you?* Trans. Sheila Fischman. Toronto: Anansi, 1971.]

Il est par là, le soleil. Montreal: Editions du Jour, 1970. [*Is it the Sun, Philibert?* Trans. Sheila Fischman. Toronto: Anansi, 1972.]

La deux-millième étage. Montreal: Editions du Jour, 1973. [*They Won't Demolish Me.* Trans. Sheila Fischman. Toronto: Anansi, 1974.]

Le jardin des délices. Montreal: Editions La Presse, 1975. [*The Garden of Delights.* Trans. Sheila Fischman. Toronto: Anansi, 1978.]

Il n'y a pas de pays sans grand-père. Montreal: Stanké, 1977. [*No Country without Grandfathers.* Trans. Sheila Fischman. Toronto: Anansi, 1981.]

Les enfants du bonhomme dans la lune. Montreal: Stanké, 1979. [*The Hockey Sweater and Other Stories.* Trans. Sheila Fischman. Toronto: Anansi, 1979.]

Les fleurs vivent-elles ailleurs que sur la terre? Montreal: Stanké, 1980.

Les voyageurs de l'arc-en-ciel. Montreal: Stanké, 1980.

La dame qui avait des chaînes aux chevilles. Montreal: Stanké, 1981.

POETRY

Les jeux incompris. Montreal: Editions Nocturne, 1956.

Cherche tes mots, cherche tes pas. Montreal: Editions Nocturne, 1958.

DRAMA

La guerre, yes sir! Montreal: Editions du Jour, 1970.

Floralie, où es-tu? Montreal: Editions du Jour, 1973.

La céleste bicyclette. Montreal: Stanké, 1980.

Le cirque noir. Montreal: Stanké, 1982.

Interviews with Roch Carrier

Conversations with Canadian Novelists. Edited by Donald Cameron. Toronto: Macmillan, 1973. Vol. 1, pp. 13-29.

Nord, 6 (Autumn, 1976), 7-31.

Mordecai Richler

"The Summer My Grandmother
Was Supposed to Die," originally
published as a piece of short fiction,

became the second chapter of
Mordecai Richler's *The Street* (1969),
a collection of stories and memoirs
inspired by his childhood. The street
is St. Urbain Street, one of five
working-class streets between the
Main and Park Avenue in Montreal,
and is the centre of the

neighborhood in which Richler grew up. "St. Urbain was, I suppose, somewhat similar to ghetto streets in New York and Chicago," the narrator of *The Street* explains. "There were a number of crucial differences, however. We were Canadians, therefore we had a king. We also had 'pea-soups,' that is to say, French Canadians, in the neighborhood."

A product of the St. Urbain Street world, Richler has spent much of his writing career chronicling, celebrating, and criticizing the Jewish Montreal of his upbringing. Whether the settings of his eight novels are St. Urbain Street itself or European capitals, he never allows his major characters to forsake the Montreal world that shaped them.

Richler left Canada in 1951, "foolishly convinced that merely by quitting the country, I could put my picayune past behind me. Like many of my contemporaries, I was mistakenly charged with scorn for all things Canadian. For the truth is if we were indeed hemmed in by the boring, the inane and the absurd, we foolishly blamed it all on Canada, failing to grasp that we would suffer from a surfeit of the boring, the inane and the absurd wherever we eventually settled and would carry Canada with us everywhere for good measure." Richler's two-decade sojourn in Europe ended in the early 1970s, when he returned to Canada to resume permanent residence in the city that permeates his fiction.

As a novelist and journalist, Richler is in the main a satirist, an artist who tries to be an honest witness of his time. "I mean to say what I feel about values and about people living in a time when to my mind there is no agreement on values." The humor and irony in his writings cannot hide his deep pain at the human condition we have brought on ourselves. "What is emerging from the social breakdown of values," he has stated, "is a much more complicated and closely-held personal standard of values. Even in small things, I think we are coming back to a very personal and basic set of values because the exterior values have failed."

In *The Street* are the boys from Fletcher's Field High School, which was "under the jurisdiction of the Montreal Protestant School Board, but had a student body that was nevertheless almost a hundred per cent Jewish. The school became something of a legend in our area." Amidst all the crowded vitality and zany fun of this region of Montreal are quieter moments of understated love and beauty. In the following selection, the narrator looks back on the time of his seventh birthday and his attitudes toward his dying grandmother. Here Richler displays his skill at capturing some of life's most tender moments. As Margaret Laurence observes, "There is another quality, not often mentioned in connection with Richler, but which nearly all his writing contains, and that is tenderness. This vital counterpoint in Richler's writing has not had the recognition or critical attention it should have had. Accompanying the genuine tenderness in his fiction,... there is a total and merciful lack of anything approaching sentimentality."

The Summer
My Grandmother
Was Supposed to Die

D r. Katzman discovered the gangrene on one of his monthly visits. "She won't last a month," he said.

He said the same the second month, the third and the fourth, and now she lay dying in the heat of the back bedroom.

"God in heaven," my mother said, "what's she holding on for?"

The summer my grandmother was supposed to die we did not chip in with the Greenbaums to take a cottage in the Laurentians. My grandmother, already bed-ridden for seven years, could not be moved again. The doctor came twice a week. The only thing was to stay in the city and wait for her to die or, as my mother said, pass away. It was a hot summer, her bedroom was just behind the kitchen, and when we sat down to eat we could smell her. The dressings on my grandmother's left leg had to be changed several times a day and, according to Dr. Katzman, any day might be her last in this world. "It's in the hands of the Almighty," he said.

"It won't be long now," my father said, "and she'll be better off, if you know what I mean?"

A nurse came every day from the Royal Victorian Order. She arrived punctually at noon and at five to twelve I'd join the rest of the boys under the outside staircase to peek up her dress as she climbed to our second-storey flat. Miss Bailey favored absolutely beguiling pink panties, edged with lace, and that was better than waiting under the stairs for Cousin Bessie, for instance, who wore enormous cotton bloomers, rain or shine.

I was sent out to play as often as possible, because my mother felt it was not good for me to see somebody dying. Usually, I would just roam the scorched streets. There was Duddy, Gas sometimes, Hershey, Stan, Arty and me.

"Before your grandmaw kicks off," Duddy said, "she's going to roll her eyes and gurgle. That's what they call the death-rattle."

"Aw, you know everything. *Putz.*"

"I read it, you jerk," Duddy said, whacking me one, "in Perry Mason."

Home again I would usually find my mother sour and spent. Sometimes she wept.

"She's dying by inches," she said to my father one stifling night, "and none of them ever come to see her. Oh, such children," she added, going on to curse them vehemently in Yiddish.

"They're not behaving right. It's certainly not according to Hoyle," my father said.

Dr. Katzman continued to be astonished. "It must be will-power alone that keeps her going," he said. "That, and your excellent care."

"It's not my mother any more in the back room, Doctor. It's an animal. I want her to die."

"Hush. You don't mean it. You're tired." Dr. Katzman dug into his black bag and produced pills for her to take. "Your wife's a remarkable woman," he told my father.

"You don't so say," my father replied, embarrassed.

"A born nurse."

My sister and I used to lie awake talking about our grandmother. "After she dies," I said, "her hair will go on growing for another twenty-four hours."

"Says who?"

"Duddy Kravitz. Do you think Uncle Lou will come from New York for the funeral?"

"I suppose so."

"Boy, that means another fiver for me. Even more for you."

"You shouldn't say things like that or her ghost will come back to haunt you."

"Well, I'll be able to go to her funeral anyway. I'm not too young any more."

I was only six years old when my grandfather died, and so I wasn't allowed to go to his funeral.

I have one imperishable memory of my grandfather. Once he called me into his study, set me down on his lap, and made a drawing of a horse for me. On the horse he drew a rider. While I watched and giggled he

gave the rider a beard and the fur-trimmed round hat of a rabbi, a
straimel, just like he wore.

My grandfather had been a Zaddik, one of the Righteous, and I've
been assured that to study Talmud with him had been an illuminating
experience. I wasn't allowed to go to his funeral, but years later I was
shown the telegrams of condolence that had come from Eire and Poland
and even Japan. My grandfather had written many books: a translation
of the Book of Splendour (the Zohar) into modern Hebrew, some
twenty years work, and lots of slender volumes of sermons, hasidic tales,
and rabbinical commentaries. His books had been published in Warsaw
and later in New York.

"At the funeral," my mother said, "they had to have six motorcycle
policemen to control the crowds. It was such a heat that twelve women
fainted—and I'm *not* counting Mrs. Waxman from upstairs. With her,
you know, *anything* to fall into a man's arms. Even Pinsky's. And did I
tell you that there was even a French Canadian priest there?"

"Aw, you're kidding me."

"The priest was some *knacker*. A bishop maybe. He used to study with
the *zeyda*. The *zeyda* was a real personality, you know. Spiritual and
worldly-wise at the same time. Such personalities they don't make any
more. Today rabbis and peanuts come in the same size."

But, according to my father, the *zeyda* (his father-in-law) hadn't
been as celebrated as all that. "There are things I could say," he told me.
"There was another side to him."

My grandfather had sprung from generations and generations of
rabbis, his youngest son was a rabbi, but none of his grandchildren
would be one. My Cousin Jerry was already a militant socialist. I once
heard him say, "When the men at the kosher bakeries went out on strike
the *zeyda* spoke up against them on the streets and in the *shuls*. It was of
no consequence to him that the men were grossly underpaid. His
superstitious followers had to have bread. Grandpappy," Jerry said,
"was a prize reactionary."

A week after my grandfather died my grandmother suffered a
stroke. Her right side was completely paralysed. She couldn't speak. At
first it's true, she could manage a coherent word or two and move her
right hand enough to write her name in Hebrew. Her name was Malka.
But her condition soon began to deteriorate.

My grandmother had six children and seven step-children, for my
grandfather had been married before. His first wife had died in the old
country. Two years later he had married my grandmother, the only
daughter of the most affluent man in the *shtetl*, and their marriage had
been a singularly happy one. My grandmother had been a beautiful girl.

She had also been a shrewd, resourceful, and patient wife. Qualities, I fear, indispensible to life with a Zaddik. For the synagogue paid my grandfather no stipulated salary and much of the money he picked up here and there he had habitually distributed among rabbinical students, needy immigrants and widows. A vice, for such it was to his impecunious family, which made him as unreliable a provider as a drinker. To carry the analogy further, my grandmother had to make hurried, surreptitious trips to the pawnbroker with her jewellery. Not all of it to be redeemed, either. But her children had been looked after. The youngest, her favorite, was a rabbi in Boston, the oldest was the actor-manager of a Yiddish theatre in New York, and another was a lawyer. One daughter lived in Montreal, two in Toronto. My mother was the youngest daughter and when my grandmother had her stroke there was a family conclave and it was decided that my mother would take care of her. This was my father's fault. All the other husbands spoke up—they protested hotly that their wives had too much work—they could never manage it—but my father detested quarrels and so he was silent. And my grandmother came to stay with us.

Her bedroom, the back bedroom, had actually been promised to me for my seventh birthday, but now I had to go on sharing a room with my sister. So naturally I was resentful when each morning before I left for school my mother insisted that I go in and kiss my grandmother goodbye.

"Bouyo-bouyo," was the only sound my grandmother could make.

During those first hopeful months—"Twenty years ago who would have thought there'd be a cure for diabetes?" my father asked. "Where there's life, you know."—my grandmother would smile and try to speak, her eyes charged with effort; and I wondered if she knew that I was waiting for her room.

Even later there were times when she pressed my hand urgently to her bosom with her surprisingly strong left arm. But as her illness dragged on and on she became a condition in the house, something beyond hope or reproach, like the leaky ice-box, there was less recognition and more ritual in those kisses. I came to dread her room. A clutter of sticky medicine bottles and the cracked toilet chair beside the bed; glazed but imploring eyes and a feeble smile, the wet smack of her crooked lips against my cheeks. I flinched from her touch. And after two years, I protested to my mother, "What's the use of telling her I'm going here or I'm going there? She doesn't even recognize me any more."

"Don't be fresh. She's your grandmother."

My uncle who was in the theatre in New York sent money regularly to help support my grandmother and, for the first few months, so did the other children. But once the initial and sustaining excitement had passed the children seldom came to our house any more. Anxious weekly visits–"And how is she today, poor lamb?"–quickly dwindled to a dutiful monthly looking in, then a semi-annual visit, and these always on the way to somewhere.

When the children did come my mother was severe with them. "I have to lift her on that chair three times a day maybe. And what makes you think I always catch her in time? Sometimes I have to change her linen twice a day. That's a job I'd like to see your wife do," she said to my uncle, the rabbi.

"We could send her to the Old People's Home."

"Now there's an idea," my father said.

"Not so long as I'm alive." My mother shot my father a scalding look, "Say something, Sam."

"Quarreling will get us nowhere. It only creates bad feelings."

Meanwhile, Dr. Katzman came once a month. "It's astonishing," he would say each time. "She's as strong as a horse."

"Some life for a person," my father said. "She can't speak–she doesn't recognize anybody–what is there for her?"

The doctor was a cultivated man; he spoke often for women's clubs, sometimes on Yiddish literature and other times, his rubicund face hot with menace, the voice taking on a doomsday tone, on the cancer threat. "Who are we to judge?" he asked.

Every evening, during the first few months of my grandmother's illness, my mother would read her a story by Sholem Aleichem. "Tonight she smiled," my mother would report defiantly. "She understood. I can tell."

Bright afternoons my mother would lift the old lady into a wheelchair and put her out in the sun and once a week she gave her a manicure. Somebody always had to stay in the house in case my grandmother called. Often, during the night, she would begin to wail unaccountably and my mother would get up and rock her mother in her arms for hours. But in the fourth year of my grandmother's illness the strain began to tell. Besides looking after my grandmother, my mother had to keep house for a husband and two children. She became scornful of my father and began to find fault with my sister and me. My father started to spend his evenings playing pinochle at Tansky's Cigar & Soda. Weekends he took me to visit his brothers and sisters. Wherever my father went people had little snippets of advice for him.

"Sam, you might as well be a bachelor. One of the other children should take the old lady for a while. You're just going to have to put your foot down for once."

"Yeah, in your face maybe."

My Cousin Libby, who was at McGill, said, "This could have a very damaging effect on the development of your children. These are their formative years, Uncle Samuel, and the omnipresence of death in the house..."

"What you need is a boy friend," my father said. *"And how."*

After supper my mother took to falling asleep in her chair, even in the middle of Lux Radio Theatre. One minute she would be sewing a patch in my breeches or making a list of girls to call for a bingo party, proceeds for the Talmud Torah, and the next she would be snoring. Then, inevitably, there came the morning she just couldn't get out of bed and Dr. Katzman had to come round a week before his regular visit. "Well, well, this won't do, will it?"

Dr. Katzman led my father into the kitchen. "Your wife's got a gallstone condition," he said.

My grandmother's children met again, this time without my mother, and decided to put the old lady in the Jewish Old People's Home on Esplanade Street. While my mother slept an ambulance came to take my grandmother away.

"It's for the best," Dr. Katzman said, but my father was in the back room when my grandmother held on tenaciously to the bedpost, not wanting to be moved by the two men in white.

"Easy does it, granny," the younger man said.

Afterwards my father did not go in to see my mother. He went out for a walk.

When my mother got out of bed two weeks later her cheeks had regained their normal pinkish hue; for the first time in months, she actually joked with me. She became increasingly curious about how I was doing in school and whether or not I shined my shoes regularly. She began to cook special dishes for my father again and resumed old friendships with the girls on the parochial school board. Not only did my father's temper improve, but he stopped going to Tansky's every night and began to come home early from work. But my grandmother's name was seldom mentioned. Until one evening, after I'd had a fight with my sister, I said, "Why can't I move into the back bedroom now?"

My father glared at me. "Big-mouth."

"It's empty, isn't it?"

The next afternoon my mother put on her best dress and coat and new spring hat.

"Don't go looking for trouble," my father said.

"It's been a month. Maybe they're not treating her right."

"They're experts."

"Did you think I was never going to visit her? I'm not inhuman, you know."

"Alright, go." But after she had gone my father stood by the window and said, "I was born lucky, and that's it."

I sat on the outside stoop watching the cars go by. My father waited on the balcony above, cracking peanuts. It was six o'clock, maybe later, when the ambulance slowed down and rocked to a stop right in front of our house. "I knew it," my father said. "I was born with all the luck."

My mother got out first, her eyes red and swollen, and hurried upstairs to make my grandmother's bed.

"You'll get sick again," my father said.

"I'm sorry, Sam, but what could I do? From the moment she saw me she cried and cried. It was terrible."

"They're recognized experts there. They know how to take care of her better than you do."

"Experts? Expert murderers you mean. She's got bedsores, Sam. Those dirty little Irish nurses they don't change her linen often enough they hate her. She must have lost twenty pounds in there."

"Another month and you'll be flat on your back again. I'll write you a guarantee, if you want."

My father became a regular at Tansky's again and, once more, I had to go in and kiss my grandmother in the morning. Amazingly, she had begun to look like a man. Little hairs had sprouted on her chin, she had grown a spiky grey moustache, and she was practically bald.

Yet again my uncles and aunts sent five dollar bills, though erratically, to help pay for my grandmother's support. Elderly people, former followers of my grandfather, came to inquire about the old lady's health. They sat in the back bedroom with her, leaning on their canes, talking to themselves and rocking to and fro. "The Holy Shakers," my father called them. I avoided the seamed, shrunken old men because they always wanted to pinch my cheeks or trick me with a dash of snuff and laugh when I sneezed. When the visit with my grandmother was over the old people would unfailingly sit in the kitchen with my mother for another hour, watching her make *lokshen*, slurping lemon tea out of a saucer. They would recall the sayings and books and charitable deeds of the late Zaddik.

"At the funeral," my mother never wearied of telling them, "they had to have six motorcycle policemen to control the crowds.

In the next two years there was no significant change in my grandmother's condition, though fatigue, ill-temper, and even morbidity enveloped my mother again. She fought with her brothers and sisters and once, after a particularly bitter quarrel, I found her sitting with her head in her hands. "If, God forbid, I had a stroke," she said, "would you send me to the Old People's Home?"

"Of course not."

"I hope that never in my life do I have to count on my children for anything."

The seventh summer of my grandmother's illness she was supposed to die and we did not know from day to day when it would happen. I was often sent out to eat at an aunt's or at my other grandmother's house. I was hardly ever at home. In those days they let boys into the left-field bleachers of Delormier Downs free during the week and Duddy, Gas sometimes, Hershey, Stan, Arty and me spent many an afternoon at the ball park. The Montreal Royals, kingpin of the Dodger farm system, had a marvellous club at the time. There was Jackie Robinson, Roy Campanella, Lou Ortiz, Red Durrett, Honest John Gabbard, and Kermit Kitman. Kitman was our hero. It used to give us a charge to watch that crafty little Jew, one of ours, running around out there with all those tall dumb southern crackers. "Hey, Kitman," we would yell, "Hey, shmohead, if your father knew you played ball on *shabus*—" Kitman, alas, was all field and no hit. He never made the majors. "There goes Kermit Kitman," we would holler, after he had gone down swinging again, "the first Jewish strike-out king of the International League." This we promptly followed up by bellowing choice imprecations in Yiddish.

It was after one of these games, on a Friday afternoon, that I came home to find a crowd gathered in front of our house.

"That's the grandson," somebody said.

A knot of old people stood staring at our front door from across the street. A taxi pulled up and my aunt hurried out, hiding her face in her hands.

"After so many years," a woman said.

"And probably next year they'll discover a cure. Isn't that always the case?"

The flat was clotted. Uncles and aunts from my father's side of the family, strangers, Dr. Katzman, neighbors, were all milling around and talking in hushed voices. My father was in the kitchen, getting out the apricot brandy. "Your grandmother's dead," he said.

"Where's Maw?"

"In the bedroom with . . . You'd better not go in."

"I want to see her."

My mother wore a black shawl and glared down at a knot of handkerchief clutched in a fist that had been cracked by washing soda.

"Don't come in here," she said.

Several bearded round-shouldered men in shiny black coats surrounded the bed. I couldn't see my grandmother.

"Your grandmother's dead."

"Daddy told me."

"Go wash your face and comb your hair."

"Yes."

"You'll have to get your own supper."

"Sure."

"One minute. The *baba* left some jewellery. The necklace is for Rifka and the ring is for your wife."

"Who's getting married?"

"Better go and wash your face. Remember behind the ears, please."

Telegrams were sent, the obligatory long distance calls were made, and all through the evening relatives and neighbors and old followers of the Zaddik poured into the house. Finally, the man from the funeral parlor arrived.

"There goes the only Jewish businessman in town," Segal said, "who wishes all his customers were German."

"This is no time for jokes."

"Listen, life goes on."

My Cousin Jerry had begun to affect a cigarette holder. "Soon the religious mumbo-jumbo starts," he said to me.

"Wha'?"

"Everybody is going to be sickeningly sentimental."

The next day was the sabbath and so, according to law, my grandmother couldn't be buried until Sunday. She would have to lie on the floor all night. Two grizzly women in white came to move and wash the body and a professional mourner arrived to sit up and pray for her. "I don't trust his face," my mother said. "He'll fall asleep."

"He won't fall asleep."

"You watch him, Sam."

"A fat lot of good prayers will do her now. Alright! Okay! I'll watch him."

My father was in a fury with Segal.

"The way he goes after the apricot brandy you'd think he never saw a bottle in his life before."

Rifka and I were sent to bed, but we couldn't sleep. My aunt was sobbing over the body in the living room; there was the old man praying, coughing and spitting into his handkerchief whenever he woke; and the hushed voices and whimpering from the kitchen, where my father and mother sat. Rifka allowed me a few drags off her cigarette.

"Well, *pisherke*, this is our last night together. Tomorrow you can take over the back room."

"Are you crazy?"

"You always wanted it for yourself, didn't you?"

"She died in there, but."

"So?"

"I couldn't sleep in there now."

"Good night and happy dreams."

"Hey, let's talk some more."

"Did you know," Rifka said, "that when they hang a man the last thing that happens is that he has an orgasm?"

"A wha'?"

"Skip it. I forgot you were still in kindergarten."

"Kiss my Royal Canadian—"

"At the funeral, they're going to open the coffin and throw dirt in her face. It's supposed to be earth from Eretz. They open it and you're going to have to look."

"Says you."

A little while after the lights had been turned out Rifka approached my bed, her head covered with a sheet and her arms raised high. "Bouyo-bouyo. Who's that sleeping in my bed? Woo-woo."

My uncle who was in the theatre and my aunt from Toronto came to the funeral. My uncle the rabbi was there too.

"As long as she was alive," my mother said, "he couldn't even send her five dollars a month. I don't want him in the house, Sam. I can't bear the sight of him."

"You're upset," Dr. Katzman said, "and you don't know what you're saying."

"Maybe you'd better give her a sedative," the rabbi said.

"Sam will you speak up for once, please."

Flushed, eyes heated, my father stepped up to the rabbi. "I'll tell you this straight to your face, Israel," he said. "You've gone down in my estimation."

The rabbi smiled a little.

"Year by year," my father continued, his face burning a brighter red, "your stock has gone down with me."

My mother began to weep and she was led unwillingly to a bed. While my father tried his utmost to comfort her, as he muttered consoling things, Dr. Katzman plunged a needle into her arm. "There we are," he said.

I went to sit on the stoop outside with Duddy. My uncle the rabbi and Dr. Katzman stepped into the sun to light cigarettes.

"I know exactly how you feel," Dr. Katzman said. "There's been a death in the family and the world seems indifferent to your loss. Your heart is broken and yet it's a splendid summer day . . . a day made for love and laughter . . . and that must seem very cruel to you."

The rabbi nodded; he sighed.

"Actually," Dr. Katzman said, "it's remarkable that she held out for so long."

"Remarkable?" the rabbi said. "It's written that if a man has been married twice he will spend as much time with his first wife in heaven as he did on earth. My father, may he rest in peace, was married to his first wife for seven years and my mother, may she rest in peace, has managed to keep alive for seven years. Today in heaven she will be able to join my father, may he rest in peace."

Dr. Katzman shook his head. "It's amazing," he said. He told my uncle that he was writing a book based on his experiences as a healer. "The mysteries of the human heart."

"Yes."

"Astonishing."

My father hurried outside. "Dr. Katzman, please. It's my wife. Maybe the injection wasn't strong enough. She just doesn't stop crying. It's like a tap. Can you come in, please?"

"Excuse me," Dr. Katzman said to my uncle.

"Of course." My uncle turned to Duddy and me. "Well, boys," he said, "what would you like to be when you grow up?"

Works by Mordecai Richler

FICTION

The Acrobats. London: Deutsch, 1954.
Son of a Smaller Hero. London: Deutsch, 1955.
A Choice of Enemies. London: Deutsch, 1957.
The Apprenticeship of Duddy Kravitz. London: Deutsch, 1959.
The Incomparable Atuk. Toronto: McClelland and Stewart, 1963.
Cocksure. Toronto: McClelland and Stewart, 1968.
The Street. Toronto: McClelland and Stewart, 1969.
Saint Urbain's Horseman. Toronto: McClelland and Stewart, 1971.
Joshua Then and Now. Toronto: McClelland and Stewart, 1980.

Jacob Two-Two Meets the Hooded Fang. Toronto: McClelland and Stewart, 1975. (children's book)

ESSAYS

Hunting Tigers Under Glass. Toronto: McClelland and Stewart, 1968.
Shovelling Trouble. Toronto: McClelland and Stewart, 1972.
Notes on an Endangered Species and Others. New York: Knopf, 1974.
The Great Comic Book Heroes and Other Essays. Toronto: McClelland and Stewart, 1978.

Interviews with Mordecai Richler

The Tamarack Review, 2 (Winter, 1957), 6-23.
Conversations with Canadian Novelists. Edited by Donald Cameron. Toronto: Macmillan, 1973. Vol. 1, pp. 114-27.
Eleven Canadian Novelists. Edited by Graeme Gibson. Toronto: Anansi, 1973, pp. 265-99.
Journal of Canadian Fiction, 3(Winter, 1974), 73-6.

Joyce Marshall

Joyce Marshall is a writer and a translator equally fluent in English and in French. Born in Montreal in 1913, she was the eldest in a family of five children. Her English-speaking family lived in Montreal and frequently vacationed in the summers in a variety of French-speaking villages along the St. Lawrence River, including Pointe Claire, which bears some resemblance to the setting of "The Accident." Marshall is a graduate of McGill University and in recent years has lived in Toronto, where she is active as a writer, translator, and free-lance editor.

Marshall is one of the most accomplished and sensitive translators of Quebec literature. Her translations include *Word from New France: The Selected Letters of Marie de l'Incarnation* (1967) and Eugène Cloutier's travel journal, *No Passport: A Discovery of Canada* (1968). Her skilled translations have captured the sensitivity of Gabrielle Roy's prose in three volumes: *The Road Past Altamont* (1967), *Windflower* (1970), and *Enchanted Summer* (1976). Her translation of the last volume won the Canada Council Translation Prize for 1976.

In her novels and short stories Marshall portrays human beings at various ages and in various settings. The folly and fragility of love, the pain of the human predicament, the

evocative power and deception of the memory–such themes recur in her fiction with its careful focus on people and their interactions.

In "The Accident," first published in 1976, the narrator, Martha, looks back on the summer when she was nine, the "last and most difficult of our three summers in the village." During that summer the young Martha received "that first sense of the true otherness of others, just as themselves"; in an instant she came to see her younger sister as an individual, a person. Looking back on the origins of this story, Marshall remarks, "I think I saw an accident. I think I saw a badly injured man. I don't know if I did or didn't." For the narrator of "The Accident," memory is the only avenue by which people can try to recapture their earlier selves and thus increase their understanding of their present selves. One of her aims is to get back to these earlier selves, "just as they were, because then perhaps I could untangle the truth of what happened or just seemed to happen."

The Accident

In that last and most difficult of our three summers in the village, I see us as trailing around endlessly together in a little string. I can almost look down and find those children, purely, without the future—all I now know or surmise about Hilary and Laura and have learned or made of myself. I would like to really get back to them, just as they were, because then perhaps I could untangle the truth of what happened or just seemed to happen—events or fancies that are linked for me always with the picture of three children moving along unwillingly and rather slowly, never side by side as I remember them but one after one after one in the distinct shapes and sizes that spaced out the five years. We were two and a half years apart, so precisely that Laura, the youngest, shared my birthday. Which was just one of many things I held against her.

The youngest except for the baby. I should make that clear. The baby, not yet called Claudia because my parents were finding it harder even than usual to agree upon a name, was never a threat. The real warfare was between us older three. And it was warfare. It was relentless. It was bitter. Yet at the time I speak of, before we were strong enough to break away (physically) from one another, we were tied together most of the day. For safety. We lived—or camped—that summer a long way back from the broadening of the St. Lawrence River we called the lake on the dirt and pebble trail known somewhat grandly as St. John's Road; for the twice-daily swims that were ritual in our family we had to cross two sets of railway tracks—each with its little station, gate

111

and roller-coaster hill– and later the main village street across to the lake side and the beginning of the gentle curve that led around to the beach.

In winter I had all the aloneness I could wish in my own class at school. And different fears and different learning. But memory is capricious. I seldom, when I look back at my childhood, connect the seasons, as if our twice-yearly upheavals of dogs and cats and children split them apart. And when I think of the struggle with my sisters, I remember chiefly the summers, which were long in our family, slow similar days stretching from May until November. And, of course, the road– that soft easy curve edging the lake. Is it still there, I wonder. Or has it been swallowed up by the airport? I have never tried to know which. It remains. My archetypal road that I dream of again and again in so many ways. I was there again last night but the lake had become an abyss, I was trying to throw an infant– a very large screaming infant– over the side; I woke in panic in what seemed for an instant an immense and hollow room. And, because I dislike those murderous dreams, which I shouldn't need any more, I began to think instead of that other safer terror, the accident, and to ask myself, as I have done so many times, whether it really happened as I seem to remember it. Did the man exist, in fact? Can it be possible that I was allowed to stand so close to him, leaning right over him as I seem to do, listening to words that like so many of my childhood words I have no means to understand? He seems real. At least the fear and horror do. Perhaps I have reached back to imagine him, harbinger. At times I can believe this and yet I do seem to see him clearly, lying there bleeding on the edge of that vanished road.

I was nine that year. This I am sure of because the sister who would not become Claudia till ten minutes or so before our grandfather, alarming in canonical robes, splashed her with water and uttered the name, was still quite new. When I see the man, I see her also, lying in her crouched baby position in our old straw carriage with its corduroy lining, under one of the trees in the bumpy ungrassed yard of that strange house. The first human being I loved. The emotion we feel for parents is a demanding, seeking. This new kind of love, which I found whole in me the moment the new little creature was laid on my arms, was a huge inner swelling almost cracking my ribs. Now I understand, I remember thinking, what they mean when they say: My heart swelled. A peremptory feeling, inexplicable, a bit frightening. I didn't know what I was going to do with it. But I rather liked it. It was magic. It still seems magic as I recall it. No later love has staled that first.

I tried to spend as much time as I could beside the baby. Serve her. Just look at her. I ran and fetched. Kept lifting the green mosquito netting tacked over her carriage for a new careful study of the always astonishing line of the cheek, tiny token fingers, bluish eyelid shells. I told myself I would die for her, this small human I didn't have to try to please, who could do nothing for me. My mother, who was almost instinctively alarmed, at least troubled, by my behavior a great part of the time, used to thrust me away when I poked my head too close as she changed or nursed the baby. Why when she was so busy was I suddenly always under her feet? Why was I so quiet? Why didn't I go and help Hilary, who was trying to teach Laura to skip hot pepper on the bit of level road in front of the house? Why didn't I have friends? (When she knew as well as I did that in this rickety farmhouse way back from the village and its few summer cottages there were no friends for me to have.)

I have called it a difficult summer. This was partly the house, not enough rooms for us and those too small, awkwardly cut up and confining with its little low windows and evil smells. And the presence of the farm's real owners in a shack at the end of the vegetable garden just back of the house. My parents, who were always slow about summer rentals, had taken the place at night, had not realized that the quarters to which the farm-family proposed to move for the summer were so close. It was disconcerting to have them all there weeding by day almost under our kitchen window and at night sitting in a row in front of their shack, rocking in unison, gazing at us. My mother, who was sociable, tried waving and gesticulating but, though they smiled and nodded always, it went no further; clearly they had a strong sense of bounds and when our dog went too close they shooed him back. There was quite a large family of half-grown children, including a girl of about my age.

"Go and play with her, Martha," my mother said to me once. "Maybe she'd like to. Poor little thing. Always working. She could help you with French. Show you the cows and chickens. Even if you can't talk much, you could. . .skip, play hopscotch."

The thought of approaching that thin fierce-looking dark girl, whose bed I perhaps slept in and who must hate me for it as I would have hated her in a similar case, filled me with terror but, because I didn't want to admit—and defend—my cowardice, I just said crossly that I didn't like her.

"Yes, she does look a bit common," my mother said.

Her answer, which should have made my not liking the girl all right, was merely puzzling. Did it mean that we were uncommon? And if so, why and how? I knew there was no use trying to find out. My mother was in a very bad mood, tied down almost all day in this poky house where diapers had to be boiled in pails on a wood-burning stove and spread over bushes and rocks to dry. She couldn't play tennis and seldom found time to wheel the carriage to the beach. No days could suddenly be declared too hot for anything but a picnic by the lake or a wild ramble across fields to find blueberries. My father was interested that year, I think, in a mining property in northern Ontario. He was away much of the time, not coming home at night to cool and calm us, change the atmosphere, sing us grand opera, substitute his sort of energy for our mother's. There wasn't even a maid to talk to. The one we'd brought with us had taken one sniff at the kitchen and, refusing even to be led up to examine the "dear little room under the eaves" where she was to sleep, demanded to be put on the very next train back to Montreal. (Our maids often left abruptly. I can't remember even one who lasted a whole summer. We liked the maids, who had fascinating lives and discussed them with us.)

My mother couldn't understand, she kept saying with one of the sideways looks that seemed to discover us for the first time, why she had let this happen. "Why did I marry and have four children?" she asked again and again as if sooner or later she'd find a reason. "I should have been a business girl." We must take a lesson from her and all be business girls. She would see to this herself. I can't remember whether we answered. Mother often complained and in a very vocal, almost automatic way. I don't think we minded being lumped together as something deplorable she had permitted to happppen to her one day when she was looking the wrong way. We were very solidly here; that was all that mattered. Our mother was quick and restless, her energies loose and untapped. In another time and place she would have been a magnificent suffragette. No force-feeding her. She would have starved to the death, no question about that. And whenever I read about Emmeline Pankhurst I see the red-gold hair, proud mouth and glinting eyes of my mother. Meanwhile we were all to be business girls, remote as that seemed. This summer we had other concerns.

The family was shifting again. I can say again, though this is the first of the shifts I really remember. We had always quarrelled, we three, sometimes savagely and physically, had fought as children have to do for position and space, had worked out certain niches for ourselves. Now there was a fourth and places no longer held. Not that we were aware of any of this except in some deep domain of blood and bone. We knew simply—at least I knew—that it was a difficult summer, hot, monotonous. This was my first experience of boredom; I hadn't known that days could simply go on and on, always very much the same. I recall them as hot and parched with a sound of rustling—from the corn perhaps, that rather spindly corn the farm-family weeded. Seldom raining but very often thundery. And no sight or sound or even smell of water. (We were water-creatures in our family, my father too. He had met my mother, we knew, in this very lake, had fallen in love with her sparkling face under the pompommed bathing-cap. We children were all carried into the water before we could walk. And to be in the country but dry, on a hill-top, with no liquid shimmer visible between trees to us was anguish.) And there my mother must stay most of the time with the occasional company of three bickering children who could seldom succeed in being what she frequently told us we ought to be, three dear little sisters. (She herself had been one of seven dear little sisters. We had seen their picture, standing in a close loving rank in front of our grandfather's old rectory at Bolton Centre, all very shiny and neat in high-necked dresses with a great many tucks. They were our despair. They had loved one another then and were still the best of friends, greeting one another after weeks with cries of delight. Children who grew up in rectories were different, it seemed to me, loved automatically, big ones liked nothing better than taking care of little ones, no one ever bit her sister. I could never live up to them.)

I was skinny and long at nine, all knobs and angles. I did not find myself appealing, could not make myself look pretty even with constant practice at the mirror. Worse, my behavior never came out quite as I wanted it to. Success in childhood, I see now, depends in large part on one's gifts as a mimic. I had none. And as I could seldom think quickly enough of a handy lie, I was obliged to try to say what I meant—and sound foolish. Hilary was an excellent mimic, stood watchful close to the grownups and learned to be charming. She was the chief of my enemies, the first usurper, rooting me out of a place I possessed and must long for still. (So that I murder her still in dreams. I'm sorry, Hilary. It's a very impersonal murder.) Not till recently did it occur to me that I was also chief of Hilary's enemies, already firmly established when she came. So that she could only become my mirror? Was obliged to be good, docile and positive because I wasn't. Did I make Hilary too in part as I struggled to make myself? I can see her trotting about that summer, more docile than ever, helping and serving, busying herself with the sort of games adults find enchanting—tucked in some little corner playing house or teacher, dressing up the cat, cuddling Laura.

For Laura, that untested child, had turned fretful, Laura for whom everything had always come easily simply because she was beautiful, in the creamy dimpled way that is the only way for children to be beautiful, and with two expressions: a touching gravity, a beguiling smile. It was hard not to hate someone who just needed to exist to delight. What Hilary thought of her I do not know; this summer she had attached herself to Laura, crooned, protected, made beds for her out of chairs, pretended to feed her. I pinched, crowded, snatched. And Laura, who seldom cried, had never told tales, not even when a blow from my croquet mallet made her bite her tongue till it bled, was now always whimpering, saw threats in shadows, screamed at thunder so that she had to be taken out of bed, rocked, called darling baby. She was called darling baby far too often, I thought. Beguiling always, she was now, it seemed to me, learning to work at being beguiling. I resented this bitterly, wanting my treasure, the real baby, to have all the love, simply because she was my chosen one. I noticed that Laura seldom looked at the baby, didn't seem even to like her. Jealous for my darling, I saw any subtraction of love from her as an insult to me. It was a trying summer as we slowly became more and more ourselves and in new ways. If it was really quite that simple. I can't be sure because, when you get down to it, I remember very little. Just a general stormy sense—that rustle, all that growly thunder—an impression of pushing and pulling, of things that ought to be clear and easy not clear or easy.

And though I would have preferred to stay at home with my darling, who was learning to smile when I lifted the netting to examine her, I was obliged to spend almost all those long summer days with two enemies. Walking with them through that village where no one ever spoke to us. Fairly well used, I suppose—and this may be a handy lesson to learn early—to a world in which many things and most people were indifferent. In the city during the winter I sometimes joined with my schoolmates to throw stones at the French children. *Pea soup. Pea soup, pea soup and Johnny cake make the Frenchie's belly ache.* I had learned these interesting taunts while I was learning "Come over, red rover" and "One two three alarie," and all were games, I thought. In this very small village, which I always recall as silent, almost painted because nothing I heard was comprehended, in some way so subtle and yet so clear I never tried to examine it, I was very definitely not at home. It must have been at about this time that I began to feel rather precarious, that finger and thumb could flick me away. (Even when I was running, pelting through fields, and should have felt most physical and real, I would begin to seem weightless, floaty.) But if we did not seem to be observed, except with some loose blanket disapproval—so much the same, always, it could be pretty well ignored—this had its good side too. We could go anywhere we liked. In a world where all the adults were enemies, leagued together by similar tastes and standards, it was a relief to find some who, however great their displeasure, would never tell our parents.

When I say we could go anywhere, I don't mean by this that there was anywhere much to go. We weren't given pocket-money, couldn't have kept track of it in our clutter of sand-pails, wadded towels, and rubber bathing-caps, and so couldn't go into the store–except on occasional Saturdays with my father–to brood over the huge glass jars that held all the marvellous candy that could be bought for a single cent. But because we were all irritable that summer we broke rules, almost without thinking. There weren't many. *Don't loiter or peer into the stores.* We loitered and peered. *Don't climb fences on St. John's Road. You might meet a bull.* We climbed fences and picked flowers almost out of the mouths of the cows, examined bluebirds' nests in rotting fence-posts, pulled long stalks of timothy to suck. And when there was a little gathering of people on the expanded sidewalk in front of the grocery-store or the butcher's, we walked right into it, trailed through it and, as it seemed, made no more impression than when we chopped through the water with our bouncing and energetic breast-stroke at our little cove. Which is why, I imagine, we could have managed, young and small as we were, to get through to the front of the crowd that pressed that day around the man who lay dying after the accident. The village people simply didn't notice us, small alien figures always roaming about.

I've thought of it all so many times, smudging it probably. But always the same details come. And the same gaps. We were on our way home from the beach, had passed the long fence of the magnificent house, fancily gabled behind trees–it had fifty-six rooms, I'd heard–and there just ahead were all those people staring at something in front of them. I suppose to us it was simply an interesting sight. We were curious. So in we went, I first because bigger and stronger, better at wriggling through, the others after.

There were often accidents at the sharp bend the road was forced to take before it slipped into its slow curve. On the north side, the side where we weren't allowed to walk, the corner of a white-plastered, rather small house jutted through the sidewalk a foot or two into the road. Some old witch-lady had lived there for years, refusing to sacrifice part of her house or let it be moved back. She believed, we had heard, that since she and her house had been there when the road was just a track, they had a right to remain. Cars often met head-on at that spot. The man in today's accident, I learned from adult discussion later, had been speeding, had been drunk, might have fallen asleep in the sun, at any rate had failed to make the sudden veer. His car was on our side of the road, against a telephone pole, he himself a few feet away. Someone must have moved him for I see him as lying straight and tidy on his back, on the grassy strip between the wooden sidewalk and the unrailed gallery of a house. The village people looked down at him as if, having done what they could, the necessary phone calls made, they sensed that he wanted to be alone and let him be. I have an impression of tremendous excitement and yet silence. He himself was not silent. He was crying as I looked into his face, very close to it, bent a little forward as I had had to do to work my way through the crowd. He was calling someone, at least speaking the same few syllables again and again. I think I imagined that he was calling a name. Have I added the blood? Transported that broken bleeding face from elsewhere? Normandy? Spain? I remember a great deal of blood, all very red. In his hair, running into his eyes. Perhaps coming from his eyes. (I seem to know that he couldn't see.) A red pool in the grass around his head as he went on calling in that very fast, bubbling sort of voice. I believe I simply stood there, stooping slightly, looking at him. Not wanting to. Unable to turn or move.

Then at some point an awareness of Laura. Right at my knee. Perhaps pulling at me, for I remember her hand, her battered yellow sand-pail and the little shovel with the paintless handle. (This must be real for I see her hand in the scale of those times, the top of her head with the glint of the sun on its crown.) She was behind me, trying to get past me, whimpering, frightened. (I asked her once. "Do you remember, Laura? A terrible accident—a man badly hurt when we were little?" "Oh yes," she said. "At one of those parades Dad used to take us to. A horse reared and fell back, crushing the rider." And looked so stricken, for Laura has grown up to be the most tender-hearted of us all, that I pressed no further. We lived different lives, our memories are loose in our own heads and seldom meet.) Hilary I haven't asked, for Hilary would maintain as she always does that she remembers nothing at all from before she was eight. Yet very clearly at my other side I can hear her high-pitched, very positive voice: "They're going to take him to the hospital. Don't worry, darling baby Laura. They're going to take him to the hospital and they're going to sew him all together again. Don't worry, Laura. They're going to—."

"Shut-up," my own voice, "oh shut up." And I looked down—again or still—at Laura's face just at my side, saw it for the first time as a human face detached from me, crumpling before something far too big for it. Saw all sorts of other things, whether or not I put them in words, and with that first sense of the true otherness of others just as themselves, had an inkling at least of all that would be required of me, willing or not, as I went on living—demands that are made of us that we must fulfil and love that can come, and does, in all sorts of forms, not only for the chosen.

I think I knew I had to get Laura away from there and did, took hold of that hand with the sand-pail and, twisting and turning as I had entered it, led her out of the crowd. But very little is sure in our memories. Of all our trudges home through the village, our walks up St. John's Road, I cannot select that one from the others. It was a difficult and edgy summer. Always thundery, always very much the same.

Works by Joyce Marshall

FICTION

Presently Tomorrow. Boston: Little,
    Brown, 1946.
Lovers and Strangers. Philadelphia:
    Lippincott, 1957.
A Private Place. Ottawa: Oberon, 1975.

Mavis Gallant

Linnet Muir, the heroine and the narrator of "In Youth Is Pleasure," leaves New York City to return to Montreal, the city of her birth. Filled with memories of Montreal past, the eighteen-year-old soon discovers that the present city is and is not the city she remembers.

Like Linnet, Mavis Gallant was born in Montreal (1922). Educated in many schools in Canada and the United States, she started publishing in 1944 when her first two short stories appeared; the same year she began work as a journalist for the *Montreal Standard*. During the following six years she wrote, in addition to her fiction, more than sixty feature articles for the *Standard* as well as photo-stories, reviews, and, for nearly two years, a weekly column about radio. According to Mordecai Richler, she is "our most compelling short-story writer since Morley Callaghan."

In 1950 she left Canada for Europe, and since that time she has made Paris her home. Frequently described as a Canadian expatriate, a term she dislikes, Gallant prides herself on her Canadian identity. "A Canadian is someone who has a logical reason to think he is one. My logical reason is that I have never been anything else, nor has it occurred to me that I might be." Like Linnet, she found herself unable to salute the American flag: "When in my American schools I refused to salute the flag, as I've described in 'In Youth Is Pleasure,' there was more to it than adolescent mulishness. I most certainly did not resent Americans. . . . It was simply that I was not an American, the Stars and Stripes was not my flag, and that was that. I resisted a change of citizenship when it was offered me because I knew the result would be fake: whatever I was called, I would continue to think of myself as Canadian."

"In Youth Is Pleasure" (1975), the first of six short stories narrated by Linnet Muir, owes its origin to the research Gallant was undertaking on Alfred Dreyfus, a French army officer unjustly court-martialled for high treason in 1894. "Gradually, as I restored his Paris, his life, I discovered something in common with that taciturn, reserved military figure: we had both resolved upon a way of life at an early age and had pursued our aims with overwhelming single-mindedness. He had been determined to become an officer in the French Army, over his family's advice and objections, just as I had been determined to write as a way of life in the face of an almost unanimous belief that I was foolish, would fail, would be sorry, and would creep back with defeat as a return ticket."

From the Paris of Dreyfus to the Montreal of Gallant's childhood was a short mental journey: "Once I had a point in common I moved with greater sureness into the book I wanted to write. I had thought of it sometimes as a river where I was drifting farther and farther from shore. At the same time–I suppose about then–there began to be restored in some underground river of the mind a lost Montreal. An image of Sherbrooke Street, at night, with the soft gaslight and leaf shadows on the sidewalk–so far back in childhood that it is more a sensation than a picture–was the starting point."

"In Youth Is Pleasure" presents the fictional world that Gallant creates so often. Her stories return to moments in memory and history, and her characters frequently learn that memory, though falsifying a former reality, also allows its reconstruction in the world of the imagination. The characters in the Linnet Muir stories, their author has commented, "are not identical with people I knew in my life. The stories are really the reconstruction of a city which no longer exists. The girl [Linnet Muir] is obviously close to me. She isn't *myself*, but a kind of summary of some of the things I once was. In real life I was far more violent and much more impulsive and not nearly so reasonable. Straight autobiography would be boring. It would bore me. It would bore the reader. The stories are a kind of reality *necessarily* transformed."

In Youth
Is
Pleasure

My father died, then my grandmother; my mother was left, but we did not get on. I was probably disagreeable with anyone who felt entitled to give me instructions and advice. We seldom lived under the same roof, which was just as well. She had found me civil and amusing until I was ten, at which time I was said to have become pert and obstinate. She was impulsive, generous, in some ways better than most other people, but without any feeling for cause and effect; this made her at the least unpredictable and at the most a serious element of danger. I was fascinated by her, though she worried me; then all at once I lost interest. I was fifteen when this happened. I would forget to answer her letters and even to open them. It was not rejection or anything so violent as dislike but a simple indifference I cannot account for. It was much the way I would be later with men I fell out of love with, but I was too young to know that then. As for my mother, whatever I thought, felt, said, wrote, and wore had always been a positive source of exasperation. From time to time she attempted to alter the form, the outward shape at least, of the creature she thought she was modelling, but at last she came to the conclusion there must be something wrong with the clay. Her final unexpected upsurge of attention coincided with my abrupt unconcern: one may well have been the reason for the other.

It took the form of digging into my diaries and notebooks and it yielded, among other documents, a two-year-old poem, Kiplingesque in its rhythms, entitled "Why I Am a Socialist." The first words of the first line were "You ask,..." then came a long answer. But it was not an answer to anything she'd wondered. Like all mothers–at least, all I have known–she was obsessed with the entirely private and possibly trivial matter of a daughter's virginity. Why I was a Socialist she rightly conceded to be none of her business. Still, she must have felt she had to say something, and the something was "You had better be clever, because you will never be pretty." My response was to take–take, not grab–the poem from her and tear it up. No voices were raised. I never mentioned the incident to anyone. That is how it was. We became, presently, mutually unconcerned. My detachment was put down to the coldness of my nature, hers to the exhaustion of trying to bring me up. It must have been a relief to her when, in the first half of Hitler's war, I slipped quietly and finally out of her life. I was now eighteen, and completely on my own. By "on my own" I don't mean a show of independence with Papa-Mama footing the bills: I mean that I was solely responsible for my economic survival and that no living person felt any duty toward me.

On a bright morning in June I arrived in Montreal, where I'd been born, from New York, where I had been living and going to school. My luggage was a small suitcase and an Edwardian picnic hamper–a preposterous piece of baggage my father had brought from England some twenty years before; it had been with me since childhood, when his death turned my life into a helpless migration. In my purse was a birth certificate and five American dollars, my total fortune, the parting gift of a Canadian actress in New York, who had taken me to see *Mayerling* before I got on the train. She was kind and good and terribly hard up, and she had no idea that apart from some loose change I had nothing more. The birth certificate, which testified I was Linnet Muir, daughter of Angus and of Charlotte, was my right of passage. I did not own a passport and possibly never had seen one. In those days there was almost no such thing as a "Canadian." You were Canadian-born, and a British subject, too, and you had a third label with no consular reality, like the racial tag that on Soviet passports will make a German of someone who has never been to Germany. In Canada you were also whatever your father happened to be, which in my case was English. He was half Scot, but English by birth, by mother, by instinct. I did not feel a scrap British or English, but I was not an American either. In American schools I had refused to salute the flag. My denial of that curiously Fascist-looking celebration, with the right arm stuck straight out, and my silence when the others intoned the trusting "...and justice for all" had never been thought offensive, only stubborn. Americans then were accustomed to gratitude from foreigners but did not demand it; they quite innocently could not imagine any country fit to live in except their own. If I could not recognize it, too bad for me. Besides, I was not a refugee–just someone from the backwoods. "You got schools in Canada?" I had been asked. "You got radios?" And once, from a teacher, "What do they major in up there? Basket-weaving?"

My travel costume was a white piqué jacket and skirt that must have been crumpled and soot-flecked, for I had sat up all night. I was reading, I think, a novel by Sylvia Townsend Warner. My hair was thick and long. I wore my grandmother's wedding ring, which was too large, and which I would lose before long. I desperately wanted to look more than my age, which I had already started to give out as twenty-one. I was travelling light; my picnic hamper contained the poems and journals I had judged fit to accompany me into my new, unfettered existence, and some books I feared I might not find again in clerical Quebec–Zinoviev and Lenin's *Against the Stream*, and a few beige pamphlets from the Little Lenin Library, purchased second hand in New York. I had a picture of Mayakovsky torn out of *Cloud in Trousers* and one of Paddy Finucane, the Irish R.A.F. fighter pilot, who was killed the following summer. I had not met either of these men, but I approved of them both very much. I had abandoned my beloved but cumbersome anthologies of American and English verse, confident that I had whatever I needed by heart. I knew every word of Stephen Vincent Benét's "Litany for Dictatorships" and "Notes to be Left in a Cornerstone," and the other one that begins:

> *They shot the Socialists at half-past five*
> *In the name of victorious Austria. . . .*

I could begin anywhere and rush on in my mind to the end. "Notes. . ." was the New York I knew I would never have again, for there could be no journeying backward; the words "but I walked it young" were already a gate shut on a part of my life. The suitcase held only the fewest possible summer clothes. Everything else had been deposited at the various war-relief agencies of New York. In those days I made symbols out of everything, and I must have thought that by leaving a tartan skirt somewhere I was shedding past time. I remember one of those wartime agencies well because it was full of Canadian matrons. They wore pearl earrings like the Duchess of Kent's and seemed to be practicing her tiny smile. Brooches pinned to their cashmere cardigans carried some daft message about the Empire. I heard one of them exclaiming, "You don't expect me, a Britisher, to drink tea made with tea bags!" Good plain girls from the little German towns of Ontario, christened probably Wilma, Jean, and Irma, they had flowing eighteenth-century names like Georgiana and Arabella now. And the Americans, who came in with their arms full of every stitch they could spare, would urge them, the Canadian matrons, to stand fast on the cliffs, to fight the fight, to slug the enemy on the landing fields, to belt him one on the beaches, to keep going with whatever iron rations they could scrape up in Bronxville and Scarsdale; and the Canadians half-shut their eyes and tipped their heads back like Gertrude Lawrence and said in thrilling Benita Hume accents that they would do that–indeed they would. I recorded "They're all trained nurses, actually. The Canadian ones have a good reputation. They managed to marry these American doctors."

Canada had been in Hitler's war from the very beginning, but America was still uneasily at peace. Recruiting had already begun; I had seen a departure from New York for Camp Stewart in Georgia, and some of the recruits' mothers crying and even screaming and trying to run alongside the train. The recruits were going off to drill with broomsticks because there weren't enough guns; they still wore old-fashioned headgear and were paid twenty-one dollars a month. There was a song about it: "For twenty-one dollars a day, once a month." As my own train crossed the border to Canada I expected to sense at once an air of calm and grit and dedication, but the only changes were from prosperous to shabby, from painted to unpainted, from smiling to dour. I was entering a poorer and a curiously empty country, where the faces of the people gave nothing away. The crossing was my sea change. I silently recited the vow I had been preparing for weeks: that I would never be helpless again and that I would not let anyone make a decision on my behalf.

When I got down from the train at Windsor Station, a man sidled over to me. He had a cap on his head and a bitter Celtic face, with deep indentations along his cheeks, as if his back teeth were pulled. I thought he was asking a direction. He repeated his question, which was obscene. My arms were pinned by the weight of my hamper and suitcase. He brushed the back of his hand over my breasts, called me a name, and edged away. The murderous rage I felt and the revulsion that followed were old friends. They had for years been my reaction to what my diaries called "their hypocrisy." "They" was a world of sly and mumbling people, all of them older than myself. I must have substituted "hypocrisy" for every sort of aggression, because fright was a luxury I could not afford. What distressed me was my helplessness–I who had sworn only a few hours earlier that I'd not be vulnerable again. The man's gaunt face, his drunken breath, the flat voice which I assigned to the graduate of some Christian Brothers teaching establishment haunted me for a long time after that. "The man at Windsor Station" would lurk in the windlowless corridors of my nightmares; he would be the passenger, the only passenger, on a dark tram. The first sight of a city must be the measure for all second looks.

But it was not my first sight. I'd had ten years of it here–the first ten. After that, and before New York (in one sense, my deliverance), there had been a long spell of grief and shadow in an Ontario city, a place full of mean judgments and grudging minds, of paranoid Protestants and slovenly Catholics. To this day I cannot bear the sight of brick houses, or of a certain kind of empty treeless street on a Sunday afternoon. My memory of Montreal took shape while I was there. It was not a random jumble of rooms and summers and my mother singing "We've Come to See Miss Jenny Jones," but the faithful record of the true survivor. I retained, I rebuilt a superior civilization. In that drowned world, Sherbrooke Street seemed to be glittering and white; the vision of a house upon that street was so painful that I was obliged to banish it from the memorial. The small hot rooms of a summer cottage became enormous and cool. If I say that Cleopatra floated down the Chateauguay River, that the Winter Palace was stormed on Sherbrooke Street, that Trafalgar was fought on Lake St. Louis, I mean it naturally; they were the natural backgrounds of my exile and fidelity. I saw now at the far end of Windsor Station–more foreign, echoing, and mysterious than any American station could be–a statue of Lord Mount Stephen, the founder of the Canadian Pacific, which everyone took to be a memorial to Edward VII. Angus, Charlotte, and the smaller Linnet had truly been: this was my proof; once upon a time my instructions had been to make my way to Windsor Station should I ever be lost and to stand at the foot of Edward VII and wait for someone to find me.

I have forgotten to say that no one in Canada knew I was there. I looked up the number of the woman who had once been my nurse, but she had no telephone. I found her in a city directory, and with complete faith that "O. Carette" was indeed Olivia and that she would recall and welcome me I took a taxi to the east end of the city–the French end, the poor end. I was so sure of her that I did not ask the driver to wait (to take me where?) but dismissed him and climbed two flights of dark-brown stairs inside a house that must have been built soon after Waterloo. That it was Olivia who came to the door, that the small grey-haired creature I recalled as dark and towering had to look up at me, that she unhesitatingly offered me shelter all seem as simple now as when I broke my fiver to settle the taxi. Believing that I was dead, having paid for years of Masses for the repose of my heretic soul, almost the first thing she said to me was *"Tu vis?"* I understood *"Tu es ici?"* We straightened it out later. She held both my hands and cried and called me *belle et grande*. *Grande* was good, for among American girls I'd seemed a shrimp. I did not see what there was to cry for; I was here. I was as naturally selfish with Olivia as if her sole reason for being was me. I stayed with her for a while and left when her affection for me made her possessive, and I think I neglected her. On her deathbed she told one of her daughters, the reliable one, to keep an eye on me forever. Olivia was the only person in the world who did not believe I could look after myself. Where she and I were concerned I remained under six.

Now, at no moment of this remarkable day did I feel anxious or worried or forlorn. The man at Windsor Station could not really affect my view of the future. I had seen some of the worst of life, but I had no way of judging it or of knowing what the worst could be. I had a sensation of loud, ruthless power, like an enormous waterfall. The past, the part I would rather not have lived, became small and remote, a dark pinpoint. My only weapons until now had been secrecy and insolence. I had stopped running away from schools and situations when I finally understood that by becoming a name in a file, by attracting attention, I would merely prolong my stay in prison–I mean, the prison of childhood itself. My rebellions then consisted only in causing people who were physically larger and legally sovereign to lose their self-control, to become bleached with anger, to shake with such temper that they broke cups and glasses and bumped into chairs. From the malleable, sunny child Olivia said she remembered, I had become, according to later chroniclers, cold, snobbish, and presumptuous. "You need an iron hand, Linnet." I can still hear that melancholy voice, which belonged to a friend of my mother's. "If anybody ever marries you he'd better have an iron hand." After today I would never need to hear this, or anything approaching it, for the rest of my life.

And so that June morning and the drive through empty, sunlit, wartime streets are even now like a roll of drums in the mind. My life was my own revolution–the tyrants deposed, the constitution wrenched from unwilling hands; I was, all by myself, the liberated crowd setting the palace on fire; I was the flags, the trees, the bannered windows, the flower-decked trains. The singing and the skyrockets of the 1848 I so trustingly believed would emerge out of the war were me, no one but me; and, as in the lyrical first days of any revolution, as in the first days of any love affair, there wasn't the whisper of a voice to tell me, "You might compromise."

If making virtue of necessity has ever had a meaning it must be here: for I was independent *inevitably*. There were good-hearted Americans who knew a bit of my story–as much as I wanted anyone to know–and who hoped I would swim and not drown, but from the moment I embarked on my journey I went on the dark side of the moon. "You seemed so sure of yourself," they would tell me, still troubled, long after this. In the cool journals I kept I noted that my survival meant nothing in the capitalist system; I was one of those not considered to be worth helping, saving, or even investigating. Thinking with care, I see this was true. What could I have turned into in another place? Why, a librarian at Omsk or a file clerk at Tomsk. Well, it hadn't happened that way; I had my private revolution and I settled in with Olivia in Montreal. Sink or swim? Of course I swam. Jobs were for the having; you could pick them up off the ground. Working for a living meant just what it says–a brisk necessity. It would be the least important fragment of my life until I had what I wanted. The cheek of it, I think now: penniless, sleeping in a shed room behind the kitchen of Olivia's cold-water flat, still I pointed across the wooden balustrade in a long open office where I was being considered for employment and said, "But I won't sit there." Girls were *there*, penned in like sheep. I did not think men better than women–only that they did more interesting work and got more money for it. In my journals I called other girls "coolies." I did not know if life made them bearers or if they had been born with a natural gift for giving in. "Coolie" must have been the secret expression of one of my deepest fears. I see now that I had an immense conceit: I thought I occupied a world other people could scarcely envision, let alone attain. It involved giddy risks and changes, stepping off the edge blindfolded, one's hand on nothing more than a birth certificate and a five-dollar bill. At this time of sitting in judgment I was earning nine dollars a week (until I was told by someone that the local minimum wage was twelve, on which I left for greener fields) and washing my white piqué skirt at night and ironing at dawn, and coming home at all hours so I could pretend to Olivia I had dined. Part of this impermeable sureness that I needn't waver or doubt came out of my having lived in New York. The first time I ever heard people laughing in a cinema was there. I can still remember the wonder and excitement and amazement I felt. I was just under fourteen and I had never heard people expressing their feelings in a public place in my life. The easy reactions, the way a poignant moment caught them, held them still–all that was new. I had come there straight from Ontario, where the reaction to a love scene was a kind of unhappy giggling, while the image of a kitten or a baby induced a long flat "Aaaah," followed by shamed silence. You could imagine them blushing in the dark for having said that–just that "Aaaah." When I heard that open American laughter I thought I could be like these people too, but had been told not to be by everyone, beginning with Olivia: *"Pas si fort"* was something she repeated to me so often when I was small that my father had made a tease out of it, called "passy four." From a tease it became oppressive too: "For the love of God, Linnet, passy four." What were these new people? Were they soft, too easily got at? I wondered that even then. Would a dictator have a field day here? Were they, as Canadian opinion had it, vulgar? Perhaps the notion of vulgarity came out of some incapacity on the part of the refined. Whatever they were, they couldn't all be daft; if they weren't I probably wasn't either. I supposed I stood as good a chance of being miserable here as anywhere, but at least I would not have to pretend to be someone else.

Now, of course there is much to be said on the other side: people who do not display what they feel have practical advantages. They can go away to be killed as if they didn't mind; they can see their sons off to war without a blink. Their upbringing is intended for a crisis. When it comes, they behave themselves. But it is murder in everyday life—truly murder. The dead of heart and spirit litter the landscape. Still, keeping a straight face makes life tolerable under stress. It makes *public* life tolerable—that is all I am saying; because in private people still got drunk, went after each other with bottles and knives, rang the police to complain that neighbors were sending poison gas over the transom, abandoned infant children and aged parents, wrote letters to newspapers in favor of corporal punishment, with inventive suggestions. When I came back to Canada that June, at least one thing had been settled: I knew that it was all right for people to laugh and cry and even to make asses of themselves. I had actually known people like that, had lived with them, and they were fine, mostly—not crazy at all. That was where a lot of my confidence came from when I began my journey into a new life and a dream past.

My father's death had been kept from me. I did not know its exact circumstances or even the date. He died when I was ten. At thirteen I was still expected to believe a fable about his being in England. I kept waiting for him to send for me, for my life was deeply wretched and I took it for granted he knew. Finally I began to suspect that death and silence can be one. How to be sure? Head-on questions got me nowhere. I had to create a situation in which some adult (not my mother, who was far too sharp) would lose all restraint and hurl the truth at me. It was easy: I was an artist at this. What I had not foreseen was the verbal violence of the scene or the effect it might have. The storm that seemed to break in my head, my need to maintain the pose of indifference

("What are you telling me that for? What makes you think I care?") were such a strain that I had physical reactions, like stigmata, which doctors would hopelessly treat on and off for years and which vanished when I became independent. The other change was that if anyone asked about my father I said, "Oh, he died." Now, in Montreal, I could confront the free adult world of falsehood and evasion on an equal footing; they would be forced to talk to me as they did to each other. Making appointments to meet my father's friends– Mr. Archie McEwen, Mr. Stephen Ross-Colby, Mr. Quentin Keller–I left my adult name, "Miss Muir." These were the men who eight, nine, ten years ago had asked, "Do you like your school?"–not knowing what else to say to children. I had curtsied to them and said, "Good night." I think what I wanted was special information about despair, but I should have known that would be taboo in a place where "like" and "don't like" were heavy emotional statements.

Archie McEwen, my father's best friend, or the man I mistook for that, kept me standing in his office on St. James Street West, he standing too, with his hands behind his back, and he said the following–not reconstructed or approximate but recalled, like "The religions of ancient Greece and Rome are extinct" or "O come, let us sing unto the Lord":

"Of course, Angus was a very sick man. I saw him walking along Sherbrooke Street. He must have just come out of hospital. He couldn't walk upright. He was using a stick. Inching along. His hair had turned grey. Nobody knew where Charlotte had got to, and we'd heard you were dead. He obviously wasn't long for this world either. He had too many troubles for any one man. I crossed the street because I didn't have the heart to shake hands with him. I felt terrible."

Savage? Reasonable? You can't tell, with those minds. Some recent threat had scared them. The Depression was too close, just at their heels. Archie McEwen did not ask where I was staying or where I had been for the last eight years; in fact, he asked only two questions. In response to the first I said, "She is married."

There came a gleam of interest–distant, amused: "So she decided to marry him, did she?"

My mother was highly visible; she had no secrets except unexpected ones. My father had nothing but. When he asked, "Would you like to spend a year in England with your Aunt Dorothy?" I had no idea what he meant and I still don't. His only brother, Thomas, who was killed in 1918, had not been married; he'd had no sisters, that anyone knew. Those English mysteries used to be common. People came out to Canada because they did not want to think about the Thomases and Dorothys anymore. Angus was a solemn man, not much of a smiler. My mother, on the other hand–I won't begin to describe her, it would never end–smiled, talked, charmed anyone she didn't happen to be related to, swam in scandal like a partisan among the people. She made herself the central figure in loud, spectacular dramas which she played with the houselights on; you could see the audience too. That was her mistake; they kept their reactions, like their lovemaking, in the dark. You can imagine what she must have been in this world where everything was hushed, muffled, disguised: she must have seemed all they had by way of excitement, give or take a few elections and wars. It sounds like a story about the old and stale, but she and my father had been quite young eight and ten years before. The dying man creeping along Sherbrooke Street was thirty-two. First it was light chatter, then darker gossip, and then it went too far (*he* was ill and he couldn't hide it; *she* had a lover and didn't try); then suddenly it became tragic, and open tragedy was disallowed. And so Mr. Archie McEwen could stand in his office and without a trace of feeling on his narrow Lowland face–not unlike my father's in shape–he could say, "I crossed the street."

Stephen Ross-Colby, a bachelor, my father's painter chum: the smell of his studio on St. Mark Street was the smell of a personal myth. I said timidly, "Do you happen to have anything of his–a drawing or anything?" I was humble because I was on a private, personal terrain of vocation that made me shy even of the dead.

He said, "No, nothing. You could ask around. She junked a lot of his stuff and he junked the rest when he thought he wouldn't survive. You might try..." He gave me a name or two. "It was all small stuff," said Ross-Colby. "He didn't do anything big." He hurried me out of the studio for a cup of coffee in a crowded place–the Honey Dew on St. Catherine Street, it must have been. Perhaps in the privacy of his studio I might have heard him thinking. Years after that he would try to call me "Lynn," which I never was, and himself "Steve." He'd come into his own as an artist by then, selling wash drawings of Canadian war graves, sun-splashed, wisteria-mauve, lime-green, with drifts of blossom across the name of the regiment; gained a reputation among the heartbroken women who bought these impersonations, had them framed–the only picture in the house. He painted the war memorial at Caen. ("Their name liveth forever.") His stones weren't stones but mauve bubbles–that is all I have against them. They floated off the page. My objection wasn't to "He didn't do anything big" but to Ross-Colby's way of turning the dead into thistledown. He said, much later, of that meeting, "I felt like a bastard, but I was broke, and I was afraid you'd put the bite on me."

Let me distribute demerits equally and tell about my father's literary

Jewish friend, Mr. Quentin Keller. He was older than the others, perhaps by some twelve years. He had a whispery voice and a long pale face and a daughter older than I. "Bossy Wendy" I used to call her when, forced by her parents as I was by mine, Bossy Wendy had to take a whole afternoon of me. She had a room full of extraordinary toys, a miniature kitchen in which everything worked, of which all I recall her saying is "Don't touch." Wendy Keller had left Smith after her freshman year to marry the elder son of a Danish baron. Her father said to me, "There is only one thing you need to know and that is that your father was a gentleman."

Jackass was what I thought. Yes, Mr. Quentin Keller was a jackass. But he was a literary one, for he had once written a play called *Forbearance*, in which I'd had a role. I had bounded across the stage like a tennis ball, into the arms of a young woman dressed up like an old one, and cried my one line: "Here I am, Granny!" Of course, he did not make his living fiddling about with amateur theatricals; thanks to our meeting I had a good look at the inside of a conservative architect's private office– that was about all it brought me.

What were they so afraid of, I wondered. I had not yet seen that I was in a false position where they were concerned; being "Miss Muir" had not made equals of us but lent distance. I thought they had read my true passport, the invisible one we all carry, but I had neither the wealth nor the influence a provincial society requires to make a passport valid. My credentials were lopsided: the important half of the scales was still in the air. I needed enormous collateral security–fame, an alliance with a powerful family, the power of money itself. I remember how Archie McEwen, trying to place me in some sensible context, to give me a voucher so he could take me home and show me to his wife, perhaps, asked his second question: "Who inherited the–?"

"The what, Mr. McEwen?"

He had not, of course, read "Why I Am a Socialist." I did not believe in inherited property. "Who inherited the–?" would not cross my mind again for another ten years, and then it would be a drawer quickly opened and shut before demons could escape. To all three men the last eight years were like minutes; to me they had been several lives. Some of my confidence left me then. It came down to "Next time I'll know better," but would that be enough? I had been buffeted until now by other people's moods, principles, whims, tantrums; I had survived, but perhaps I had failed to grow some outer skin it was now too late to acquire. Olivia thought that; she was the only one. Olivia knew more about the limits of nerve than I did. Her knowledge came out of the clean, swept, orderly poverty that used to be tucked away in the corners of cities. It didn't spill out then, or give anyone a bad conscience. Nobody took its picture. Anyway, Olivia would not have sat for such a portrait. The fringed green rug she put over her treadle sewing machine was part of a personal fortune. On her mantelpiece stood a copper statuette of Voltaire in an armchair. It must have come down to her from some robustly anticlerical ancestor. "Who is he?" she said to me. "You've been to school in a foreign country." "A governor of New France," I replied. She knew Voltaire was the name of a bad man and she'd have thrown the figurine out, and it would have made one treasure less in the house. Olivia's maiden name was Ouvrardville, which was good in Quebec, but only really good if you were one of the rich ones. Because of her maiden name she did not want anyone ever to know she had worked for a family; she impressed this on me delicately—it was like trying to understand what a dragonfly wanted to tell. In the old days she had gone home every weekend, taking me with her if my parents felt my company was going to make Sunday a very long day. Now I understood what the weekends were about: her daughters, Berthe and Marguerite, for whose sake she worked, were home from their convent schools Saturday and Sunday and had to be chaperoned. Her relatives pretended not to notice that Olivia was poor or even that she was widowed, for which she seemed grateful. The result of all this elegant sham was that Olivia did not say, "I was afraid you'd put the bite on me," or keep me standing. She dried her tears and asked if there was a trunk to follow. No? She made a pot of tea and spread a starched cloth on the kitchen table and we sat down to a breakfast of toast and honey. The honey tin was a ten-pounder decorated with bees the size of hornets. Lifting it for her, I remarked, "*C'est collant*, a word out of a frozen language that started to thaw when Olivia said, '*Tu vis?*''

On the advice of her confessor, who was to be my rival from now on, Olivia refused to tell me whatever she guessed or knew, and she was far too dignified to hint. Putting together the three men's woolly stories, I arrived at something about tuberculosis of the spine and a butchery of an operation. He started back to England to die there but either changed his mind or was too ill to begin the journey; at Quebec City, where he was to have taken ship, he shot himself in a public park at five o'clock in the morning. That was one version; another was that he died at sea and the gun was found in his luggage. The revolver figured in all three accounts. It was an officer's weapon from the Kaiser's war, that had belonged to his brother. Angus kept it at the back of a small drawer in the tall chest used for men's clothes and known in Canada as a highboy. In front of the revolver was a pigskin stud box and a pile of ironed handkerchiefs. Just describing that drawer dates it. How I happen to know the revolver was loaded and how I learned never to point a gun even in play is another story. I can tell you that I never again in my life looked inside a drawer that did not belong to me.

I know a woman whose father died, she thinks, in a concentration camp. Or was he shot in a schoolyard? Or hanged and thrown in a ditch? Were the ashes that arrived from some eastern plain his or another prisoner's? She invents different deaths. Her inventions have become her conversation at dinner parties. She takes on a child's voice and says, "My father died at Buchenwald." She chooses and rejects elements of the last act; one avoids mentioning death, shooting, capital punishment, cremation, deportation, even fathers. Her inventions are not thought neurotic or exhibitionist but something sanctioned by history. Peacetime casualties are not like that. They are lightning bolts out of a sunny sky that strike only one house. All around the ashy ruin lilacs blossom, leaves gleam. Speculation in public about the disaster would be indecent. Nothing remains but a silent, recurring puzzlement to the survivors: Why here and not there? Why this and not that? Before July was out I had settled his fate in my mind and I never varied: I thought he had died of homesickness; sickness for England was the consumption, the gun, the everything. "Everything" had to take it all in, for people in Canada then did not speak of irrational endings to life, and newspapers did not print that kind of news: this was because of the spiritual tragedy for Catholic families, and because the act had long been considered a criminal one in British law. If Catholic feelings were spared it gave the impression no one but Protestants ever went over the edge, which was unfair; and so the possibility was eliminated, and people came to a natural end in a running car in a closed garage, hanging from a rafter in the barn, in an icy lake with a canoe left to drift empty. Once I had made up my mind, the whole story somehow became none of my business: I had looked in a drawer that did not belong to me. More, if I was to live my own life I had to let go. I wrote in my journal that "they" had got him but would not get me, and after that there was scarcely ever a mention.

My dream past evaporated. Montreal, in memory, was a leafy citadel where I knew every tree. In reality I recognized nearly nothing and had to start from scratch. Sherbrooke Street had been the dream street, pure white. It was the avenue poor Angus descended leaning on a walking stick. It was a moat I was not allowed to cross alone; it was lined with gigantic spreading trees through which light fell like a rain of coins. One day, standing at a corner, waiting for the light to change, I understood that the Sherbrooke Street of my exile–my Mecca, my Jerusalem–was this. It had to be: there could not be two. It was *only* this. The limitless green where in a perpetual spring I had been taken to play was the campus of McGill University. A house, whose beauty had brought tears to my sleep, to which in sleep I'd returned to find it inhabited by ugly strangers, gypsies, was a narrow stone thing with a shop on the ground floor and offices above–if that was it, for there were several like it. Through the bare panes of what might have been the sitting room, with its deep private window seats, I saw neon striplighting along a ceiling. Reality, as always, was narrow and dull. And yet what dramatic things had taken place on this very corner: Once Satan had approached me–furry dark skin, claws, red eyes, the lot. He urged me to cross the street and I did, in front of a car that braked in time. I explained, ''The Devil told me to.'' I had no idea until then that my parents did not believe what I was taught in my convent school. (Satan is not bilingual, by the way; he speaks Quebec French.) My parents had no God and therefore no Fallen Angel. I was scolded for lying, which was a thing my father detested, and which my mother regularly did but never forgave in others.

Why these two nonbelievers wanted a strong religious education for me is one of the mysteries. (Even in loss of faith they were unalike, for he was ex-Anglican and she was ex-Lutheran and that is not your same atheist–no, not at all.) ''To make you tolerant'' was a lame excuse, as was ''French,'' for I spoke fluent French with Olivia, and I could read in two languages before I was four. Discipline might have been one reason–God knows, the nuns provided plenty of that–but according to Olivia I did not need any. It cannot have been for the quality of the teaching, which was lamentable. I suspect that it was something like sending a dog to a trainer (they were passionate in their concern for animals, especially dogs), but I am not certain it ever brought me to heel. The first of my schools, the worst, the darkest, was on Sherbrooke Street too. When I heard, years later, it had been demolished, it was like the burial of a witch. I had remembered it penitentiary size, but what I found myself looking at one day was simply a very large stone house. A crocodile of little girls emerged from the front gate and proceeded along the street–white-faced, black-clad, eyes cast down. I knew they were bored, fidgety, anxious, and probably hungry. I should have felt pity, but at eighteen all that came to me was thankfulness that I had been correct about one thing throughout my youth, which I now considered ended: time had been on my side, faithfully, and unless you died you were always bound to escape.

Works by Mavis Gallant

FICTION

The Other Paris. Boston: Houghton
    Mifflin, 1956.
Green Water, Green Sky. Boston:
    Houghton Mifflin, 1959; Toronto:
    Macmillan, 1983.
My Heart Is Broken. New York: Random
    House, 1964.
A Fairly Good Time. New York: Random
    House, 1970; Toronto: Macmillan,
    1983.
The Pegnitz Junction. New York: Random
    House, 1973.
The End of the World and Other Stories.
    Toronto: McClelland and Stewart,
    1974.
From the Fifteenth District. Toronto:
    Macmillan, 1979.
Home Truths: Selected Canadian Stories.
    Toronto: Macmillan, 1981.

Interview with Mavis Gallant

Canadian Fiction Magazine, vol. 28 (1978),
    19-67.

Alice Munro

The creation of a work of art is mysterious, as Alice Munro acknowledges: "When I write a story I want to make a certain kind of structure, and I know the feeling I want to get from being inside that structure. This is the hard part of the explanation, where I have to use a word like 'feeling,' which is not very precise, because if I attempt to be more intellectually respectable I will have to be dishonest. 'Feeling' will have to do."

From the "feeling" comes the shape of the work of art. "I've got to make, I've got to build up, a house, a story, to fit around the indescribable 'feeling' that is like the soul of the story, and which I must insist upon in a dogged, embarrassed way, as being no more definable than that. And I don't know where it comes from. It seems to be already there, and some unlikely clue, such as a shop window or a bit of conversation, makes me aware of it."

Munro has set her five volumes of fiction primarily in southwestern Ontario, where she was born and raised and where she lives. Though she lived for nearly twenty years in Vancouver and Victoria, settings that do appear in some of her stories, her artistic home remains small-town southwestern Ontario. She writes out of the world she knows well, taking the ordinary, everyday world around her and transforming it in fiction.

Born in 1931 in Wingham, Ontario, Munro grew up there "outside the whole social structure because we didn't live in the town and we didn't live in the country. We lived in this kind of little ghetto where all the bootleggers and prostitutes and hangers-on lived. Those were the people I knew. It was a community of outcasts." When Munro was about twelve, her mother contracted Parkinson's disease; she suffered from this condition until her death in 1959. Her mother, Munro recalls, "was totally off on her own. She needed love so badly, but I was a teenager, so I couldn't afford to love anybody but myself. You don't realize until years later what you could have done. Maybe you couldn't have. But that doesn't mean you won't have an awful stab of pain all through your life."

Munro's second book, *Lives of Girls and Women* (1971), is "autobiographical in form but not in fact. My family, neighbors and friends did not serve as models." Her closest approach to autobiography, however, is "The Ottawa Valley," the final story in the collection *Something I've Been Meaning to Tell You* (1974). Here she returns to one of her most frequent themes, the complexity of the relationship between mother and daughter. "The Ottawa Valley," though exploring Munro's relationship with her own mother, is more than autobiographical notes or reminiscences. In this "series of snapshots, like the brownish snapshots with fancy borders that my parents' old camera used to take," the writer tries to distance herself from her own experiences in order to transform them into art. Constantly she intervenes, as she does so poignantly at the end of the story, to underscore her personal relationship to the fiction on the page.

The
Ottawa
Valley

I think of my mother sometimes in department stores. I don't know why, I was never in one with her; their plenitude, their sober bustle, it seems to me, would have satisfied her. I think of her of course when I see somebody on the street who has Parkinson's disease, and more and more often lately when I look in the mirror. Also in Union Station, Toronto, because the first time I was there I was with her, and my little sister. It was one summer during the War, we waited between trains; we were going home with her, with my mother, to her old home in the Ottawa Valley.

A cousin she was planning to meet, for a between-trains visit, did not show up. "She probably couldn't get away," said my mother, sitting in a leather chair in the darkly paneled Ladies' Lounge, which is now boarded up. "There was probably something to do that she couldn't leave to anybody else." This cousin was a legal secretary, and she worked for a senior partner in what my mother always called, in her categorical way, "the city's leading law firm." Once she had come to visit us, wearing a large black hat and a black suit, her lips and nails like rubies. She did not bring her husband. He was an alcoholic. My mother always mentioned that her husband was an alcoholic, immediately after she had stated that she held an important job with the city's leading law firm. The two things were seen to balance each other, to be tied together in some inevitable and foreboding way. In the same way my mother would say of a family we knew that they had everything money could buy but their only son was an epileptic, or that the parents of the only person from our town who had become moderately famous, a pianist

141

named Mary Renwick, had said that they would give all their daughter's fame for a pair of baby hands. *A pair of baby hands?* Luck was not without its shadow, in her universe.

My sister and I went out into the station which was like a street with its lighted shops and like a church with its high curved roof and great windows at each end. It was full of the thunder of trains hidden, it seemed, just behind the walls, and an amplified voice, luxuriant, power-ful, reciting place names that could not quite be understood. I bought a movie magazine and my sister bought chocolate bars with the money we had been given. I was going to say to her, "Give me a bite or I won't show you the way back," but she was so undone by the grandeur of the place, or subdued by her dependence on me, that she broke off a piece without being asked.

Late in the afternoon we got on the Ottawa train. We were sur-rounded by soldiers. My sister had to sit on my mother's knee. A soldier sitting in front of us turned around and joked with me. He looked very much like Bob Hope. He asked me what town I came from, and then he said, "Have they got the second storey on there yet?" in just the sharp, unsmiling, smart-alecky way that Bob Hope would have said it. I thought that maybe he really was Bob Hope, traveling around incognito in a soldier's uniform. That did not seem unlikely to me. Outside of my own town—this far outside it, at least—all the bright and famous people in the world seemed to be floating around free, ready to turn up anywhere.

Aunt Dodie met us at the station in the dark and drove us to her house, miles out in the country. She was small and sharp-faced and laughed at the end of every sentence. She drove an old square-topped car with a running board.

"Well, did Her Majesty show up to see you?"

She was referring to the legal secretary, who was in fact her sister. Aunt Dodie was not really our aunt at all but our mother's cousin. She and her sister did not speak.

"No, but she must have been busy," said my mother neutrally.

"Oh, busy," said Aunt Dodie. "She's busy scraping the chicken dirt off her boots. Eh?" She drove fast, over washboard and potholes.

My mother waved at the blackness on either side of us. "Children! Children, this is the Ottawa Valley!"

It was no valley. I looked for mountains, or at least hills, but in the morning all it was was fields and bush, and Aunt Dodie outside the window holding a milk pail for a calf. The calf was butting its head into the pail so hard it slopped the milk out, and Aunt Dodie was laughing and scolding and hitting it, trying to make it slow down. She called it a bugger. "Greedy little bugger!"

She was dressed in her milking outfit, which was many-layered and -colored and ragged and flopping like the clothes a beggarwoman might wear in a school play. A man's hat without a crown was shoved–for what purpose?–on her head.

My mother had not led me to believe we were related to people who dressed like that or who used the word bugger. "I will not tolerate filth," my mother always said. But apparently she tolerated Aunt Dodie. She said they had been like sisters, when they were growing up. (The legal secretary, Bernice, had been older and had left home early.) Then my mother usually said that Aunt Dodie had had a tragic life.

Aunt Dodie's house was bare. It was the poorest house I had ever been in, to stay. From this distance, our own house–which I had always thought poor, because we lived too far out of town to have a flush toilet or running water, and certainly we had no real touches of luxury, like Venetian blinds–looked very comfortably furnished, with its books and piano and good set of dishes and one rug that was bought, not made out of rags. In Aunt Dodie's front room there was one overstuffed chair and a magazine rack full of old Sunday school papers. Aunt Dodie lived off her cows. Her land was not worth farming. Every morning, after she finished milking and separating, she loaded the cans in the back of her pickup truck and drove seven miles to the cheese factory. She lived in dread of the milk inspector, who went around declaring cows tubercular, we understood, for no reason but spite, and to put poor farmers out of business. Big dairy interests paid him off, Aunt Dodie said.

The tragedy in her life was that she had been jilted. "Did you know," she said, "that I was jilted?" My mother had said we were never to mention it, and there was Aunt Dodie in her own kitchen, washing the noon dishes, with me wiping and my sister putting away (my mother had to go and have her rest), saying "jilted" proudly, as somebody would say, "Did you know I had polio?" or some such bad important disease.

"I had my cake baked," she said. "I was in my wedding dress."

"Was it satin?"

"No, it was a nice dark red merino wool, because of it being a late fall wedding. We had the minister here. All prepared. My dad kept running out to the road to see if he could see him coming. It got dark, and I said, time to go out and do the milking! I pulled off my dress and I never put it back on. I gave it away. Lots of girls would've cried, but me, I laughed."

My mother telling the same story said, "When I went home two years after that, and I was staying with her, I used to wake up and hear her crying in the night. Night after night.''

> *There was I*
> *Waiting at the church,*
> *Waiting at the church,*
> *Waiting at the church.*
> *And when I found*
> *He'd left me in the lurch,*
> *Oh, how it did upset me.*

Aunt Dodie sang this at us, washing the dishes at her round table covered with scrubbed oilcloth. Her kitchen was as big as a house, with a back door and a front door; always a breeze blew through. She had a homemade icebox, such as I had never seen, with a big chunk of ice in it that she would haul in a child's wagon from the ice-house. The ice-house itself was remarkable, a roofed dugout where ice cut from the lake in winter lasted the summer, in sawdust.

"Of course it wasn't," she said, "in my case, it wasn't the church."

Across the fields from Aunt Dodie on the next farm lived my mother's brother, Uncle James, and his wife, Aunt Lena, and their eight children. That was the house where my mother had grown up. It was a bigger house with more furniture but still unpainted outside, dark grey. The furniture was mostly high wooden beds, with feather ticks and dark carved headboards. Under the beds were pots not emptied every day. We visited there but Aunt Dodie did not come with us. She and Aunt Lena did not speak. But Aunt Lena did not speak much to anybody. She had been a sixteen-year-old girl, straight out of the backwoods, said my mother and Aunt Dodie (which left you to wonder, where was this?), when Uncle James married her. At this time, she would have been married ten or twelve years. She was tall and straight, flat as a board front and back–even though she would bear her ninth child before Christmas–darkly freckled, with large dark slightly inflamed eyes, animal's eyes. All the children had got those, instead of Uncle James's mild blue ones.

"When your mother was dying," said Aunt Dodie, "Oh, I can hear her. Don't touch that towel! Use your own towel! Cancer, she thought you could catch it like the measles. She was that ignorant."

"I can't forgive her."

"And wouldn't let any of the kids go near her. I had to go over myself and give your mother her wash. I saw it all."

"I can never forgive her."

Aunt Lena was stiff all the time with what I now recognize as terror. She would not let her children swim in the lake for fear they would drown, she would not let them go tobogganing in winter for fear they would fall off the toboggan and break their necks, she would not let them learn to skate for fear they would break their legs and be crippled for life. She beat them all the time for fear they would grow up to be lazy, or liars, or clumsy people who broke things. They were not lazy but they broke things anyway; they were always darting and grabbing; and, of course, they were all liars, even the little ones, brilliant, instinctive liars who lied even when it was not necessary, just for the practice, and maybe the pleasure, of it. They were always telling and concealing, making and breaking alliances; they had the most delicate and ruthless political instincts. They howled when they were beaten. Pride was a luxury they had discarded long ago, or never considered. If you did not howl for Aunt Lena, when would she ever stop? Her arms were as long and strong as a man's, her face set in an expression of remote unanswerable fury. But five minutes, three minutes, afterwards, her children would have forgotten. With me, such a humiliation could last for weeks, or forever.

Uncle James kept the Irish accent my mother had lost and Aunt Dodie had halfway lost. His voice was lovely, saying the children's names. Mar-ie, Ron-ald, Ru-thie. So tenderly, comfortingly, reproachfully he said their names, as if the names, or the children themselves, were jokes played on him. But he never held them back from being beaten, never protested. You would think all this had nothing to do with him. You would think Aunt Lena had nothing to do with him.

The youngest child slept in the parents' bed until a new baby displaced it.

"He used to come over and see me," Aunt Dodie said. "We used to have some good laughs. He used to bring two, three of the kids but he quit that. I know why. They'd tell on him. Then he quit coming himself. She lays down the law. But he gets it back on her, doesn't he?"

Aunt Dodie did not get a daily paper, just a weekly that was published in the town where she had picked us up.

"There's a mention in here about Allen Durrand."

"Allen Durrand?" said my mother doubtfully.

"Oh, he's a big Holstein man now. He married a West."

"What's the mention?"

"It's the Conservative Association. I bet he wants to get nominated. I bet."

She was in the rocker, with her boots off, laughing. My mother was sitting with her back against a porch post. They were cutting up yellow beans, to can.

"I was thinking about the time we gave him the lemonade," Aunt Dodie said, and turned to me. "He was just a French Canadian boy then, working here for a couple of weeks in the summer."

"Only his name was French," my mother said. "He didn't even speak it."

"You'd never know now. He turned his religion too, goes to St. John's."

"He was always intelligent."

"You bet he is. Oh, intelligent. But we got him with the lemonade.

"You picture the hottest possible day in summer. Your mother and I didn't mind it so much, we could stay in the house. But Allen had to be in the mow. You see they were getting the hay in. My dad was bringing it in and Allen was spreading it out. I bet James was over helping too."

"James was pitching on," my mother said. "Your dad was driving, and building the load."

"And they put Allen in the mow. You've no idea what a mow is like on that kind of a day. It's a hell on earth. So we thought it would be a nice idea to take him some lemonade–No. I'm getting ahead of myself. I meant to tell about the overalls first.

"Allen had brought me these overalls to fix just when the men were sitting down to dinner. He had a heavy pair of old suit pants on, and a work shirt, must have been killing him, though the shirt I guess he took off when he got in the barn. But he must've wanted the overalls on because they'd be cooler, you know, the circulation. I forget what had to be fixed on them, just some little thing. He must have been suffering bad in those old pants just to bring himself to ask, because he was awful shy. He'd be–what, then?"

"Seventeen," my mother said.

"And us two eighteen. It was the year before you went away to Normal. Yes. Well, I took and fixed his pants, just some little thing to do to them while you served up dinner. There I was sitting in the corner of the kitchen at the sewing machine when I had my inspiration, didn't I? I called you over. Pretended I was calling you to hold the material straight for me. So's you could see what I was doing. And neither one of us cracked a smile or dared look sideways at each other, did we?"

"No."

"Because my inspiration was to sew up his fly!

"So then, you see, a little bit on in the afternoon, with them out to work again, we got the idea for the lemonade. We made two pailfuls. One we took out to the men working in the field; we yelled to them and set it under a tree. And the other we took up to the mow and offered it to him. We'd used up every lemon we had, and even so it was weak. I remember was had to put vinegar in. But he wouldn't've noticed. I never saw a person so thirsty in my life as him. He drank by the dipperful, and then he just tipped up the pail. Drank it all down. Us standing there watching. How did we keep a straight face?"

"I'll never know," my mother said.

"Then we took the pail and made for the house and waited about two seconds before we came sneaking back. We hid ourselves up in the granary. That was like an oven, too. I don't know how we stood it. But we climbed up on the sacks of feed and each found ourselves a crack or knothole or something to look through. We knew the corner of the barn the men always peed in. They peed down the shovel if they were upstairs. Down in the stable I guess they peed in the gutter. And soon enough, soon enough, he starts strolling over in that direction. Dropped his fork and starts strolling over. Puts his hand up to himself as he went. Sweat running down our faces from the heat and the way we had to keep from laughing. Oh, the cruelty of it! First he was just going easy, wasn't he? Then thinking about it I guess the need gets stonger; he looked down wondering what was the matter, and soon he's fairly clawin' and yankin' every which way, trying all he can to get himself free. But I'd sewed him up good and strong. I wonder when it hit him, what'd been done?"

"Right then, I'd think. He was never stupid."

"He never was. So he must've put it all together. The lemonade and all. The one thing I don't guess he ever thought of was us hid up in the granary. Or else would he've done what he did next?"

"He wouldn't have," said my mother firmly.

"I don't know though. He might've been past caring. Eh? He just finally went past caring and gave up and ripped down his overalls altogether and let'er fly. We had the full view."

"He had his back to us."

"He did not! When he shot away there wasn't a thing we couldn't see. He turned himself sideways."

"I don't remember that."

"Well, I do. I haven't seen so many similar sights that I can afford to forget."

"Dodie!" said my mother, as if at this too-late point to issue a warning.

(Another thing my mother quite often said was, "I will never listen to smut.")

"Oh, you! You didn't run away yourself. Did you? Kept your eye to the knothole!"

My mother looked from me to Aunt Dodie and back with an unusual expression on her face: helplessness. I won't say she laughed. She just looked as if there was a point at which she might give up.

> *The onset is very slow and often years may pass before the patient or his family observes that he is becoming disabled. He shows slowly increasing bodily rigidity, associated with tremors of the head and limbs. There may be various tics, twitches, muscle spasms, and other involuntary movements. Salivation increases and drooling is common. Scientifically the disease is known as* paralysis agitans. *It is also called Parkinson's disease or shaking palsy.* Paralysis agitans *affects first a single arm or leg, then the second limb on the same side and finally those on the other side. The face begins to lose its customary expressiveness and changes slowly or not at all with passing moods. The disease is typically one of elderly people, striking mostly persons in their sixties and seventies. No recoveries are recorded. Drugs are available to control the tremor and excess salivation. The benefits of these, however, are limited.* [Fishbein, *Medical Encyclopedia.*]

My mother, during this summer, would have been forty-one or forty-two years old, I think, somewhere around the age that I am now.

Just her left forearm trembled. The hand trembled more than the arm. The thumb knocked ceaselessly against the palm. She could, however, hide it in her fingers, and she could hold the arm still by stiffening it against her body.

Uncle James drank porter after supper. He let me taste it, black and bitter. Here was a new contradiction. "Before I married your father," my mother had told me, "I asked him to promise me that he would never drink, and he never has." But Uncle James her brother could drink without apologies.

On Saturday night we all went into town. My mother and my sister went in Aunt Dodie's car. I was with Uncle James and Aunt Lena and the children. The children claimed me. I was a little older than the oldest of them, and they treated me as if I were a trophy, someone for whose favor they could jostle and compete. So I was riding in their car, which was high and old and square-topped, like Aunt Dodie's. We were coming home, we had the windows rolled down for coolness, and unexpectedly Uncle James began to sing.

He had a fine voice of course, a fine sad, lingering voice. I can remember perfectly well the tune of the song he sang, and the sound of his voice rolling out the black windows, but I can remember only bits of the words, here and there, though I have often tried to remember more, because I liked the song so well.

As I was a-goen over Kil-i-kenny Mountain . . .

I think that was the way it started.

Then further along something about *pearly*, or *early* and *Some take delight in*—various things, and finally the strong but sad-sounding line:

But I take delight in the water of the barley.

There was silence in the car while he was singing. The children were not squabbling and being hit, some of them were even falling asleep. Aunt Lena with the youngest on her knee was an unthreatening dark shape. The car bounced along as if it would go forever through a perfectly black night with its lights cutting a frail path; and there was a jack rabbit on the road, leaping out of our way, but nobody cried out to notice it, nobody broke the singing, its booming tender sadness.

But I take delight in THE WATER OF THE BARLEY.

We got to church early, so that we could go and look at the graves. St. John's was a white wooden church on the highway, with the graveyard behind it. We stopped at two stones, on which were written the words *Mother* and *Father*. Underneath in much smaller letters the names and dates of my mother's parents. Two flat stones, not very big, lying like paving stones in the clipped grass. I went off to look at things more interesting—urns and praying hands and angels in profile.

Soon my mother and Aunt Dodie came too.

"Who needs all this fancy folderol?" said Aunt Dodie, waving.

My sister, who was just learning to read, tried reading the inscriptions.

Until the Day Break

He is not Dead but Sleepeth

In Pacem

"What is *pacem*?"

"Latin," said my mother approvingly.

"A lot of these people put up these fancy stones and it is all show, they are still paying for them. Some of them still trying to pay for the plots and not even started on the stones. Look at that for instance." Aunt Dodie pointed to a large cube of dark blue granite, flecked white like a cooking pot, balanced on one corner.

"How modern," said my mother absently.

"That is Dave McColl's. Look at the size of it. And I know for a fact they told her if she didn't hurry up and pay something on the plot they were going to dig him up and pitch him out on the highway."

"It that Christian?" my mother wondered.

"Some people don't deserve Christian."

I felt something slithering down from my waist and realized that the elastic of my underpants had broken. I caught my hands to my sides in time—I had no hips then to hold anything up—and said to my mother in an angry whisper, "I have to have a safety pin."

"What do you want a safety pin for?" said my mother, in a normal, or louder than normal, voice. She could always be relied upon to be obtuse at such moments.

I would not answer, but glared at her beseechingly, threateningly.

"I bet her panties bust," Aunt Dodie laughed.

"Did they?" said my mother sternly, still not lowering her voice.

"*Yes*."

"Well, take them off then," said my mother.

"Not right here, though," said Aunt Dodie. "There is the Ladies."

Behind St. John's Church, as behind a country school, were two wooden toilets.

"Then I wouldn't have anything on," I said to my mother, scandalized. I couldn't imagine walking into church in a blue taffeta dress and no pants. Rising to sing the hymns, sitting down, in *no pants*. The smooth cool boards of the pew and *no pants*.

Aunt Dodie was looking through her purse. "I wish I had one to give you but I haven't. You just run and take them off and nobody's going to know the difference. Lucky there's no wind."

I didn't move.

"Well I do have one pin," said my mother doubtfully. "But I can't take it out. My slip strap broke this morning when I was getting dressed and I put a pin in to hold it. But I can't take that out."

My mother was wearing a soft grey dress covered with little flowers which looked as if they had been embroidered on, and a grey slip to match, because you could see through the material. Her hat was a dull rose color, matching the color of some of the flowers. Her gloves were almost the same rose and her shoes were white, with open toes. She had brought this whole outfit with her, had assembled it, probably, especially to wear when she walked into St. John's Church. She might have imagined a sunny morning, with St. John's bell ringing, just as it was ringing now. She must have planned this and visualized it just as I now plan and visualize, sometimes, what I will wear to a party.

"I can't take it out for you or my slip will show."

"People going in," Aunt Dodie said.

"Go to the Ladies and take them off. If you won't do that, go sit in the car."

I started for the car. I was halfway to the cemetery gate when my mother called my name. She marched ahead of me to the ladies' toilet, where without a word she reached inside the neck of her dress and brought out the pin. Turning my back—and not saying thank-you, because I was too deep in my own misfortune and too sure of my own rights—I fastened together the waistband of my pants. Then my mother walked ahead of me up the toilet path and around the side of the church. We were late, everybody had gone in. We had to wait while the choir, with the minister trailing, got themselves up the aisle at their religious pace.

> *All things bright and beautiful,*
> *All creatures great and small,*
> *All things wise and wonderful,*
> *The Lord God made them all.*

When the choir was in place and the minister had turned to face the congregation, my mother set out boldly to join Aunt Dodie and my sister in a pew near the front. I could see that the grey slip had slid down half an inch and was showing in a slovenly way at one side.

After the service my mother turned in the pew and spoke to people. People wanted to know my name and my sister's name and then they said, "She does look like you." "No, maybe this one looks more like you"; or, "I see your own mother in this one." They asked how old we were and what grade I was in at school and whether my sister was going to school. They asked her when she was going to start and she said, "I'm not," which was laughed at and repeated. (My sister often made people laugh without meaning to; she had such a firm way of publicizing her misunderstandings. In this case it turned out that she really did think she was not going to school because the primary school near where we lived was being torn down, and nobody had told her she would go on a bus.)

Two or three people said to me, "Guess who taught me when *I* went to school? Your Momma!"

"She never learned me much," said a sweaty man, whose hand I could tell she did not want to shake, "but she was the best-lookin' one I ever had!"

"Did my slip show?"

"How could it? You were standing in the pew."

"When I was walking down the aisle, I wonder?"

"Nobody could see. They were all still standing for the hymn."

"They could have seen, though."

"Only one thing surprises me. Why didn't Allen Durrand come over and say hello?"

"Was he there?"

"Didn't you see him? Over in the Wests' pew, under the window they put in for the father and mother."

"I didn't see him. Was his wife?"

"Ah, you must have seen *her*! All in blue with a hat like a buggy wheel. She's very dressy. But not to be compared to you, today."

Aunt Dodie herself was wearing a navy blue straw hat with some droopy cloth flowers, and a button-down-the-front slub rayon dress.

"Maybe he didn't know me. Or didn't see me."

"He couldn't very well not have seen you."

"Well."

"And he's turned out such a good-looking man. That counts if you go into politics. And the height. You very seldom see a short man get elected."

"What about Mackenzie King?"

"I meant around here. We wouldn't've elected *him*, from around here."

"Your mother's had a little stroke. She says not, but I've seen too many like her.

"She's had a little one, and she might have another little one, and another, and another. Then some day she might have the big one. You'll have to learn to be the mother, then.

"Like me. My mother took sick when I was only ten. She died when I was fifteen. In between, what a time I had with her! She was all swollen up; what she had was dropsy. They came one time and took it out of her by the pailful."

"Took what out?"

"*Fluid*.

"She sat up in her chair till she couldn't any more, she had to go to bed. She had to lie on her right side all the time to keep the fluid pressure off her heart. What a life. She developed bedsores, she was in misery. So one day she said to me, Dodie, please, just turn me on to my other side for just a little while, just for the relief. She begged me. I got hold of her and turned her—she was a weight! I turned her on her heart side, and the minute I did, she died.

"What are you crying about? I never meant to make you cry! Well you are a big baby, if you can't stand to hear about Life."

Aunt Dodie laughed at me, to cheer me up. In her thin brown face her eyes were large and hot. She had a scarf around her head that day and looked like a gypsy woman, flashing malice and kindness at me, threatening to let out more secrets than I could stand.

"Did you have a stroke?" I said sullenly.

"What?"

"Aunt Dodie said you had a stroke."

"Well, I didn't. I told her I didn't. The doctor says I didn't. She thinks she knows everything, Dodie does. She thinks she knows better than a doctor."

"Are you going to have a stroke?"

"No. I have low blood pressure. That is just the opposite of what gives you strokes."

"So, are you not going to get sick at all?" I said, pushing further. I was very much relieved that she had decided against strokes, and that I would not have to be the mother, and wash and wipe and feed her lying in bed, as Aunt Dodie had had to do with her mother. For I did feel it was she who decided, she gave her consent. As long as she lived, and through all the changes that happened to her, and after I had received the medical explanations of what was happening, I still felt secretly that she had given her consent. For her own purposes, I felt she did it: display, of a sort; revenge of a sort as well. More, that nobody could ever understand.

She did not answer me, but walked on ahead. We were going from Aunt Dodie's place to Uncle James's, following a path through the humpy cow pasture that made the trip shorter than going by the road.

"Is your arm going to stop shaking?" I pursued recklessly, stubbornly.

I demanded of her now, that she turn and promise me what I needed.

But she did not do it. For the first time she held out altogether against me. She went on as if she had not heard, her familiar bulk ahead of me

turning strange, indifferent. She withdrew, she darkened in front of me,
though all she did in fact was keep on walking along the path that she
and Aunt Dodie had made when they were girls running back and forth
to see each other; it was still there.

One night my mother and Aunt Dodie sat on the porch and recited
poetry. How this started I forget; with one of them thinking of a
quotation, likely, and the other one matching it. Uncle James was
leaning against the railing, smoking. Because we were visiting, he had
permitted himself to come.

   "How can a man die better," cried Aunt Dodie cheerfully,

> *Than facing fearful odds,*
> *For the ashes of his fathers*
> *And the temples of his gods?*

"And all day long the noise of battle rolled," my mother declared,

> *Among the mountains by the winter sea.*

> *Not a drum was heard, not a funeral note,*
> *As his corpse to the ramparts we hurried. . . .*

> *For I am going a long way*
> *To the island-valley of Avalon*
> *Where falls not hail, or rain, or any snow. . . .*

My mother's voice had taken on an embarrassing tremor, so I was glad
when Aunt Dodie interrupted.

   "Heavens, wasn't it all sad, the stuff they put in the old readers?"

   "I don't remember a bit of it," said Uncle James. "Except–" and he
recited without a break:

> *Along the line of smoky hills*
> *The crimson forest stands*
> *And all day long the bluejay calls*
> *Throughout the autumn lands.*

"Good for you," said Aunt Dodie, and she and my mother joined in, so
they were all reciting together, and laughing at each other:

> *Now by great marshes wrapped in mist,*
> *Or past some river's mouth,*
> *Throughout the long still autumn day*
> *Wild birds are flying south.*

"Though when you come to think of it, even that has kind of a sad ring," Aunt Dodie said.

If I had been making a proper story out of this, I would have ended it, I think, with my mother not answering and going ahead of me across the pasture. That would have done. I didn't stop there, I suppose, because I wanted to find out more, remember more. I wanted to bring back all I could. Now I look at what I have done and it is like a series of snapshots, like the brownish snapshots with fancy borders that my parents' old camera used to take. In these snapshots Aunt Dodie and Uncle James and even Aunt Lena, even her children, come out clear enough. (All these people dead now except the children, who have turned into decent friendly wage earners, not a criminal or as far as I know even a neurotic among them.) The problem, the only problem, is my mother. And she is the one of course that I am trying to get; it is to reach her that this whole journey has been undertaken. With what purpose? To mark her off, to describe, to illumine, to celebrate, to *get rid*, of her; and it did not work, for she looms too close, just as she always did. She is heavy as always, she weighs everything down, and yet she is indistinct, her edges melt and flow. Which means she has stuck to me as close as ever and refused to fall away, and I could go on, and on, applying what skills I have, using what tricks I know, and it would always be the same.

Works by Alice Munro

FICTION

Dance of the Happy Shades. Toronto: Ryerson, 1968.
Lives of Girls and Women. Toronto: McGraw-Hill Ryerson, 1971.
Something I've Been Meaning to Tell You. Toronto: McGraw-Hill Ryerson, 1974.
Who Do You Think You Are? Toronto: Macmillan, 1978.
The Moons of Jupiter. Toronto: Macmillan, 1982.

Interviews with Alice Munro

Journal of Canadian Fiction, 1 (Fall, 1972), 54-62.
Eleven Canadian Novelists. Edited by Graeme Gibson. Toronto: Anansi, 1973, pp. 237-64.
For Openers. Edited by Alan Twigg. Madeira Park, B.C.: Harbour, 1981, pp. 13-20.

Margaret Laurence

Born in Neepawa, Manitoba, in 1926, Margaret Laurence spent many years far from her home town before returning to it. Neepawa became a model for her fictional town of Manawaka, the initial setting for her five books of Canadian fiction, *The Stone Angel* (1964), *A Jest of God* (1966), *The Fire-Dwellers* (1969), *A Bird in the House* (1970), and *The Diviners* (1974). In each of these books the female protagonist is raised in and shaped by the small prairie town.

Laurence spent the early 1950s with her husband in Africa, first in Somaliland (now Somali Republic) and later in the Gold Coast (now Ghana). Her African sojourn introduced her to that world's culture and art; she translated some Nigerian literature, wrote critical studies of African writings, and set her first novel, *This Side Jordan* (1960), and her first collection of short stories, *The Tomorrow-Tamer* (1963), in Africa. Though she had returned to Canada in 1957, she continued for a time to set her fiction in Africa, not Canada. "I was fortunate in going to Africa when I did—in my early twenties—because for some years I was so fascinated by the African scene that I was in this way prevented from writing an autobiographical first novel. I don't

157

say there is anything wrong in autobiographical novels, but it would not have been the right thing for me–my view of the prairie from which I had come was still too prejudiced and distorted by closeness.''

In 1962 Laurence and her children moved to England. At this time she began writing *The Stone Angel*, and in 1964 she published the short story, ''A Bird in the House.'' Six years later she included this as the title story in a collection that comprises the adult Vanessa MacLeod's memories of growing up in Manawaka.

To the question whether what she writes is autobiographical, Laurence answers, ''It isn't, except in the case of the stories in *A Bird in the House*, which are directly drawn from my own childhood although even there fictionalized–but nothing I have written is directly autobiographical at all. The thing that *is* autobiographical is not the events, not the characters, but some of the underlying responses toward life, where you're really saying what you really feel about various situations.''

Like Vanessa, Laurence did not experience a painless childhood. When she was only five, her mother died suddenly. The following year her father married her mother's elder sister, and four years later he also died. At that time she moved into her grandfather's house. That house and the prairie town of Neepawa left an indelible image on the writer and her fiction. ''Having grown up in...a fairly stultifying community in some ways, and yet having come from...Scots ancestors who certainly were extremely

independent if not bloody-minded, and equally bloody-minded Irish ancestors–including my grandfather about whom I've written in *A Bird in the House*, who was a terrible old man, but who had an enormous sense of his own independence–it seems to me that these two things probably have worked in kind of juxtaposition in my life: on the one hand a repressed community, on the other hand a community in which the values of the individual were extraordinarily strongly recognized....'' Through the creation of Vanessa, Laurence came to a new understanding of her upbringing. Referring to her grandfather, she recalls, ''I really hated him as a kid, and I think with some reason: he was in some ways eminently hateable.'' But on finishing the Vanessa stories, ''I realized that in point of fact, I was an awful lot like him in this way. I had been so rebellious against him because that very tenacity which he had, I *also* had. I feel passionate about people trying not to manipulate other people, not to force other people, and yet with my grandfather's awful example in front of me and knowing that I had the same desire for a kind of personal independence as he had, I feel that this is something in myself that I have to watch.''

In this selection from *A Bird in the House*, Vanessa looks back on moments in her childhood, each moment tracing some growth of understanding in the child Vanessa as recalled and interpreted by the adult. The maturing protagonist comes to see her parents and her grandmother in a new perspective.

A Bird
in
the House

‌

T‌he parade would be almost over by now, and I had
not gone. My mother had said in a resigned voice, "All right, Vanessa, if
that's the way you feel," making me suffer twice as many jabs of guilt as
I would have done if she had lost her temper. She and Grandmother
MacLeod had gone off, my mother pulling the low box-sleigh with
Roddie all dolled up in his new red snowsuit, just the sort of little kid
anyone would want people to see. I sat on the lowest branch of the birch
tree in our yard, not minding the snowy wind, even welcoming its
punishment. I went over my reasons for not going, trying to believe they
were good and sufficient, but in my heart I felt I was betraying my
father. This was the first time I had stayed away from the Remembrance
Day parade. I wondered if he would notice that I was not there, standing
on the sidewalk at the corner of River and Main while the parade passed,
and then following to the Court House grounds where the service was
held.

I could see the whole thing in my mind. It was the same every year.
The Manawaka Civic Band always led the way. They had never been
able to afford full uniforms, but they had peaked navy-blue caps and
sky-blue chest ribbons. They were joined on Remembrance Day by the
Salvation Army band, whose uniforms seemed too ordinary for a
parade, for they were the same ones the bandsmen wore every Saturday
night when they played "Nearer My God to Thee" at the foot of River
Street. The two bands never managed to practise quite enough together,
so they did not keep in time too well. The Salvation Army band
invariably played faster, and afterwards my father would say irritably,

159

"They play those marches just like they do hymns, blast them, as though they wouldn't get to heaven if they didn't hustle up." And my mother, who had great respect for the Salvation Army because of the good work they did, would respond chidingly, "Now, now, Ewen–" I vowed I would never say "Now, now" to my husband or children, not that I ever intended having the latter, for I had been put off by my brother Roderick, who was now two years old with wavy hair, and everyone said what a beautiful child. I was twelve, and no one in their right mind would have said what a beautiful child, for I was big-boned like my Grandfather Connor and had straight lanky black hair like a Blackfoot or Cree.

After the bands would come the veterans. Even thinking of them at this distance, in the white and withdrawn quiet of the birch tree, gave me a sense of painful embarrassment. I might not have minded so much if my father had not been among them. How could he go? How could he not see how they all looked? It must have been a long time since they were soldiers, for they had forgotten how to march in step. They were old–that was the thing. My father was bad enough, being almost forty, but he wasn't a patch on Howard Tully from the drugstore, who was completely grey-haired and also fat, or Stewart MacMurchie, who was bald at the back of his head. They looked to me like imposters, plump or spindly caricatures of past warriors. I almost hated them for walking in that limping column down Main. At the Court House, everyone would sing *Lord God of Hosts, be with us yet, lest we forget, lest we forget.* Will Masterson would pick up his old Army bugle and blow the Last Post. Then it would be over and everyone could start gabbling once more and go home.

I jumped down from the birch bough and ran to the house, yelling, making as much noise as I could.

> *I'm a poor lonesome cowboy*
> *An' a long way from home–*

I stepped inside the front hall and kicked off my snow boots. I slammed the door behind me, making the dark ruby and emerald glass shake in the small leaded panes. I slid purposely on the hall rug, causing it to bunch and crinkle on the slippery polished oak of the floor. I seized the newel post, round as a head, and spun myself to and fro on the bottom stair.

> *I ain't got no father*
> *To buy the clothes I wear.*
> *I'm a poor lonesome–*

At this moment my shoulders were firmly seized and shaken by a pair of hands, white and delicate and old, but strong as talons.

"Just what do you think you're doing, young lady?" Grandmother MacLeod enquired, in a voice like frost on a windowpane, infinitely cold and clearly etched.

I went limp and in a moment she took her hands away. If you struggled, she would always hold on longer.

"Gee, I never knew you were home yet."

"I would have thought that on a day like this you might have shown a little respect and consideration," Grandmother MacLeod said, "even if you couldn't make the effort to get cleaned up enough to go to the parade."

I realised with surprise that she imagined this to be my reason for not going. I did not try to correct her impression. My real reason would have been even less acceptable.

"I'm sorry," I said quickly.

In some families, *please* is described as the magic word. In our house, however, it was *sorry*.

"This isn't an easy day for any of us," she said.

Her younger son, my Uncle Roderick, had been killed in the Great War. When my father marched, and when the hymn was sung, and when that unbearably lonely tune was sounded by the one bugle and everyone forced themselves to keep absolutely still, it would be that boy of whom she was thinking. I felt the enormity of my own offence.

"Grandmother—I'm sorry."

"So you said."

I could not tell her I had not really said it before at all. I went into the den and found my father there. He was sitting in the leather-cushioned armchair beside the fireplace. He was not doing anything, just sitting and smoking. I stood beside him, wanting to touch the light-brown hairs on his forearm, but thinking he might laugh at me or pull his arm away if I did.

"I'm sorry," I said, meaning it.

"What for, honey?"

"For not going."

"Oh—that. What was the matter?"

I did not want him to know, and yet I had to tell him, make him see.

"They look silly," I blurted. "Marching like that."

For a minute I thought he was going to be angry. It would have been a relief to me if he had been. Instead, he drew his eyes away from mine and fixed them above the mantelpiece where the sword hung, the handsome and evil-looking crescent in its carved bronze sheath that some ancestor had once brought from the Northern Frontier of India.

"Is that the way it looks to you?" he said.

I felt in his voice some hurt, something that was my fault. I wanted to make everything all right between us, to convince him that I understood, even if I did not. I prayed that Grandmother MacLeod would stay put in her room, and that my mother would take a long time in the kitchen, giving Roddie his lunch. I wanted my father to myself, so I could prove to him that I cared more about him than any of the others did. I wanted to speak in some way that would be more poignant and comprehending than anything of which my mother could possibly be capable. But I did not know how.

"You were right there when Uncle Roderick got killed, weren't you?" I began uncertainly.

"Yes."

"How old was he, Dad?"

"Eighteen," my father said.

Unexpectedly, that day came into intense being for me. He had had to watch his own brother die, not in the antiseptic calm of some hospital, but out in the open, the stretches of mud I had seen in his snapshots. He would not have known what to do. He would just have had to stand there and look at it, whatever that might mean. I looked at my father with a kind of horrified awe, and then I began to cry. I had forgotten about impressing him with my perception. Now I needed him to console me for this unwanted glimpse of the pain he had once known.

"Hey, cut it out, honey," he said, embarrassed. "It was bad, but it wasn't all as bad as that part. There were a few other things."

"Like what?" I said, not believing him.

"Oh—I don't know," he replied evasively. "Most of us were pretty young, you know, I and the boys I joined up with. None of us had ever been away from Manawaka before. Those of us who came back mostly came back here, or else went no further away from town than Winnipeg. So when we were overseas—that was the only time most of us were ever a long way from home."

"Did you want to be?" I asked, shocked.

"Oh well—" my father said uncomfortably. "It was kind of interesting to see a few other places for a change, that's all."

Grandmother MacLeod was standing in the doorway.

"Beth's called you twice for lunch, Ewen. Are you deaf, you and Vanessa?"

"Sorry," my father and I said simultaneously.

Then we went upstairs to wash our hands.

That winter my mother returned to her old job as nurse in my father's medical practice. She was able to do this only because of Noreen.

"Grandmother MacLeod says we're getting a maid," I said to my father, accusingly, one morning. "We're not, are we?"

"Believe you me, on what I'm going to be paying her," my father growled, "she couldn't be called anything as classy as a maid. Hired girl would be more like it."

"Now, now, Ewen," my mother put in, "it's not as if we were cheating her or anything. You know she wants to live in town, and I can certainly see why, stuck out there on the farm, and her father hardly ever letting her come in. What kind of life is that for a girl?"

"I don't like the idea of your going back to work, Beth," my father said. "I know you're fine now, but you're not exactly the robust type."

"You can't afford to hire a nurse any longer. It's all very well to say the Depression won't last forever–probably it won't, but what else can we do for now?"

"I'm damned if I know," my father admitted. "Beth–"

"Yes?"

They both seemed to have forgotten about me. It was at breakfast, which we always ate in the kitchen, and I sat rigidly on my chair, pretending to ignore and thus snub their withdrawal from me. I glared at the window, but it was so thickly plumed and scrolled with frost that I could not see out. I glanced back to my parents. My father had not replied, and my mother was looking at him in that anxious and half-frowning way she had recently developed.

"What is it, Ewen?" Her voice had the same nervous sharpness it bore sometimes when she would say to me, "For mercy's sake, Vanessa, what is it *now*?" as though whatever was the matter, it was bound to be the last straw.

My father spun his sterling silver serviette ring, engraved with his initials, slowly around on the table.

"I never thought things would turn out like this, did you?"

"Please–" my mother said in a low strained voice, "please, Ewen, let's not start all this again. I can't take it."

"All right," my father said. "Only–"

"The MacLeods used to have money and now they don't," my mother cried. "Well, they're not alone. Do you think all that matters to me, Ewen? What I can't bear is to see you forever reproaching yourself. As if it were your fault."

"I don't think it's the comedown," my father said. "If I were somewhere else, I don't suppose it would matter to me, either, except where you're concerned. But I suppose you'd work too hard wherever you were–it's bred into you. If you haven't got anything to slave away at, you'll sure as hell invent something."

"What do you think I should do, let the house go to wrack and ruin? That would go over well with your mother, wouldn't it?"

"That's just it," my father said. "It's the damned house all the time. I haven't only taken on my father's house, I've taken on everything that goes with it, apparently. Sometimes I really wonder–"

"Well, it's a good thing I've inherited some practicality even if you haven't," my mother said. "I'll say that for the Connors–they aren't given to brooding, thank the Lord. Do you want your egg poached or scrambled?"

"Scrambled," my father said. "All I hope is that this Noreen doesn't get married straightaway, that's all."

"She won't," my mother said. "Who's she going to meet who could afford to marry?"

"I marvel at you, Beth," my father said. "You look as though a puff of wind would blow you away. But underneath, by God, you're all hardwood."

"Don't talk stupidly," my mother said. "All I hope is that she won't object to taking your mother's breakfast up on a tray."

"That's right," my father said angrily. "Rub it in."

"Oh Ewen, I'm sorry!" my mother cried, her face suddenly stricken. "I don't know why I say these things. I didn't mean to."

"I know," my father said. "Here, cut it out, honey. Just for God's sake please don't cry."

"I'm sorry," my mother repeated, blowing her nose.

"We're both sorry," my father said. "Not that that changes anything."

After my father had gone, I got down from my chair and went to my mother.

"I don't want you to go back to the office. I don't want a hired girl here. I'll hate her."

My mother sighed, making me feel that I was placing an intolerable burden on her, and yet making me resent having to feel this weight. She looked tired, as she often did these days. Her tiredness bored me, made me want to attack her for it.

"Catch me getting along with a dumb old hired girl," I threatened.

"Do what you like," my mother said abruptly. "What can I do about it?"

And then, of course, I felt bereft, not knowing which way to turn.

My father need not have worried about Noreen getting married. She was, as it turned out, interested not in boys but in God. My mother was relieved about the boys but alarmed about God.

"It isn't natural," she said, "for a girl of seventeen. Do you think she's all right mentally, Ewen?"

When my parents, along with Grandmother MacLeod, went to the United Church every Sunday, I was made to go to Sunday school in the church basement, where there were small red chairs which humiliatingly resembled kindergarten furniture, and pictures of Jesus wearing a white sheet and surrounded by a whole lot of well-dressed kids whose mothers obviously had not suffered them to come unto Him until every face and ear was properly scrubbed. Our religious observances also included grace at meals, when my father would mumble "For what we are about to receive the Lord make us truly thankful Amen," running the words together as though they were one long word. My mother approved of these rituals, which seemed decent and moderate to her. Noreen's religion, however, was a different matter. Noreen belonged to the Tabernacle of the Risen and Reborn, and she had got up to testify no less than seven times in the past two years, she told us. My mother, who could not imagine anyone's voluntarily making a public spectacle of themselves, was profoundly shocked by this revelation.

"Don't worry," my father soothed her. "She's all right. She's just had kind of a dull life, that's all."

My mother shrugged and went on worrying and trying to help Noreen without hurting her feelings, by tactful remarks about the advisability of modulating one's voice when singing hymns, and the fact that there was plenty of hot water so Noreen really didn't need to hesitate about taking a bath. She even bought a razor and a packet of blades and whispered to Noreen that any girl who wore transparent blouses so much would probably like to shave under her arms. None of these suggestions had the slightest effect on Noreen. She did not cease belting out hymns at the top of her voice, she bathed once a fortnight, and the sorrel-colored hair continued to bloom like a thicket of Indian paintbrush in her armpits.

Grandmother MacLeod refused to speak to Noreen. This caused Noreen a certain amount of bewilderment until she finally hit on an answer.

"Your poor grandma," she said. "She is deaf as a post. These things are sent to try us here on earth, Vanessa. But if she makes it to Heaven, I'll bet you anything she will hear clear as a bell."

Noreen and I talked about Heaven quite a lot, and also Hell. Noreen had an intimate and detailed knowledge of both places. She not only knew what they looked like–she even knew how big they were. Heaven was seventy-seven thousand miles square and it had four gates, each one made out of a different kind of precious jewel. The Pearl Gate, the Topaz Gate, the Amethyst Gate, the Ruby Gate–Noreen would reel them off, all the gates of Heaven. I told Noreen they sounded like poetry, but she was puzzled by my reaction and said I shouldn't talk that way. If you said poetry, it sounded like it was just made up and not really so, Noreen said.

Hell was larger than Heaven, and when I asked why, thinking of it as something of a comedown for God, Noreen said naturally it had to be bigger because there were a darn sight more people there than in Heaven. Hell was one hundred and ninety million miles deep and was in perpetual darkness, like a cave or under the sea. Even the flames (this was the awful thing) *did not give off any light.*

I did not actually believe in Noreen's doctrines, but the images which they conjured up began to inhabit my imagination. Noreen's fund of exotic knowledge was not limited to religion, although in a way it all seemed related. She could do many things which had a spooky tinge to them. Once when she was making a cake, she found we had run out of eggs. She went outside and gathered a bowl of fresh snow and used it instead. The cake rose like a charm, and I stared at Noreen as though she were a sorceress. In fact, I began to think of her as a sorceress, someone not quite of this earth. There was nothing unearthly about her broad shoulders and hips and her forest of dark red hair, but even these features took on a slightly sinister significance to me. I no longer saw her through the eyes or the expressed opinions of my mother and father, as a girl who had quit school at grade eight and whose life on the farm had been endlessly drab. I knew the truth–Noreen's life had not been drab at all, for she dwelt in a world of violent splendors, a world filled with angels whose wings of delicate light bore real feathers, and saints shining like the dawn, and prophets who spoke in ancient tongues, and the ecstatic souls of the saved, as well as denizens of the lower regions–mean-eyed imps and crooked cloven-hoofed monsters and beasts with the bodies of swine and the human heads of murderers, and lovely depraved jezebels torn by dogs through all eternity. The middle layer of Creation, our earth, was equally full of grotesque presences, for Noreen believed strongly in the visitation of ghosts and the communication with spirits. She could prove this with her Ouija board. We would both place our fingers lightly on the indicator, and it would skim across the board and spell out answers to our questions. I did not believe wholeheartedly in the Ouija board, either, but I was cautious about the kind of question

I asked, in case the answer would turn out unfavorable and I would be unable to forget it.

One day Noreen told me she could also make a table talk. We used the small table in my bedroom, and sure enough, it lifted very slightly under our fingertips and tapped once for *Yes*, twice for *No*. Noreen asked if her Aunt Ruthie would get better from the kidney operation, and the table replied *No*. I withdrew my hands.

"I don't want to do it any more."

"Gee, what's the matter, Vanessa?" Noreen's plain placid face creased in a frown. "We only just begun."

"I have to do my homework."

My heart lurched as I said this. I was certain Noreen would know I was lying, and that she would know not by any ordinary perception, either. But her attention had been caught by something else, and I was thankful, at least until I saw what it was.

My bedroom window was not opened in the coldest weather. The storm window, which was fitted outside as an extra wall against the winter, had three small circular holes in its frame so that some fresh air could seep into the house. The sparrow must have been floundering in the new snow on the roof, for it had crawled in through one of these holes and was now caught between the two layers of glass. I could not bear the panic of the trapped bird, and before I realised what I was doing, I had thrown open the bedroom window. I was not releasing the sparrow into any better a situation, I soon saw, for instead of remaining quiet and allowing us to catch it in order to free it, it began flying blindly around the room, hitting the lampshade, brushing against the walls, its wings seeming to spin faster and faster.

I was petrified. I thought I would pass out if those palpitating wings touched me. There was something in the bird's senseless movements that revolted me. I also thought it was going to damage itself, break one of those thin wing-bones, perhaps, and then it would be lying on the floor, dying, like the pimpled and horribly featherless baby birds we saw sometimes on the sidewalks in the spring when they had fallen out of their nests. I was not any longer worried about the sparrow. I wanted only to avoid the sight of it lying broken on the floor. Viciously, I thought that if Noreen said, *God sees the little sparrow fall*, I would kick her in the shins. She did not, however, say this.

"A bird in the house means a death in the house," Noreen remarked.

Shaken, I pulled my glance away from the whirling wings and looked at Noreen.

"What?"

"That's what I've heard said, anyhow."

The sparrow had exhausted itself. It lay on the floor, spent and trembling. I could not bring myself to touch it. Noreen bent and picked it up. She cradled it with great gentleness between her cupped hands. Then we took it downstairs, and when I had opened the back door, Noreen set the bird free.

"Poor little scrap," she said, and I felt struck to the heart, knowing she had been concerned all along about the sparrow, while I, perfidiously, in the chaos of the moment, had been concerned only about myself.

"Wanna do some with the Ouija board, Vanessa?" Noreen asked.

I shivered a little, perhaps only because of the blast of cold air which had come into the kitchen when the door was opened.

"No thanks, Noreen. Like I said, I got my homework to do. But thanks all the same."

"That's okay," Noreen said in her guileless voice. "Any time."

But whenever she mentioned the Ouija board or the talking table, after that, I always found some excuse not to consult these oracles.

"Do you want to come to church with me this evening, Vanessa?" my father asked.

"How come you're going to the evening service?" I enquired.

"Well, we didn't go this morning. We went snowshoeing instead, remember? I think your grandmother was a little bit put out about it. She went alone this morning. I guess it wouldn't hurt you and me, to go now."

We walked through the dark, along the white streets, the snow squeaking dryly under our feet. The streetlights were placed at long intervals along the sidewalks, and around each pole the circle of flimsy light created glistening points of blue and crystal on the crusted snow. I would have liked to take my father's hand, as I used to do, but I was too old for that now. I walked beside him, taking long steps so he would not have to walk more slowly on my account.

The sermon bored me, and I began leafing through the Hymnary for entertainment. I must have drowsed, for the next thing I knew, my father was prodding me and we were on our feet for the closing hymn.

> *Near the Cross, near the Cross,*
> *Be my glory ever,*
> *Till my ransomed soul shall find*
> *Rest beyond the river.*

I knew the tune well, so I sang loudly for the first verse. But the music to that hymn is sombre, and all at once the words themselves seemed too dreadful to be sung. I stopped singing, my throat knotted. I thought I was going to cry, but I did not know why, except that the song recalled to me my Grandmother Connor, who had been dead only a year now. I wondered why her soul needed to be ransomed. If God did not think she was good enough just as she was, then I did not have much use for His opinion. *Rest beyond the river*—was that what had happened to her? She had believed in Heaven, but I did not think that rest beyond the river was quite what she had in mind. To think of her in Noreen's flashy Heaven, though—that was even worse. Someplace where nobody ever got annoyed or had to be smoothed down and placated, someplace where there were never any family scenes—that would have suited my Grandmother Connor. Maybe she wouldn't have minded a certain amount of rest beyond the river, at that.

When we had the silent prayer, I looked at my father. He sat with his head bowed and his eyes closed. He was frowning deeply, and I could see the pulse in his temple. I wondered then what he believed. I did not have any real idea what it might be. When he raised his head, he did not look uplifted or anything like that. He merely looked tired. Then Reverend McKee pronounced the benediction, and we could go home.

"What do you think about all that stuff, Dad?" I asked hesitantly, as we walked.

"What stuff, honey?"

"Oh, Heaven and Hell, and like that."

My father laughed. "Have you been listening to Noreen too much? Well, I don't know. I don't think they're actual places. Maybe they stand for something that happens all the time here, or else doesn't happen. It's kind of hard to explain. I guess I'm not so good at explanations."

Nothing seemed to have been made any clearer to me. I reached out and took his hand, not caring that he might think this a babyish gesture.

"I hate that hymn!"

"Good Lord," my father said in astonishment. "Why, Vanessa?"

But I did not know and so could not tell him.

Many people in Manawaka had flu that winter, so my father and Dr. Cates were kept extremely busy. I had flu myself, and spent a week in bed, vomiting only the first day and after that enjoying poor health, as my mother put it, with Noreen bringing me ginger ale and orange juice, and each evening my father putting a wooden tongue-depressor into my mouth and peering down my throat, then smiling and saying he thought I might live after all.

Then my father got sick himself, and had to stay at home and go to bed. This was such an unusual occurrence that it amused me.

"Doctors shouldn't get sick," I told him.

"You're right," he said. "That was pretty bad management."

"Run along now, dear," my mother said.

That night I woke and heard voices in the upstairs hall. When I went out, I found my mother and Grandmother MacLeod, both in their dressing-gowns. With them was Dr. Cates. I did not go immediately to my mother, as I would have done only a year before. I stood in the doorway of my room, squinting against the sudden light.

"Mother—what is it?"

She turned, and momentarily I saw the look on her face before she erased it and put on a contrived calm.

"It's all right," she said. "Dr. Cates has just come to have a look at Daddy. You go on back to sleep."

The wind was high that night, and I lay and listened to it rattling the storm windows and making the dry and winter-stiffened vines of the Virginia creeper scratch like small persistent claws against the red brick. In the morning, my mother told me that my father had developed pneumonia.

Dr. Cates did not think it would be safe to move my father to the hospital. My mother began sleeping in the spare bedroom, and after she had been there for a few nights, I asked if I could sleep in there too. I thought she would be bound to ask me why, and I did not know what I would say, but she did not ask. She nodded, and in some way her easy agreement upset me.

That night Dr. Cates came again, bringing with him one of the nurses from the hospital. My mother stayed upstairs with them. I sat with Grandmother MacLeod in the living room. That was the last place in the world I wanted to be, but I thought she would be offended if I went off. She sat as straight and rigid as a totem pole, and embroidered away at the needlepoint cushion cover she was doing. I perched on the edge of the chesterfield and kept my eyes fixed on *The White Company* by Conan Doyle, and from time to time I turned a page. I had already read it three times before, but luckily Grandmother MacLeod did not know that. At nine o'clock she looked at her gold brooch watch, which she always wore pinned to her dress, and told me to go to bed, so I did that.

I wakened in darkness. At first, it seemed to me that I was in my own bed, and everything was as usual, with my parents in their room, and Roddie curled up in the crib in his room, and Grandmother MacLeod sleeping with her mouth open in her enormous spool bed, surrounded by half a dozen framed photos of Uncle Roderick and only one of my father, and Noreen snoring fitfully in the room next to mine, with the dark flames of her hair spreading out across the pillow, and the pink and silver motto cards from the Tabernacle stuck with adhesive tape onto the wall beside her bed—*Lean on Him, Emmanuel Is My Refuge, Rock of Ages Cleft for Me.*

Then in the total night around me, I heard a sound. It was my mother, and she was crying, not loudly at all, but from somewhere very deep inside her. I sat up in bed. Everything seemed to have stopped, not only time but my own heart and blood as well. Then my mother noticed that I was awake.

I did not ask her, and she did not tell me anything. There was no need. She held me in her arms, or I held her, I am not certain which. And after a while the first mourning stopped, too, as everything does sooner or later, for when the limits of endurance have been reached, then people must sleep.

In the days following my father's death, I stayed close beside my mother, and this was only partly for my own consoling. I also had the feeling that she needed my protection. I did not know from what, nor what I could possibly do, but something held me there. Reverend McKee called, and I sat with my grandmother and my mother in the living room. My mother told me I did not need to stay unless I wanted to, but I refused to go. What I thought chiefly was that he would speak of the healing power of prayer, and all that, and it would be bound to make my mother cry again. And in fact, it happened in just that way, but when it actually came, I could not protect her from this assault. I could only sit there and pray my own prayer, which was that he would go away quickly.

My mother tried not to cry unless she was alone or with me. I also tried, but neither of us was entirely successful. Grandmother MacLeod, on the other hand, was never seen crying, not even the day of my father's funeral. But that day, when we had returned to the house and she had taken off her black velvet overshoes and her heavy sealskin coat with its black fur that was the softest thing I had ever touched, she stood in the hallway and for the first time she looked unsteady. When I reached out instinctively towards her, she sighed.

"That's right," she said. "You might just take my arm while I go upstairs, Vanessa."

That was the most my Grandmother MacLeod ever gave in, to anyone's sight. I left her in her bedroom, sitting on the straight chair beside her bed and looking at the picture of my father that had been taken when he graduated from medical college. Maybe she was sorry now that she had only the one photograph of him, but whatever she felt, she did not say.

I went down into the kitchen. I had scarcely spoken to Noreen since my father's death. This had not been done on purpose. I simply had not seen her. I had not really seen anyone except my mother. Looking at Noreen now, I suddenly recalled the sparrow. I felt physically sick, remembering the fearful darting and plunging of those wings, and the fact that it was I who had opened the window and let it in. Then an inexplicable fury took hold of me, some terrifying need to hurt, burn, destroy. Absolutely without warning, either to her or to myself, I hit Noreen as hard as I could. When she swung around, appalled, I hit out at her once more, my arms and legs flailing. Her hands snatched at my wrists, and she held me, but still I continued to struggle, fighting blindly, my eyes tightly closed, as though she were a prison all around me and I was battling to get out. Finally, too shocked at myself to go on, I went limp in her grasp and she let me drop to the floor.

"Vanessa! I never done one single solitary thing to you, and here you go hitting and scratching me like that! What in the world has got into you?"

I began to say I was sorry, which was certainly true, but I did not say it. I could not say anything.

"You're not yourself, what with your dad and everything," she excused me. "I been praying every night that your dad is with God, Vanessa. I know he wasn't actually saved in the regular way, but still and all—"

"Shut up," I said.

Something in my voice made her stop talking. I rose from the floor and stood in the kitchen doorway.

"He didn't need to be saved," I went on coldly, distinctly. "And he is not in Heaven, because there is no Heaven. And it doesn't matter, see? *It doesn't matter!*"

Noreen's face looked peculiarly vulnerable now, her high wide cheekbones and puzzled childish eyes, and the thick russet tangle of her hair. I had not hurt her much before, when I hit her. But I had hurt her now, hurt her in some inexcusable way. Yet I sensed, too, that already she was gaining some satisfaction out of feeling sorrowful about my disbelief.

I went upstairs to my room. Momentarily I felt a sense of calm, almost of acceptance. *Rest beyond the river*. I knew now what that meant. It meant Nothing. It meant only silence, forever.

Then I lay down on my bed and spent the last of my tears, or what seemed then to be the last. Because, despite what I had said to Noreen, it did matter. It mattered, but there was no help for it.

Everything changed after my father's death. The MacLeod house could not be kept up any longer. My mother sold it to a local merchant who subsequently covered the deep red of the brick over with yellow stucco. Something about the house had always made me uneasy–that tower room where Grandmother MacLeod's potted plants drooped in a lethargic and lime-green confusion, those long stairways and hidden places, the attic which I had always imagined to be dwelt in by the spirits of the family dead, that gigantic portrait of the Duke of Wellington at the top of the stairs. It was never an endearing house. And yet when it was no longer ours, and when the Virginia creeper had been torn down and the dark walls turned to a light marigold, I went out of my way to avoid walking past, for it seemed to me that the house had lost the stern dignity that was its very heart.

Noreen went back to the farm. My mother and brother and myself moved into Grandfather Connor's house. Grandmother MacLeod went to live with Aunt Morag in Winnipeg. It was harder for her than for anyone, because so much of her life was bound up with the MacLeod house. She was fond of Aunt Morag, but that hardly counted. Her men were gone, her husband and her sons, and a family whose men are gone is *no family at all.* The day she left, my mother and I did not know what to say. Grandmother MacLeod looked even smaller than usual in her fur coat and her black velvet toque. She became extremely agitated about trivialities, and fussed about the possibility of the taxi not arriving on time. She had forbidden us to accompany her to the station. About my father, or the house, or anything important, she did not say a word. Then, when the taxi had finally arrived, she turned to my mother.

"Roddie will have Ewen's seal ring, of course, with the MacLeod crest on it," she said. "But there is another seal as well, don't forget, the larger one with the crest and motto. It's meant to be worn on a watch chain. I keep it in my jewel-box. It was Roderick's. Roddie's to have that, too, when I die. Don't let Morag talk you out of it."

During the Second World War, when I was seventeen and in love with an airman who did not love me, and desperately anxious to get away from Manawaka and from my grandfather's house, I happened one day to be going through the old mahogany desk that had belonged to my father. It had a number of small drawers inside, and I accidentally pulled one of these all the way out. Behind it there was another drawer, one I had not known about. Curiously, I opened it. Inside there was a letter written on almost transparent paper in a cramped angular handwriting. It began–*Cher Monsieur Ewen*–That was all I could make out, for the writing was nearly impossible to read and my French was not good. It was dated 1919. With it, there was a picture of a girl, looking absurdly old-fashioned to my eyes, like the faces on long-discarded calendars or chocolate boxes. But beneath the dated quality of the photograph, she seemed neither expensive nor cheap. She looked like what she probably had been–an ordinary middle-class girl, but in another country. She wore her hair in long ringlets, and her mouth was shaped into a sweetly sad posed smile like Mary Pickford's. That was all. There was nothing else in the drawer.

I looked for a long time at the girl, and hoped she had meant some momentary and unexpected freedom. I remembered what he had said to me, after I hadn't gone to the Remembrance Day parade.

"What are you doing, Vanessa?" my mother called from the kitchen.

"Nothing," I replied.

I took the letter and picture outside and burned them. That was all I could do for him. Now that we might have talked together, it was many years too late. Perhaps it would not have been possible anyway. I did not know.

As I watched the smile of the girl turn into scorched paper, I grieved for my father as though he had just died now.

Works by Margaret Laurence

FICTION

This Side Jordan. Toronto: McClelland and Stewart, 1960.
The Tomorrow-Tamer. Toronto: McClelland and Stewart, 1963.
The Stone Angel. Toronto: McClelland and Stewart, 1964.
A Jest of God. Toronto: McClelland and Stewart, 1966.
The Fire-Dwellers. Toronto: McClelland and Stewart, 1969.
A Bird in the House. Toronto: McClelland and Stewart, 1970.
The Diviners. Toronto: McClelland and Stewart, 1974.

Jason's Quest. Toronto: McClelland and Stewart, 1970. (children's novel)
Six Darn Cows. Toronto: Lorimer, 1979. (children's book)
The Olden Days Coat. Toronto: McClelland and Stewart, 1979. (children's book)
The Christmas Birthday Story. Toronto: McClelland and Stewart, 1980. (children's book)

AUTOBIOGRAPHY

The Prophet's Camel Bell. Toronto: McClelland and Stewart, 1963.

ESSAYS AND CRITICISM

Long Drums and Cannons: Nigerian Dramatists and Novelists. London: Macmillan, 1968.
Heart of a Stranger. Toronto: McClelland and Stewart, 1976.

Interviews with Margaret Laurence

Eleven Canadian Novelists. Edited by Graeme Gibson. Toronto: Anansi, 1973, pp. 185-208.
Conversations with Canadian Novelists. Edited by Donald Cameron. Toronto: Macmillan, 1973. Vol. 1, pp. 96-115.
For Openers. Edited by Alan Twigg. Madeira Park, B.C.: Harbour, 1981, pp. 261-71.

Morley Callaghan

The author of twelve novels and more than a hundred shorter pieces of fiction, Morley Callaghan is Canada's first professional writer, the first artist to devote his life to the vocation of writing fiction. Born in Toronto in 1903, he is a graduate of the University of Toronto and Osgoode Hall Law School. In 1928 his first novel, *Strange Fugitive*, was published; the same year he was called to the bar, but fiction commanded his complete attention and he never practised law.

While in college, Callaghan had taken a summer position at the *Toronto Daily Star*, "in those days... as aggressive and raffish a newspaper as you could find in any North American city." He continued working at the *Star* for four summers. In April, 1929, Callaghan travelled with his wife to Paris, where their literary circle of friends included Hemingway, F. Scott Fitzgerald, James Joyce, and many other writers. The following autumn he returned to Toronto, which has been and remains his physical and literary home.

In his fiction, Callaghan takes the drama of ordinary life and shapes it into a novel or a short story. The only difference between these forms, he believes, is that a novel "just seems longer, that's all, a story that seems too long to be short. A short story seems to be something that you just see, right there, in a sort of flash. A long story, a novel, is a number of flashes. You see the thing going right on, or you may be dealing with something that you know you just can't do in ten pages.

"The art of fiction is the greatest of all arts," Callaghan believes, "because the writer has for his material the ways of men and women in their relationship to each other." To delineate such relationships, Callaghan writes a prose that presents the material without stylistic embellishments; he removes himself from the narrative completely. In his early years as a writer, Callaghan learned that "writing had to do with the right relationship between the words and the thing or person being described: the words should be as transparent as glass, and every time a writer used a brilliant phrase to prove himself witty or clever he merely took the mind of the reader away from the object and directed it to himself; he became simply a performer."

In his short stories, Callaghan illuminates the essence of a character or characters through the careful and sensitive depiction of a revealing incident. "When a story came easily," he recalls, "I had suddenly found a structure, or an incident that drew out of me an emotion or a view of things that I had been nursing for a long time...there had to be a total poignant impact, and first, of course, this impact had to be in me." In "A Cap for Steve," first published in 1952, the incident of the lost baseball cap leads Steve and his father to understand each other a little more tenderly and offers the reader a glimpse into the workings of the Diamond family.

A Cap
for
Steve

Dave Diamond, a poor man, a carpenter's assistant, was a small, wiry, quick-tempered individual who had learned how to make every dollar count in his home. His wife, Anna, had been sick a lot, and his twelve-year-old son, Steve, had to be kept in school. Steve, a big-eyed, shy kid, ought to have known the value of money as well as Dave did. It had been ground into him.

But the boy was crazy about baseball, and after school, when he could have been working as a delivery boy or selling papers, he played ball with the kids. His failure to appreciate that the family needed a few extra dollars disgusted Dave. Around the house he wouldn't let Steve talk about baseball, and he scowled when he saw him hurrying off with his glove after dinner.

When the Phillies came to town to play an exhibition game with the home team and Steve pleaded to be taken to the ball park, Dave, of course, was outraged. Steve knew they couldn't afford it. But he had got his mother on his side. Finally Dave made a bargain with them. He said that if Steve came home after school and worked hard helping to make some kitchen shelves, he would take him that night to the ball park.

Steve worked hard, but Dave was still resentful. They had to coax him to put on his good suit. When they started out Steve held aloof, feeling guilty, and they walked down the street like strangers; then Dave glanced at Steve's face and, half-ashamed, took his arm more cheerfully.

As the game went on Dave had to listen to Steve's recitation of the batting average of every Philly that stepped up to the plate; the time the boy must have wasted learning these averages began to appall him. He showed it so plainly that Steve felt guilty again and was silent.

After the game Dave let Steve drag him on to the field to keep him company while he tried to get some autographs from the Philly players, who were being hemmed in by gangs of kids blocking the way to the club-house. But Steve, who was shy, let the other kids block him off from the players. Steve would push his way in, get blocked out, and come back to stand mournfully beside Dave. And Dave grew impatient. He was wasting valuable time. He wanted to get home; Steve knew it and was worried.

Then the big, blond Philly outfielder, Eddie Condon, who had been held up by a gang of kids tugging at his arm and thrusting their score cards at him, broke loose and made a run for the club-house. He was jostled, and his blue cap with the red peak, tilted far back on his head, fell off. It fell at Steve's feet, and Steve stooped quickly and grabbed it. "Okay, son," the outfielder called, turning back. But Steve, holding the hat in both hands, only stared at him.

"Give him his cap, Steve," Dave said, smiling apologetically at the big outfielder who towered over them. But Steve drew the hat closer to his chest. In an awed trance he looked up at big Eddie Condon. It was an embarrassing moment. All the other kids were watching. Some shouted, "Give him his cap."

"My cap, son," Eddie Condon said, his hand out.

"Hey, Steve," Dave said, and he gave him a shake. But he had to jerk the cap out of Steve's hands.

"Here you are," he said.

The outfielder, noticing Steve's white worshipping face and pleading eyes, grinned and then shrugged. "Aw, let him keep it," he said.

"No, Mister Condon, you don't need to do that," Steve protested.

"It's happened before. Forget it," Eddie Condon said, and he trotted away to the club-house.

Dave handed the cap to Steve; envious kids circled around them and Steve said, "He said I could keep it, Dad. You heard him, didn't you?"

"Yeah, I heard him," Dave admitted. The wonder in Steve's face made him smile. He took the boy by the arm and they hurried off the field.

On the way home Dave couldn't get him to talk about the game; he couldn't get him to take his eyes off the cap. Steve could hardly believe in his own happiness. "See," he said suddenly, and he showed Dave that Eddie Condon's name was printed on the sweatband. Then he went on dreaming. Finally he put the cap on his head and turned to Dave with a slow, proud smile. The cap was away too big for him; it fell down over his ears. "Never mind," Dave said. "You can get your mother to take a tuck in the back."

When they got home Dave was tired and his wife didn't understand the cap's importance, and they couldn't get Steve to go to bed. He swaggered around wearing the cap and looking in the mirror every ten minutes. He took the cap to bed with him.

Dave and his wife had a cup of coffee in the kitchen, and Dave told her again how they had got the cap. They agreed that their boy must have an attractive quality that showed in his face, and that Eddie Condon must have been drawn to him—why else would he have singled Steve out from all the kids?

But Dave got tired of the fuss Steve made over that cap, and of the way he wore it from the time he got up in the morning until the time he went to bed. Some kid was always coming in, wanting to try on the cap. It was childish, Dave said, for Steve to go around assuming that the cap made him important in the neighborhood, and to keep telling them how he had become a leader in the park a few blocks away, where he played ball in the evenings. And Dave wouldn't stand for Steve's keeping the cap on while he was eating. He was always scolding his wife for accepting Steve's explanation that he'd forgotten he had it on. Just the same, it was remarkable what a little thing like a ball cap could do for a kid, Dave admitted to his wife as he smiled to himself.

One night Steve was late coming home from the park. Dave didn't realize how late it was until he put down his newspaper and watched his wife at the window. Her restlessness got on his nerves. "See what comes from encouraging the boy to hang around with those park loafers," he said. "I don't encourage him," she protested. "You do," he insisted irritably, for he was really worried now. A gang hung around the park until midnight. It was a bad park. It was true that on one side there was a good district with fine, expensive apartment houses, but the kids from that neighborhood left the park to the kids from the poorer homes. When his wife went out and walked down to the corner it was his turn to wait and worry and watch at the open window. Each waiting moment tortured him. At last he heard his wife's voice and Steve's voice, and he relaxed and sighed; then he remembered his duty and rushed angrily to meet them.

"I'll fix you, Steve, once and for all," he said. "I'll show you you can't start coming into the house at midnight."

"Hold your horses, Dave," his wife said. "Can't you see the state he's in?" Steve looked utterly exhausted and beaten.

"What's the matter?" Dave asked quickly.

"I lost my cap," Steve whispered; he walked past his father and threw himself on the couch in the living-room and lay with his face hidden.

"Now, don't scold him, Dave," his wife said.

"Scold him. Who's scolding him?" Dave asked, indignantly. "It's his cap, not mine. If it's not worth his while to hang on to it, why should I scold him?'' But he was implying resentfully that he alone recognized the cap's value.

"So you are scolding him," his wife said. "It's his cap. Not yours. What happened, Steve?"

Steve told them he had been playing ball and he found that when he ran the bases the cap fell off; it was still too big, despite the tuck his mother had taken in the band. So the next time he came to bat he tucked the cap in his hip pocket. Someone had lifted it, he was sure.

"And he didn't even know whether it was still in his pocket," Dave said sarcastically.

"I wasn't careless, Dad," Steve said. For the last three hours he had been wandering around to the homes of the kids who had been in the park at the time; he wanted to go on, but he was too tired. Dave knew the boy was apologizing to him, but he didn't know why it made him angry.

"If he didn't hang on to it, it's not worth worrying about now," he said, and he sounded offended.

After that night they knew that Steve didn't go to the park to play ball; he went to look for the cap. It irritated Dave to see him sit around listlessly, or walk in circles, trying to force his memory to find a particular incident which would suddenly recall to him the moment when the cap had been taken. It was no attitude for a growing, healthy boy to take, Dave complained. He told Steve firmly once and for all that he didn't want to hear any more about the cap.

One night, two weeks later, Dave was walking home with Steve from the shoemaker's. It was a hot night. When they passed an ice-cream parlor Steve slowed down. "I guess I couldn't have a soda, could I?" Steve said. "Nothing doing," Dave said firmly. "Come on now," he added as Steve hung back, looking in the window.

"Dad, look!" Steve cried suddenly, pointing at the window. "My cap! There's my cap! He's coming out!"

A well-dressed boy was leaving the ice-cream parlor; he had on a blue ball cap with a red peak, just like Steve's cap. "Hey, you!" Steve cried, and he rushed at the boy, his small face fierce and his eyes wild. Before the boy could back away Steve had snatched the cap from his head. "That's my cap!" he shouted.

"What's this?" the bigger boy said. "Hey, give me my cap or I'll give you a poke on the nose."

Dave was surprised that his own shy boy did not back away. He watched him clutch the cap in his left hand, half crying with excitement as he put his head down and drew back his right fist: he was willing to fight. And Dave was proud of him.

"Wait, now," Dave said. "Take it easy, son," he said to the other boy, who refused to back away.

"My boy says it's his cap," Dave said.

"Well, he's crazy. It's my cap."

"I was with him when he got this cap. When the Phillies played here. It's a Philly cap."

"Eddie Condon gave it to me," Steve said. "And you stole it from me, you jerk."

"Don't call me a jerk, you little squirt. I never saw you before in my life."

"Look," Steve said, pointing to the printing on the cap's sweatband. "It's Eddie Condon's cap. See? See, Dad?"

"Yeah. You're right, Son. Ever see this boy before, Steve?"

"No," Steve said reluctantly.

The other boy realized he might lose the cap. "I bought it from a guy," he said. "I paid him. My father knows I paid him." He said he got the cap at the ball park. He groped for some magically impressive words and suddenly found them. "You'll have to speak to my father," he said.

"Sure, I'll speak to your father," Dave said. "What's your name? Where do you live?"

"My name's Hudson. I live about ten minutes away on the other side of the park." The boy appraised Dave, who wasn't any bigger than he was and who wore a faded blue windbreaker and no tie. "My father is a lawyer," he said boldly. "He wouldn't let me keep the cap if he didn't think I should."

"Is that a fact?"Dave asked belligerently. "Well, we'll see. Come on. Let's go." And he got between the two boys and they walked along the street. They didn't talk to each other. Dave knew the Hudson boy was waiting to get the protection of his home, and Steve knew it, too, and he looked up apprehensively at Dave. And Dave, reaching for his hand, squeezed it encouragingly and strode along, cocky and belligerent, knowing that Steve relied on him.

The Hudson boy lived in that row of fine apartment houses on the other side of the park. At the entrance to one of these houses Dave tried not to hang back and show he was impressed, because he could feel Steve hanging back. When they got into the small elevator Dave didn't know why he took off his hat. In the carpeted hall on the fourth floor the Hudson boy said, "Just a minute," and entered his own apartment. Dave and Steve were left alone in the corridor, knowing that the other boy was preparing his father for the encounter. Steve looked anxiously at his father, and Dave said, "Don't worry, Son," and he added resolutely, "No one's putting anything over on us."

A tall balding man in a brown velvet smoking-jacket suddenly opened the door. Dave had never seen a man wearing one of those jackets, although he had seen them in department-store windows. "Good evening," he said, making a deprecatory gesture at the cap Steve still clutched tightly in his left hand. "My boy didn't get your name. My name is Hudson."

"Mine's Diamond."

"Come on in," Mr. Hudson said, putting out his hand and laughing good-naturedly. He led Dave and Steve into his living-room. "What's this about that cap?" he asked. "The way kids can get excited about a cap. Well, it's understandable, isn't it?"

"So it is," Dave said, moving closer to Steve, who was awed by the broadloom rug and the fine furniture. He wanted to show Steve he was at ease himself, and he wished Mr. Hudson wouldn't be so polite. That meant Dave had to be polite and affable, too, and it was hard to manage when he was standing in the middle of the floor in his old windbreaker.

"Sit down, Mr. Diamond," Mr. Hudson said. Dave took Steve's arm and sat him down beside him on the chesterfield. The Hudson boy watched his father. And Dave looked at Steve and saw that he wouldn't face Mr. Hudson or the other boy; he kept looking up at Dave, putting all his faith in him.

"Well, Mr. Diamond, from what I gathered from my boy, you're able to prove this cap belonged to your boy."

"That's a fact," Dave said.

"Mr. Diamond, you'll have to believe my boy bought that cap from some kid in good faith."

"I don't doubt it," Dave said. "But no kid can sell something that doesn't belong to him. You know that's a fact, Mr. Hudson."

"Yes, that's a fact," Mr. Hudson agreed. "But that cap means a lot to my boy, Mr. Diamond."

"It means a lot to my boy, too, Mr. Hudson."

"Sure it does. But supposing we call in a policeman. You know what he'd say? He'd ask you if you were willing to pay my boy what he paid for the cap. That's usually the way it works out," Mr. Hudson said, friendly and smiling, as he eyed Dave shrewdly.

"But that's not right. It's not justice," Dave protested. "Not when it's my boy's cap."

"I know it isn't right. But that's what they do."

"All right. What did you say your boy paid for the cap?" Dave said reluctantly.

"Two dollars."

"Two dollars!" Dave repeated. Mr. Hudson's smile was still kindly, but his eyes were shrewd, and Dave knew the lawyer was counting on his not having the two dollars. Mr. Hudson thought he had Dave sized up; he had looked at him and decided he was broke. Dave's pride was hurt, and he turned to Steve. What he saw in Steve's face was more powerful than the hurt to his pride: it was the memory of how difficult it had been to get an extra nickel, the talk he heard about the cost of food, the worry in his mother's face as she tried to make ends meet, and the bewildered embarrassment that he was here in a rich man's home, forcing his father to confess that he couldn't afford to spend two dollars. Then Dave grew angry and reckless. "I'll give you the two dollars," he said.

Steve looked at the Hudson boy and grinned brightly. The Hudson boy watched his father.

"I suppose that's fair enough," Mr. Hudson said. "A cap like this can be worth a lot to a kid. You know how it is. Your boy might want to sell– I mean be satisfied. Would he take five dollars for it?"

"Five dollars?" Dave repeated. "Is it worth five dollars, Steve?" he asked uncertainly.

Steve shook his head and looked frightened.

"No, thanks, Mr. Hudson," Dave said firmly.

"I'll tell you what I'll do," Mr. Hudson said. "I'll give you ten dollars. The cap has a sentimental value for my boy, a Philly cap, a big-leaguer's cap. It's only worth about a buck and a half really," he added. But Dave shook his head again. Mr. Hudson frowned. He looked at his own boy with indulgent concern, but now he was embarrassed. "I'll tell you what I'll do," he said. "This cap– well, it's worth as much as a day at the circus to my boy. Your boy should be recompensed. I want to be fair. Here's twenty dollars," and he held out two ten-dollar bills to Dave.

That much money for a cap, Dave thought, and his eyes brightened. But he knew what the cap had meant to Steve; to deprive him of it now that it was within his reach would be unbearable. All the things he needed in his life gathered around him; his wife was there, saying he couldn't afford to reject the offer, he had no right to do it; and he turned to Steve to see if Steve thought it wonderful that the cap could bring them twenty dollars.

"What do you say, Steve?" he asked uneasily.

"I don't know," Steve said. He was in a trance. When Dave smiled, Steve smiled too, and Dave believed that Steve was as impressed as he was, only more bewildered, and maybe even more aware that they could not possibly turn away that much money for a ball cap.

"Well, here you are," Mr. Hudson said, and he put the two bills in Steve's hand. "It's a lot of money. But I guess you had a right to expect as much."

With a dazed, fixed smile Steve handed the money slowly to his father, and his face was white.

Laughing jovially, Mr. Hudson led them to the door. His own boy followed a few paces behind.

In the elevator Dave took the bills out of his pocket. "See, Stevie," he whispered eagerly. "That windbreaker you wanted! And ten dollars for your bank! Won't Mother be surprised?"

"Yeah," Steve whispered, the little smile still on his face. But Dave had to turn away quickly so their eyes wouldn't meet, for he saw that it was a scared smile.

Outside, Dave said, "Here, you carry the money home, Steve. You show it to your mother."

"No, you keep it," Steve said, and then there was nothing to say. They walked in silence.

"It's a lot of money," Dave said finally. When Steve didn't answer him, he added angrily, "I turned to you, Steve. I asked you, didn't I?"

"That man knew how much his boy wanted that cap," Steve said.

"Sure. But he recognized how much it was worth to us."

"No, you let him take it away from us," Steve blurted.

"That's unfair," Dave said. "Don't dare say that to me."

"I don't want to be like you," Steve muttered, and he darted across the road and walked along on the other side of the street.

"It's unfair," Dave said angrily, only now he didn't mean that Steve was unfair, he meant that what had happened in the prosperous Hudson home was unfair, and he didn't know quite why. He had been trapped, not just by Mr. Hudson, but by his own life. Across the road Steve was hurrying along with his head down, wanting to be alone. They walked most of the way home on opposite sides of the street, until Dave could stand it no longer. "Steve," he called, crossing the street. "It was very unfair. I mean, for you to say..." but Steve started to run. Dave walked as fast as he could and Steve was getting beyond him, and he felt enraged and suddenly he yelled, "Steve!" and he started to chase his son. He wanted to get hold of Steve and pound him, and he didn't know why. He gained on him, he gasped for breath and he almost got him by the shoulder. Turning, Steve saw his father's face in the street light and was terrified; he circled away, got to the house, and rushed in, yelling, "Mother!"

"Son, Son!" she cried, rushing from the kitchen. As soon as she threw her arms around Steve, shielding him, Dave's anger left him and he felt stupid. He walked past them into the kitchen.

"What happened?" she asked anxiously. "Have you both gone crazy? What did you do, Steve?"

"Nothing," he said sullenly.

"What did your father do?"

"We found the boy with my ball cap, and he let the boy's father take it from us."

"No, no," Dave protested. "Nobody pushed us around. The man didn't put anything over on us." He felt tired and his face was burning. He told what had happened; then he slowly took the two ten-dollar bills out of his wallet and tossed them on the table and looked up guiltily at his wife.

It hurt him that she didn't pick up the money, and that she didn't rebuke him. "It is a lot of money, Son," she said slowly. "Your father was only trying to do what he knew was right, and it'll work out, and you'll understand." She was soothing Steve, but Dave knew she felt that she needed to be gentle with him, too, and he was ashamed.

When she went with Steve to his bedroom, Dave sat by himself. His son had contempt for him, he thought. His son, for the first time, had seen how easy it was for another man to handle him, and he had judged him and had wanted to walk alone on the other side of the street. He looked at the money and he hated the sight of it.

His wife returned to the kitchen, made a cup of tea, talked soothingly, and said it was incredible that he had forced the Hudson man to pay him twenty dollars for the cap, but all Dave could think of was *Steve was scared of me*.

Finally, he got up and went into Steve's room. The room was in darkness, but he could see the outline of Steve's body on the bed, and he sat down beside him and whispered, "Look, Son, it was a mistake. I know why. People like us—in circumstances where money can scare us. No, no," he said, feeling ashamed and shaking his head apologetically; he was taking the wrong way of showing the boy they were together; he was covering up his own failure. For the failure had been his, and it had come out of being so separated from his son that he had been blind to what was beyond price in a boy's life. He longed now to show Steve he could be with him from day to day. His hand went out hesitantly to Steve's shoulder. "Steve, look," he said eagerly. "The trouble was I didn't realize how much I enjoyed it that night at the ball park. If I had watched you playing for your own team—the kids around here say you could be a great pitcher. We could take that money and buy a new pitcher's glove for you, and a catcher's mitt. Steve, Steve, are you listening? I could catch for you, work with you in the lane. Maybe I could be your coach...watch you become a great pitcher." In the half-darkness he could see the boy's pale face turn to him.

Steve, who had never heard his father talk like this, was shy and wondering. All he knew was that his father, for the first time, wanted to be with him in his hopes and adventures. He said, "I guess you do know how important that cap was." His hand went out to his father's arm. "With that man the cap was—well it was just something he could buy, eh Dad?" Dave gripped his son's hand hard. The wonderful generosity of childhood—the price a boy was willing to pay to be able to count on his father's admiration and approval—made him feel humble, then strangely exalted.

Works by Morley Callaghan

FICTION

Strange Fugitive. New York: Scribner's, 1928.

A Native Argosy. Toronto: Macmillan, 1929.

It's Never Over. Toronto: Macmillan, 1930.

No Man's Meat. Paris: Black Manikin, 1931.

A Broken Journey. Toronto: Macmillan, 1932.

Such Is My Beloved. Toronto: Macmillan, 1934.

They Shall Inherit the Earth. Toronto: Macmillan, 1935.

Now That April's Here and Other Stories. Toronto: Macmillan, 1936.

More Joy in Heaven. Toronto: Macmillan, 1937.

Luke Baldwin's Vow. Toronto: Winston, 1948.

The Varsity Story. Toronto: Macmillan, 1948.

The Loved and the Lost. Toronto: Macmillan, 1951.

Morley Callaghan's Stories. Toronto: Macmillan, 1959.

The Many Colored Coat. Toronto: Macmillan, 1960.

A Passion in Rome. Toronto: Macmillan, 1961.

A Fine and Private Place. Toronto: Macmillan, 1975.

Close to the Sun Again. Toronto: Macmillan, 1977.

No Man's Meat and The Enchanted Pimp. Toronto: Macmillan, 1978.

A Time for Judas. Toronto: Macmillan, 1983.

AUTOBIOGRAPHY

That Summer in Paris. Toronto: Macmillan, 1963.

DRAMA

Season of the Witch. Toronto: House of Exile, 1976.

Interviews with Morley Callaghan

The Tamarack Review, 7 (Spring, 1958), 3-29.

Conversations with Canadian Novelists. Edited by Donald Cameron. Toronto: Macmillan, 1973. Vol. 2, pp. 17-33.

Margaret Atwood

Novelist and poet, critic and
cartoonist, Margaret Atwood is one
of the most prolific and important
writers of contemporary Canada.
Equally acclaimed as a writer of both
fiction and poetry, she devotes much
of her creative energy to giving
literary shape to her country's
aspirations, fears, and foibles.

Born in Ottawa in 1939, Atwood
spent her early years in the bush
country of Quebec and northern
Ontario. When she was seven years
old, her family settled in the Leaside

area of Toronto, where the narrator of *Lady Oracle* spends her childhood years. After attending Leaside High School, Atwood majored in English at the University of Toronto. She pursued graduate studies at Harvard University where she embarked on a doctoral dissertation on romance fiction in Victorian England.

Lady Oracle, Atwood's third and most comic novel, is the moving yet hilarious autobiography of Joan Foster, a famous Canadian author who secretly writes costume Gothic romances under the pseudonym of Louisa K. Delacourt. Joan's fame rests on a feminist novel called *Lady Oracle*, which she wrote in a trance as an experiment in automatic writing. When a blackmailer threatens to expose Joan's dual identity, she stages her own death, a false drowning. As the novel opens after her supposed drowning, Joan is living in an Italian town, looking back honestly on the various identities she has been supporting.

Some of the scenes of *Lady Oracle* are reconstructions from Atwood's own life. And the childhood settings resemble Atwood's childhood world: "I used settings I was familiar with, you always do. Otherwise you'd be writing science fiction." Beyond such comparisons the correspondences are limited.

Atwood grew up, as she notes, "isolated from society in a kind and non-violent family of scientists." Her parents bear no resemblance to the aggressive and unhappy mother and the passive father of Joan Foster. "My father was from a rural generation that did everything themselves," Atwood recalls. "If they needed a house they built it, if they needed wood they cut it, if they needed something to eat they shot it. They were self-sufficient." Her real mother is nothing like the monstrous mother who iced chocolate cakes with melted Ex-Lax to make her obese daughter, Joan, lose weight. "My mother came from a tiny village in Nova Scotia. She was the village tomboy. She became a teacher because her father, who was a stern Nova Scotia doctor, considered that she was too frivolous and fun-loving to deserve to be sent to college. He sent her sister instead. So my mother went to a normal school and became a teacher. Then she saved the money and sent herself to college. She got a scholarship, demonstrating that although she was frivolous and fun-loving she could also get an education."

In this chapter from *Lady Oracle*, Joan is looking back on the years when she was thirteen and fifteen, when she turned to eating as an escape from her routine world and as a weapon in her struggle against her mother. In writing *Lady Oracle* Atwood was determined "to make the character physically unidentifiable with myself, so I made her very fat and I gave her red hair—I had a friend with marvellous red hair that I always envied, so I took her hair and stuck it onto this character. What happens when I read these chapters to an audience? Someone immediately sticks up a hand and says, *How did you manage to lose all that weight?*"

Lady Oracle

One of the bad dreams I used to have about my mother was this. I would be walking across the bridge and she would be standing in the sunlight on the other side of it, talking to someone else, a man whose face I couldn't see. When I was halfway across, the bridge would start to collapse, as I'd always feared it would. Its rotten planks buckled and split, it tilted over sideways and began to topple slowly into the ravine. I would try to run but it would be too late, I would throw myself down and grab onto the far edge as it rose up, trying to slide me off. I called out to my mother, who could still have saved me, she could have run across quickly and reached out her hand, she could have pulled me back with her to firm ground–But she didn't do this, she went on with her conversation, she didn't notice that anything unusual was happening. She didn't even hear me.

In the other dream I would be sitting in a corner of my mother's bedroom, watching her put on her makeup. I did this often as a small child: it was considered a treat, a privilege, by both my mother and myself, and refusing to let me watch was one of my mother's ways of punishing me. She knew I was fascinated by her collection of cosmetics and implements: lipsticks, rouges, perfume in dainty bottles which I longed to have, bright red nail polish (sometimes, as an exceptional bribe, I was allowed to have some brushed on my toes, but never on my fingers: "You're not old enough," she'd say), little tweezers, nail files and emery boards. I was forbidden to touch any of these things. Of course I did, when she was out, but they were arranged in such rigid rows both on the dressertop and in the drawers that I had to be very careful to put them back exactly where I'd found them. My mother had a hawk's eye

190

for anything out of place. I later extended this habit of snooping through her drawers and cupboards until I knew everything that each of them contained; finally I would do it not to satisfy my curiosity–I already knew everything–but for the sense of danger. I only got caught twice, early on: once when I ate a lipstick (even then, at the age of four, I was wise enough to replace the cover on the tube and the tube in the drawer, and to wash my mouth carefully; how did she know it was me?), and once when I couldn't resist covering my entire face with blue eye shadow, to see how I would look blue. That got me exiled for weeks. I almost gave the whole game away the day I found a curious object, like a rubber clamshell, packed away neatly in a box. I was dying to ask her what it was, but I didn't dare.

"Sit there quietly, Joan, and watch Mother put on her face," she'd say on the good days. Then she would tuck a towel around her neck and go to work. Some of the things she did seemed to be painful; for instance, she would cover the space between her eyebrows with what looked like brown glue, which she heated in a little pot, then tear it off, leaving a red patch; and sometimes she'd smear herself with pink mud which would harden and crack. She often frowned at herself, shaking her head as if she was dissatisfied; and occasionally she'd talk to herself as if she'd forgotten I was there. Instead of making her happier, these sessions appeared to make her sadder, as if she saw behind or within the mirror some fleeting image she was unable to capture or duplicate; and when she was finished she was always a little cross.

I would stare at the proceedings, fascinated and mute. I thought my mother was very beautiful, even more beautiful when she was colored in. And this was what I did in the dream: I sat and stared. Although her vanity tables became more grandiose as my father got richer, my mother always had a triple mirror, so she could see both sides as well as the front of her head. In the dream, as I watched, I suddenly realized that instead of three reflections she had three actual heads, which rose from her toweled shoulders on three separate necks. This didn't frighten me, as it seemed merely a confirmation of something I'd always known; but outside the door there was a man, a man who was about to open the door and come in. If he saw, if he found out the truth about my mother, something terrible would happen, not only to my mother but to me. I wanted to jump up, run to the door, and stop him, but I couldn't move and the door would swing slowly inward....

As I grew older, this dream changed. Instead of wanting to stop the mysterious man, I would sit there wishing for him to enter. I wanted him to find out her secret, the secret that I alone knew: my mother was a monster.

I can never remember calling her anything but Mother, never one of those childish diminutives; I must have, but she must have discouraged it. Our relationship was professionalized early. She was to be the manager, the creator, the agent; I was to be the product. I suppose one of the most important things she wanted from me was gratitude. She wanted me to do well, but she wanted to be responsible for it.

Her plans for me weren't specific. They were vague but large, so that whatever I did accomplish was never the right thing. But she didn't push all the time; for days and even weeks she would seem to forget me altogether. She would become involved in some other project of hers, like redecorating her bedroom or throwing a party. She even took a couple of jobs: she was a travel agent, for instance, and she once worked for an interior decorator, searching out lamps and carpets that would match living-room color designs. But none of these jobs lasted long, she would get discouraged, they weren't enough for her and she would quit.

It wasn't that she was aggressive and ambitious, although she was both these things. Perhaps she wasn't aggressive or ambitious enough. If she'd ever decided what she really wanted to do and had gone out and done it, she wouldn't have seen me as a reproach to her, the embodiment of her own failure and depression, a huge edgeless cloud of inchoate matter which refused to be shaped into anything for which she could get a prize.

In the image of her that I carried for years, hanging from my neck like an iron locket, she was sitting in front of her vanity table, painting her fingernails a murderous red and sighing. Her lips were thin but she made a larger mouth with lipstick over and around them, like Bette Davis, which gave her a curious double mouth, the real one showing through the false one like a shadow. She was an attractive woman, even into her late thirties, she had kept her figure, she had been popular in her youth. In her photograph album there were snapshots of her in party dresses and bathing suits, with various young men, her looking at the camera, the young men looking at her. One young man recurred often, in white flannels, with a big motor car. She said she'd been engaged to him, more or less.

There were no pictures of her as a girl though, none of her parents, none of the two brothers and the sister I later found out she had. She almost never talked about her family or her early life, though I was able to piece a little of it together. Her parents had both been very strict, very religious. They hadn't been rich; her father had been a stationmaster for the CPR. She'd done something that offended them—what it was I never learned—and she'd run away from home at the age of sixteen and never gone back. She'd worked at various jobs, clerking in Kresge's, waitressing. When she was eighteen she'd been a waitress at a resort in Muskoka, which was where she later met my father. The young men in the pictures were guests at the resort. She could only wear the party dresses and the bathing suits on her day off.

My father hadn't been staying at the resort; it wasn't the kind of thing he would do. He met my mother by accident, when he'd dropped by to visit a friend. There were a couple of pictures of them before the wedding, in which my father looked embarrassed. My mother held his arm as if it were a leash. Then the wedding portrait. After that some photos of my mother alone, which my father must have taken. Then nothing but me, drooling on rugs, eating stuffed animals or fists; my father had gone off to the war, leaving her pregnant, with nobody to take pictures of her.

My father didn't come back until I was five, and before that he was only a name, a story which my mother would tell me and which varied considerably. Sometimes he was a nice man who was coming home soon, bringing with him all kinds of improvements and delightful surprises: we would live in a bigger house, eat better, have more clothes, and the landlord would be put in his place once and for all. At other times, when I was getting out of hand, he was retribution personified, the judgment day that would catch up with me at last; or (and I think this was closest to her true feelings) he was a heartless wretch who had abandoned her, leaving her to cope with everything all by herself. The day he finally returned I was almost beside myself, torn between hope and fear: what would he bring me, what would he do to me? Was he a bad man or a nice man? (My mother's two categories: nice men did things for you, bad men did things to you.) But when the time came, a stranger walked through the door, kissed my mother and then me, and sat down at the table. He seemed very tired and said little. He brought nothing and did nothing, and that remained his pattern.

Most of the time he was simply an absence. Occasionally, though, he would stroll back into reality from wherever he had been, and he even had his moments of modest drama. I was thirteen, it must have been 1955, it was a Sunday. I was sitting in the kitchenette, eating half of an orange layer cake, for which I would later be scolded. But I'd already eaten one piece and I knew the number of words for that one piece would be as great as for half a cake, so I ate on, speedily, trying to get it all down before being discovered.

By this time I was eating steadily, doggedly, stubbornly, anything I could get. The war between myself and my mother was on in earnest; the disputed territory was my body. I didn't quite know this though I sensed it in a hazy way; but I reacted to the diet booklets she left on my pillow, to the bribes of dresses she would give me if I would reduce to fit them–formal gowns with layers of tulle and wired busts, perky little frocks, skirts with slim waists and frothy crinolines–to her cutting remarks about my size, to her pleas about my health (I would die of a heart attack, I would get high blood pressure), to the specialists she sent me to and the pills they prescribed, to all of these things, with another Mars Bar or a double helping of french fries. I swelled visibly, relentlessly, before her very eyes, I rose like dough, my body advanced inch by inch towards her across the dining-room table, in this at least I was undefeated. I was five feet four and still growing, and I weighed a hundred and eighty-two pounds.

Anyway: I was sitting in the kitchenette, eating half of an orange layer cake. It was a Sunday in 1955. My father was in the living room, sitting in an easy chair reading a murder mystery, his favorite way of relaxing. My mother was on the chesterfield, pretending to read a book on child psychology–she put in a certain amount of time demonstrating that, God knew, she was doing her best–but actually reading *The Fox*, an historical novel about the Borgias. I had already finished it, in secret. The chesterfield had a diminutive purple satin cushion at either end, and these two cushions were sacrosanct, ritual objects which were not to be moved. The chesterfield itself was dull pink, a nubby material shot through with silver threads. It had a covering of transparent plastic, which was removed for entertaining. The rug, which picked up the purple of the cushions, was also covered with a sheet of plastic, heavier in texture. The lampshades were protected with cellophane. On each of my father's feet was a slipper of maroon leather. My mother's feet and my own were similarly encased, as by this time my mother had made it a rule that no shoes were to be allowed inside the house. It was a new house and she had just finished getting it into shape; now that it was finally right she didn't want anything touched, she wanted it static and dustless and final, until that moment when she would see what a mistake she had made and the painters or movers would arrive once more, trailing disruption.

(My mother didn't want her living rooms to be different from everyone else's, or even very much better. She wanted them to be acceptable, the same as everybody else's, although her idea of everybody else changed as my father's salary increased. Perhaps this was why they looked like museum displays or, more accurately, like the show windows of Eaton's and Simpson's, those magic downtown palaces I would approach, with Aunt Lou, every December along a vista of streetcar tracks. We didn't go to see the furniture though, we were heading for the other windows, where animals, fairies and red-cheeked dwarfs twirled mechanically to the sound of tinkle bells. When I was old enough to go Christmas shopping it was Aunt Lou who took me. One year I announced I wasn't going to get my mother a Christmas present. "But, dear," Aunt Lou said, "you'll hurt her feelings." I didn't think she had any, but I gave in and bought her some bubble bath, enclosed in a lovely pink squeezable swan. She never used it, but I knew in advance she wouldn't. I ended up using it myself.)

I finished the slab of leftover cake and rose to my feet, my stomach bumping the table. My slippers were large and furry; they made my feet look twice as big. I clomped in them sullenly through the dining room, into the living room and past my parents and their books, without saying anything. I had developed the habit of clomping silently but very visibly through rooms in which my mother was sitting; it was a sort of fashion show in reverse, it was a display, I wanted her to see and recognize what little effect her nagging and pleas were having.

I intended to go into the hall, then up the stairs with a sasquatch-like, banister-shaking tread, and along the hall to my room, where I was going to put on an Elvis Presley record and turn the volume up just loud enough so she would repress the desire to complain. She was beginning to worry about her ability to communicate with me. I didn't have any intentional plans, I was merely acting according to a dimly felt, sluggish instinct. I was aware only of a wish to hear "Heartbreak Hotel" at the maximum volume possible without reprisals.

But when I was halfway across the room there was a sudden pounding at the front door. Someone was hammering on it with balled fists; then there was the thud of a hurled body and a hoarse voice, a man's voice, screaming, "I'll kill you! You bastard, I'll kill you!"

I froze. My father leapt from his chair and doubled over in a kind of wrestler's crouch. My mother put a bookmark between the pages of her book and closed it; then she removed her reading glasses, which she wore on a silver chain around her neck, and looked at my father with irritation. It was obviously his fault: who would call her a bastard? My father straightened up and went to the door.

"Oh, it's you, Mr. Currie," he said. "I'm glad to see you're up and about again."

"I'll sue you," the voice shouted. "I'll sue you within an inch of your life! Why couldn't you just leave me alone? You've ruined everything!" The voice broke into long, raucous sobs.

"You're a little upset right now," my father's voice said.

The other voice wept, "You messed it up! I did it right this time and you messed it up! I don't want to live...."

"Life is a gift," my father said with quiet dignity but a slight edge of reprimand, like the kindly dentist who demonstrated about cavities on the television set we'd acquired two years before. "You should be grateful for it. You should respect it."

"What do you know?" the voice roared. Then there was a scuffling sound and the voice receded into the distance, trailing muffled words behind it like a string of bubbles underwater. My father shut the door quietly and came back to the living room.

"I don't know why you do it," my mother said. "They're never grateful."

"Do what?" I said, bulgy-eyed, breaking my vow of silence in my eagerness to know. I had never heard a man cry before and the knowledge that they sometimes did was electrifying.

"When people try to kill themselves," my mother said, "your father brings them to life again."

"Not always, Frances," my father said sadly.

"Often enough," my mother said, opening her book. "I'm tired of getting abusive phone calls in the middle of the night. I really wish you would stop."

My father was an anesthetist at the Toronto General Hospital. He had studied to be one at my mother's urging, as she felt specialization was the coming thing, everyone said that specialists did better than family doctors. She had even been willing to make the necessary financial sacrifices while he was training. But I thought all my father did was put people to sleep before operations. I didn't know about this resurrection- ist side of his personality.

"Why do people try to kill themselves?" I asked. "How do you bring them to life again?"

"My father ignored the first part of this question, it was far too complicated for him. "I'm testing experimental methods," he said. "They don't always work. But they only give me the hopeless cases, when they've tried everything else." Then he said, to my mother rather than to me, "You'd be surprised how many of them are glad. That they've been able to...come back, have another chance."

"Well," said my mother, "I only wish the ones who aren't so glad would keep it to themselves. It's a waste of time, if you ask me. They'll simply try all over again. If they were serious they'd just stick a gun in their mouth and pull the trigger. That takes the chance out of it."

"Not everyone," said my father, "has your determination."

Two years later, I learned something else about my father. We were in another house, with a bigger dining room, wood-paneled and impres- sive. My mother was having a dinner party, entertaining two couples whom she claimed privately to dislike. According to her, it was necessary to have them to dinner because they were my father's colleagues, important men at the hospital, and she was trying to help him with his career. She paid no attention when he said that it didn't matter one iota to his career whether she had these people to dinner or not; she went ahead and did it anyway. When she finally realized he'd been telling the truth, she stopped giving dinner parties and began drinking a little more heavily. But she must have already started by this evening, for which I can remember the menu: chicken breasts in cream sauce with wild rice and mushrooms, individual jellied salads with cranberries and celery, topped with mayonnaise, Duchess potatoes, and a complex dessert with mandarin oranges, ginger sauce and some kind of sherbet.

I was in the kitchen. I was fifteen, and I'd reached my maximum growth: I was five feet eight and I weighed two hundred and forty-five, give or take a few pounds. I no longer attended my mother's dinner parties; she was tired of having a teenaged daughter who looked like a beluga whale and never opened her mouth except to put something into it. I cluttered up her gracious-hostess act. On my side, much as I would have welcomed the chance to embarrass her, strangers were different, they saw my obesity as an unfortunate handicap, like a hump or a club foot, rather than the refutation, the victory it was, and watching myself reflected in their eyes shook my confidence. It was only in relation to my mother that I derived a morose pleasure from my weight; in relation to everyone else, including my father, it made me miserable. But I couldn't stop.

I was in the kitchen then, eavesdropping through the passageway and devouring spare parts and leftovers. They had reached the dessert, so I was making away with the extra chicken and cranberry salads and Duchess potatoes, and listening to the conversation in the other room halfheartedly, as if to a tepid radio drama. One of the visiting doctors had been in the war, mostly in Italy as it turned out; the other one had enlisted but had never made it farther than England. Then of course there was my father, who apart from acknowledging that he had been over there too, never said much about it. I'd listened in on conversations like this before and they didn't interest me. From the war movies I'd seen, there was nothing much for women to do in wars except the things they did anyway.

The man who had served in Italy finished recounting one of his exploits, and after a chorus of ruminative murmurs, asked, "Where were you stationed, Phil?"

"Oh, um," said my father.

"In France," my mother said.

"Oh, you mean after the invasion," said the other man.

"No," said my mother, and giggled; a danger sign. She had taken to giggling during dinner parties lately. The giggle, which had a bleary, uncontrolled quality, had replaced the high, gay company laugh she used to wield as purposefully as a baseball bat.

"Oh," said the Italy man politely, "what were you doing?"

"Killing people," said my mother promptly and with relish, as if she were enjoying a private joke.

"Fran," said my father. It was a warning, but the tone was also imploring; something new and rare. I was gnawing the last shreds off the carcass of a breast, but I stopped in order to listen more closely.

"Well, everyone kills a few people in a war, I guess," said the second man.

"Up close?" said my mother. "I bet you didn't kill them up close."

There was a silence, of the kind that comes into a room when everyone knows that something exciting and probably unpleasant is going to happen. I could picture my mother looking around at the attentive faces, avoiding my father's eyes.

"He was in Intelligence," she said importantly. "You wouldn't think it to look at him, would you? They dropped him in behind the lines and he worked with the French underground. You wouldn't ever hear it from him, but he can speak French like a native; he gets it from his last name."

"My," said one of the women, "I've always wanted to go to Paris. Is it as beautiful as they say?"

"His job was to kill the people they thought were fakes," my mother continued. "He had to just take them out and shoot them. In cold blood. Sometimes he wouldn't even know if he'd shot the right one. Isn't that something?" Her voice was thrilled and admiring. "The funny thing is, he doesn't like me to mention it...the funny thing is, he told me once that the frightening thing about it was, he started to *enjoy* it."

One of the men laughed nervously. I got up and retreated on my furry slippered feet to the stairs (I could walk quietly enough when I wanted to) and lowered myself down halfway up. Sure enough, a moment later my father marched through the swinging door into the kitchen, followed by my mother. She must have realized she had pushed it too far.

"There's nothing *wrong* with it," she said. "It was in a good cause. You never make the most of yourself."

"I asked you not to talk about it," my father said. He sounded very angry, enraged. It was the first time I realized he could feel rage; he was usually very calm. "You have no idea what it was like."

"I think it's great," said my mother, earnestly. "It took real courage, I don't see what's wrong with...."

"Shut up," said my father.

Those are stories from later; earlier he wasn't there, which is probably why I remember him as nicer than my mother. And after that he was busy studying, he was someone who was not to be disturbed, and then he was at the hospital a lot. He didn't know quite what to make of me, ever; though I never felt he was hostile, only bemused.

The few things we did together were wordless things. Such as: he took to growing house plants—vines and spider plants and ferns and begonias. He liked to tinker with them, snipping off cuttings and repotting and planting, on Saturday afternoons if he had the free time, listening to the Texaco Company Metropolitan Opera broadcasts on the radio, and he would let me help him with the plants. As he never said much of anything, I would pretend his voice was the voice of Milton Cross, kindly and informed, describing the singers' costumes and the passionate, tragic and preposterous events in which they were involved. There he would be, puffing away on the pipe he took up after he quit cigarettes, poking at his house plants and conversing to me about lovers being stabbed and abandoned or betrayed, about jealousy and madness, about unending love triumphing over the grave; and then those chilling voices would drift into the room, raising the hair on the back of my neck, as if he had evoked them. He was a conjuror of spirits, a shaman with the voice of a dry, detached old opera commentator in a tuxedo. Or that's how I imagined him sounding, when I thought up the conversations I would have liked to have had with him but never did. I wanted him to tell me the truth about life, which my mother would not tell me and which he must have known something about, as he was a doctor and had been in the war, he'd killed people and raised the dead. I kept waiting for him to give me some advice, warn me, instruct me, but he never did any of these things. Perhaps he felt as if I weren't really his daughter; he'd seen me for the first time five years after I was born, and he treated me more like a colleague than a daughter, more like an accomplice. But what was our conspiracy? Why hadn't he come back on leave during those five years? A question my mother asked also. Why did they both act as though he owed my mother something?

Then there were those other conversations I overheard. I used to go into the upstairs bathroom, lock the door, and turn on the tap so they would think I was brushing my teeth. Then I would arrange the bath mat on the floor so my knees wouldn't get cold, put my head into the toilet, and listen to them through the pipes. It was almost a direct line to the kitchen, where they had most of their fights, or rather my mother had them. She was a lot easier to hear than my father.

"Why don't you try doing something with her for a change, she's your daughter, too. I'm really at the end of my rope."

My father: silence.

"You don't know what it was like, all alone with her to bring up while you were over there enjoying yourself."

My father: "I didn't enjoy myself."

And once: "It's not as though I wanted to have her. It's not as though I wanted to marry you. I had to make the best of a bad job if you ask me."

My father: "I'm sorry it hasn't worked out for you."

And once, when she was very angry: "You're a doctor, don't tell me you couldn't have done something."

My father: (inaudible).

"Don't give me that crap, you killed a lot of people. Sacred my foot."

At first I was shocked, mainly by my mother's use of the word *crap*. She tried so hard to be a lady in front of other people, even me. Later I tried to figure out what she'd meant, and when she'd say, "If it wasn't for me you wouldn't be here," I didn't believe her.

I ate to defy her, but I also ate from panic. Sometimes I was afraid I wasn't really there, I was an accident; I'd heard her call me an accident. Did I want to become solid, solid as a stone so she wouldn't be able to get rid of me? What had I done? Had I trapped my father, if he really was my father, had I ruined my mother's life? I didn't dare to ask.

For a while I wanted to be an opera singer. Even though they were fat they could wear extravagant costumes, nobody laughed at them, they were loved and praised. Unfortunately I couldn't sing. But it always appealed to me: to be able to stand up there in front of everyone and shriek as loud as you could, about hatred and love and rage and despair, scream at the top of your lungs and have it come out music. That would be something.

Works by Margaret Atwood

FICTION

The Edible Woman. Toronto: McClelland
and Stewart, 1969.
Surfacing. Toronto: McClelland and
Stewart, 1972.
Lady Oracle. Toronto: McClelland and
Stewart, 1976.
Dancing Girls. Toronto: McClelland and
Stewart, 1977.
Life Before Man. Toronto: McClelland and
Stewart, 1979.
Bodily Harm. Toronto: McClelland and
Stewart, 1981.
Murder in the Dark. Toronto: Coach
House, 1983.
Bluebeard's Egg. Toronto: McClelland and
Stewart, 1983.

Up in the Tree. Toronto: McClelland and
Stewart, 1978. (children's book)
Anna's Pet (with Joyce Barkhouse).
Toronto: Lorimer, 1980. (children's
book)

POETRY

The Circle Game. Toronto: Contact, 1966.
The Animals in That Country. Toronto:
Oxford University Press, 1968.
The Journals of Susanna Moodie. Toronto:
Oxford University Press, 1970.
Procedures for Underground. Toronto:
Oxford University Press, 1970.
Power Politics. Toronto: Anansi, 1971.
You Are Happy. Toronto: Oxford
University Press, 1974.
Selected Poems. Toronto: Oxford
University Press, 1976.
Two-Headed Poems. Toronto: Oxford
University Press, 1978.
True Stories. Toronto: Oxford University
Press, 1981.

CRITICISM

*Survival: A Thematic Guide to Canadian
Literature.* Toronto: Anansi, 1972.
Second Words. Toronto: Anansi, 1982.

Interviews with Margaret Atwood

Eleven Canadian Novelists. Edited by
Graeme Gibson. Toronto: Anansi,
1973, pp. 1-31.
Room of One's Own, 1, 2 (Summer, 1975),
66-70.
Essays on Canadian Writing, 6 (Spring,
1977), 18-27.
The Malahat Review, 41 (January, 1977),
7-27.
For Openers. Edited by Alan Twigg.
Madeira Park, B.C.: Harbour, 1981,
pp. 219-30.

James Reaney

The area in and around Stratford, Ontario, has played a central role in the life and the writings of James Reaney. Born on a farm outside Stratford in 1926, Reaney attended Elmhurst Public School, a one-room country school; in 1939 he set off to attend Stratford Collegiate and Vocational Institute. Upon graduation from high school he won an entrance scholarship to University College at the University of Toronto. During his undergraduate years he wrote many poems and short stories, and the year after he received his bachelor's degree he won the Governor General's Award for his first volume of poetry.

From 1949 until 1960, with the exception of two years of doctoral studies at the University of Toronto, Reaney taught English at the University of Manitoba. In 1960 he accepted an invitation to join the Department of English at the University of Western Ontario. And so he returned to the area of his childhood and the inspiration of so much of his art.

Primarily known as a poet and a playwright, Reaney has often sought to document and depict the life of southern or southwestern Ontario and to transform this material imaginatively into the realm of myth. Turning to the world of his

203

childhood, he does not seek to explore its individual, personal significance. Instead he shapes details from childhood into patterns of behavior that transcend time and place. For example, he wrote the original version of his first play, *The Sun and the Moon*, with the Stratford Festival Theatre stage in mind. In the play he treats elements of his own background as if they were the source of a Shakespearean drama. Thus Reaney's own experiences– "the essence of country life in Ontario as I know it"–become the stuff of theatre, and the world of Stratford and vicinity is reshaped as myth.

For Reaney, it is through the world of the imagination that such changes can take place. The realm of the imagination provides a setting for transforming reality, sometimes for moving even beyond reality. This world is not always a happy one; especially in Reaney's early writings, it is filled with isolated human beings, spiritual exiles, orphans, and misfits. As Reaney's vision develops, imagination, often in the form of verbal magic and even dreams, is seen as a means for human salvation. "Horror remains and evil is still a presence, but a way past the world, the flesh and the devil is now possible," Margaret Atwood notes in describing Reaney's artistic vision. "It is the individual's inner vision, not the external social order, that must change if anything is to be salvaged."

"The Bully" is autobiographical in setting, though not in details; Partridge resembles the world of Stratford that haunts Reaney's art. The boy's final dream is the kind of imaginative transformation that occurs in so many of his plays and poems. In the dream itself the boy's inner vision changes so that he is able to come to terms with the fears of the waking world.

The Bully

As a child I lived on a farm not far from a small town called Partridge. In the countryside about Partridge, thin roads of gravel and dust slide in and out among the hollows and hills. As roads go, they certainly aren't very brave, for quite often they go round a hill instead of up it and even in the flattest places they will jog and hesitate absurdly. But then this latter tendency often comes from some blunder a surveying engineer made a hundred years ago. And although his mind has long ago dissolved, its forgetfulness still pushes the country people crooked where they might have gone straight.

Some of the farm houses on these ill-planned roads are made of red brick and have large barns and great cement silos and soft large straw-stacks behind them. And other farm houses are not made of brick, but of frame and clap-board that gleam with the silver film unpainted wood attains after years of wild rain and shrill wind beating upon it. The house where I was born was such a place, and I remember that whenever it rained, from top to bottom the whole outside of the house would turn jet-black as if it were blushing in shame or anger.

Perhaps it blushed because of my father, who was not a very good farmer. He was what is known as an afternoon farmer. He could never get out into the fields till about half-past eleven in the morning and he never seemed to be able to grow much of anything except buckwheat which as everyone knows is the lazy farmer's crop. If you could make a living out of playing checkers and talking, then my father would have made enough to send us all to college, but as it was he did make enough to keep us alive, to buy tea and coffee, cake and pie, boots and stockings, and a basket of peaches once every summer. So it's really hard to begrudge him a few games of checkers or a preference for talking instead of a preference for ploughing.

When I was six, my mother died of T.B. and I was brought up by my Aunt Coraline and by my two older sisters, Noreen and Kate. Noreen, the oldest of us, was a very husky, lively girl. She was really one of the liveliest girls I have ever seen. She rode every horse we had bare-back, sometimes not with a bridle at all but just by holding on to their manes. When she was fifteen, in a single day she wall-papered both our kitchen and our living-room. And when she was sixteen she helped my father draw in hay just like a hired man. When she was twelve she used to tease me an awful lot. Sometimes when she had teased me too much, I would store away scraps of food for days, and then go off down the side-road with the strong idea in my head that I was not going to come back. But then Noreen and Kate would run after me with tears in their eyes and, having persuaded me to throw away my large collection of break-fast toast crusts and agree to come back, they would both promise never to tease me again. Although Kate, goodness knows, had no need to promise that for she was always kind, would never have thought of teasing me. Kate was rather like me in being shy and in being rather weak. Noreen's strength and boldness made her despise Kate and me, but she was like us in some ways. For instance Noreen had a strange way of feeding the hens. Each night she would sprinkle the grain out on the ground in the shape of a letter or some other pattern, so that when the hens ate the grain, they were forced to spell out Noreen's initials or to form a cross and a circle. There were just enough hens to make this rather an interesting game. Sometimes, I know, Noreen spelt out whole sentences in this way, a letter or two each night, and I often wondered to whom she was writing up in the sky.

Aunt Coraline, who brought me up, was most of the time sick in bed and as a result was rather pettish and ill-tempered. In the summer time, she would spend most of the day in her room making bouquets out of any flowers we could bring her; even dandelions, Shepherd's Purse, or Queen Anne's Lace. She was very skilful at putting letters of the alphabet into a bouquet, with two kinds of flowers, you know, one for the letters and one for the background. Aunt Coraline's room was filled with all sorts of jars and bottles containing bouquets, some of them very ancient so that her room smelt up a bit, especially in the hot weather. She was the only one of us who had a room to herself. My father slept in the kitchen. Aunt Coraline's days were devoted to the medicine-bottle and the pill-box, making designs in bouquets, telling us stories, and bringing us up; her nights were spent in trying to get to sleep and crying softly to herself.

When we were children we never were worked to death, but still we didn't play or read books all of the time. In the summer we picked strawberries, currants, and raspberries. Sometimes we picked wild berries into milkpails for money, but after we had picked our pails full, before we could get the berries to the woman who had commissioned them, the berries would settle down in the pails and of course the woman would refuse then to pay what she had promised because we hadn't brought her full pails. Sometimes our father made us pick potato beetles off the potato plants. We would tap the plants on one side with a shingle and hold out a tin can on the other side to catch the potato bugs as they fell. And we went for cows and caught plough-horses for our father.

Every Saturday night we children all took turns bathing in the dish-pan and on Sundays, after Sunday-school, we would all sit out on the lawn and drink the lemonade that my father would make in a big glass pitcher. The lemonade was always slightly green and sour like the moon when it's high up in a summer sky. While we were drinking the lemonade, we would listen to our victrola gramophone which Noreen would carry out of the house along with a collection of records. These were all very old, very thick records and their names were: *I Know Where the Flies Go*, *The Big Rock Candy Mountain*, *Hand Me Down My Walking Cane*, and a dialogue about some people in a boarding-house that went like this:

"Why can't you eat this soup?"

Various praising replies about the soup and its fine, fine qualities by all the fifteen members of the boarding-house. Then:

"So WHY can't you eat this soup?"

And the non-appreciative boarder replies:

"Because I ain't got a spoon."

Even if no one laughed, and of course we always did, the Record Company had thoughtfully put in some laughter just to fill up the centre. Those Sunday afternoons are all gone now and if I had known I was never to spend any more like them, I would have spent them more slowly.

We began to grow up. Noreen did so gladly but Kate and I secretly hated to. We were much too weak to face things as they were. We were weak enough to prefer what we had been as children rather than what we saw people often grew up to be, people who worked all day at dull, senseless things and slept all night and worked all day and slept all night and so on until they died. I think Aunt Coraline must have felt the same when she was young and decided to solve the problem by being ill. Unfortunately for us, neither Kate nor I could quite bring ourselves to take this line. I don't know what Kate decided, but at the age of eleven I decided that school-teaching looked neither too boring nor too hard so a schoolteacher I would be. It was my one chance to escape what my father had fallen into. To become a teacher one had to go to high school five years and go one year to Normal School. Two miles away in the town of Partridge there actually stood a high school.

It was not until the summer after I had passed my Entrance Examination that I began to feel rather frightened of the new life ahead of me. That spring, Noreen had gone into town to work for a lady as a housemaid. At my request, she went to look at the high school. It was situated right next the jail, and Noreen wrote home that of the two places she'd much rather go to the jail, even although they had just made the gates of the jail three feet higher. Of that summer I particularly remember one sultry Sunday afternoon in August when I walked listlessly out to the mail-box and, leaning against it, looked down the road in the general direction of town. The road went on past our house and then up a hill and then not over the top of the hill for it went crooked a bit, wavered and disappeared, somehow, on the other side. Somewhere on that road stood a huge building which would swallow me up for five years. Why I had ever wanted to leave all the familiar things around me, I could hardly understand. Why people had to grow up and leave home I could not understand either. I looked first at the road and then into the dull sky as I wondered at this. I tried to imagine what the high school would really be like, but all I could see or feel was a strong tide emerging from it to sweep me into something that would give me a good shaking up.

Early every morning, I walked into high school with my lunch-box and my school-books under my arm. And I walked home again at night. I have none of the textbooks now that were used at that school, for I sold them when I left. And I can't remember very much about them except that the French book was fat and blue. One took fifteen subjects in all: Business Practice (in this you learned how to write out cheques and pay electric light bills, a knowledge that so far has been of no use to me); there was English, Geography, Mathematics, French, Spelling, History, Physical Training, Music, Art, Science (here one was taught how to light a Bunsen Burner) and there must have been other subjects for I'm sure there were fifteen of them. I never got used to high school. There were so many rooms, so many people, so many teachers. The teachers were watchful as heathen deities and it was painful to displease them. Almost immediately I became the object of everyone's disgust and rage. The Geography teacher growled at me, the English teacher stood me up in corners. The History teacher denounced me as an idiot. The French teacher cursed my accent. In Physical Training I fell off innumerable parallel-bars showing, as the instructor remarked, that I could not and never would co-ordinate my mind with my body. My platoon of the cadet corps discovered that the only way to make progress possible in drill was to place me deep in the centre of the ranks away from all key positions. In Manual Training I broke all sorts of precious saws and was soundly strapped for something I did to the iron-lathe. For no reason that I could see, the Art teacher went purple in the face at me, took me out into the hall and struck my defenceless hands with a leather thong. The French teacher once put me out into the hall, a far worse fate than that of being put in a corner, for the halls were hourly stalked by the principal in search of game; anyone found in the halls he took off with him to his office where he administered a little something calculated to keep the receiver out of the halls thereafter.

Frankly, I must have been, and I was, a simpleton, but I did the silly things I did mainly because everyone expected me to do them. Very slowly I began to be able to control myself and give at least some sort of right answer when questioned. Each night when I came home at first, Kate would ask me how I liked high school. I would reply as stoutly as I could that I was getting on all right. But gradually I did begin to get along not too badly and might have been a little happy if something not connected with my studies had not thrown me back into a deeper misery.

This new unhappiness had something to do with the place where those students who came from the country ate their lunch. This place was called a cafeteria and was divided into a girls' cafeteria and a boys' one. After about a month of coming to the boys' cafeteria to eat my lunch, I noticed that a certain young man (he couldn't be called a boy) always sat near me with his back to me at the next long table. The cafeteria was a basement room filled with three long tables and rows of wire-mended chairs. Now my lunch always included a small bottle of milk. The bottle had originally been a vinegar bottle and was very difficult to drink from unless you put your head away back and gulped it fast. One day when I had finished my sandwiches and was drinking my milk, he turned around and said quietly: "Does baby like his bottle?"

I blushed and immediately stopped drinking. Then I waited until he would finish his lunch and go away. While I waited with downcast eyes and a face red with shame, I felt a furious rush of anger against Kate and Aunt Coraline for sending milk for my lunch in a vinegar bottle. Finally, I began to see that he had finished his lunch and was not going to leave until I did. I put the vinegar bottle back in my lunch-box and walked as quickly as I could out of the boys' cafeteria, upstairs into the classroom left open during the noon-hour so that the country people could study there. He followed me there and sat in the seat opposite me with what I managed to discover in the two times I looked at him, a derisive smile upon his face. He had a carved face, mysteriously and perpetually tanned, with heavy lips, and he wore a dark green shirt. With him sitting beside me, I had no chance of ever getting the products of New Zealand and Australia off by heart and so I failed the Geography test we had that afternoon. Day after day he tormented me. He never hit me. He would always just stay close to me, commenting on how I ate my food or didn't drink my vinegar and once he pulled a chair from beneath me. Since our first meeting I never drank anything while he was near me. Between him and my friends the teachers, my life in first form at high school was a sort of Hell with too many tormenting fiends and not enough of me to go round so they could all get satisfaction. If I'd had the slightest spark of courage I'd have burnt the high school down at least.

At last, in the middle of November, I hit upon the plan of going over to the public library after I had eaten my lunch. Lots of other country students went there too. Most of them either giggled at magazines or hunted up art prints and photographs of classical sculpture on which they made obscene additions, or if more than usually clever, obscene comments. For over one happy week the Bully seemed to have lost me, for he did not appear at the library. Then I looked up from a dull book I was reading and there he was. He had my cap in his hand and would not give it back to me. How he had got hold of it I couldn't imagine. How I was to get it back from him, I couldn't imagine either. He must have given it back to me, I can't remember just how. Of course it wasn't the sort of hat anyone else wore, as you might expect. It was a toque, a red-and-white woollen one that Noreen used to wear. Every other boy at school wore a fedora or at least a helmet.

During the library period of my bullying he sat as close up against me as he could and whispered obscenities in my ear. After two weeks of this, being rather desperate, I did not go to the boys' cafeteria to eat my lunch but took my books and my lunch and went out into the streets. This was in early December and there was deep snow everywhere. I ran past the jail, down into the civic gardens, across the river, under a bridge, and down the other side of the river as fast as I could go. I had no idea where I was going to eat my lunch until I saw the town cemetery just ahead of me. It seemed fairly safe. I could eat my sandwiches under a tree and then keep warm by reading the inscriptions on gravestones and walking about.

The second day or the third, I discovered that the doors of the cemetery's mausoleum were open and that there were two benches inside where you can be buried in a marble pigeon-hole instead of the cold ground. To this place I came day after day, and I revelled in the morbid quiet of the place. I sat on one of the walnut benches and whispered irregular French verbs to myself or memorized the mineral resources of Turkey or the history of the Upper Canada Rebellion. All around and all above me dead citizens lay in their coffins, their rings flashing in the darkness, their finger-nails grown long like white thin carrots, and the hair of the dead men grown out long and wild to their shoulders. No one ever disturbed me. People's finger-nails and hair do keep on growing after they're dead, you know. Aunt Coraline read it in a book.

No one ever disturbed me at the mausoleum. The wind howled about that dismal place but no other voice howled. Only once I had some trouble in getting the heavy doors open when the factory whistles blew and it was time to start walking back to school. I usually arrived back at school at twenty minutes after one. But one day the wind weakened the sound of the whistles and I arrived at school just at half-past one. If it had been allowed, I might have run in the girls' door and not been late. But it was not allowed and since the boys' door was at the other end of the building, by the time I had run to it, I was quite late and had to stay after four.

Just before Christmas they had an At Home at the school. The emphasis in pronouncing At Home is usually put on the AT. Everyone goes to the AT Home. The tickets are usually old tickets that weren't sold for last year's operetta, cut in half. Noreen forced me to take her because she wanted to see what an AT Home was like. She did not mind that I could not dance. She only wanted to sip at second-hand what she supposed to be the delightful joys of higher education. We first went into the rooms where school-work was exhibited. Noreen kept expecting some of my work to be up and kept being disappointed. I was very nervous with a paint-brush so none of my drawings were up in the art display. At the writing exhibit none of my writing was up. I had failed to master the free-hand stroke, although away from the writing teacher I could draw beautiful writing that looked as if it had been done by the freest hand imaginable. At the Geography exhibit not one of my charts of national resources had been pinned up. Noreen was heart-broken. I had learned not to care. For instance, almost everyone's window-stick got into the Manual Training show. Mine didn't because I had planed it down until it was about a quarter of an inch thick, and as the Manual Training teacher pointed out, it couldn't have held up a feather. But I didn't care.

Noreen and I went into the girls' gymnasium where we saw a short, brown-colored movie that showed Dutch gardeners clipping hedges into the shapes of geese and chickens, ducks and peacocks. The Dutch gardeners cut away with their shears so fast that the ducks and peacocks seemed fairly to leap out of the hedges at you. Noreen and I wondered how these gardeners were going to keep employed if they carved up things that fast. Then we went into the boys' gym where young men stripped almost naked and covered with gold paint pretended to be statues. After watching them for a while Noreen and I went up to the Assembly Hall where dancing was in progress and young girls hovered shyly at the edge of the floor. Some of these shy young girls were dressed in handmade evening gowns that seemed to be made out of very thin mosquito netting coated with icing sugar. Noreen had one of her employer's old dresses on. It was certainly an old dress, made about 1932 I guess, for it had a hunch-back sack of cloth flying out of the middle of the back. Noreen, I know, thought she looked extremely distinctive. I only thought she looked extremely extraordinary.

And she did so want to dance. So we went up to the third floor and there Noreen tried to teach me how to dance in one lesson, but it was no use. She asked me to introduce her to some of my friends who danced. I had no friends but there was one boy who borrowed everything I owned almost daily. Here was a chance for him to repay me if he could dance. We soon captured him, but although Noreen clung tightly to him for a good deal of the evening and although we led him to the mouth of the Assembly Hall, all the time proclaiming quite loudly how nice it must be to dance, he didn't ask Noreen for a dance. So we went down into the basement to the Domestic Science Room where punch was being served and thin cookies with silver beads in the middle of them. There was a great crowd of people in the Domestic Science Room and before we knew it, he had given us the slip. Then Noreen said, "Where do you eat your lunch? Kate was telling me how she makes it every night for you."

I replied that I ate it in the boys' cafeteria.

"Oh, what's that? Come on. Show me."

"It's not very interesting," I said.

"But show me it. Show me it," Noreen insisted stubbornly.

"It's down here," I said.

We went past the furnace room.

"That's the furnace room, Noreen. There's the girls' cafeteria. Here's the—"

It was dark inside the boys' cafeteria and I felt along the wall just inside the door for a light button. I could hear someone climbing in one of the windows. Someone who didn't want to buy a ticket, I supposed. Probably someone who came here regularly at noon and thought of leaving a window open for himself. Before I could tell her not to, Noreen had found the light switch ahead of me and turned it on. The person climbing in the window turned out to be my friend the Bully. Like a wild animal he stared for a second at us and then jumped back through the window.

"Well, who on earth was that?" asked Noreen.

"I don't know," I said, trembling all over.

"Don't tremble like a leaf!" said Noreen scornfully. "Why you look and act exactly like you'd seen a ghost. What was so frightening about him?"

"Nothing," I said, leaning against the wall and putting my hand to my forehead. "Nothing."

The Christmas holidays were haunted for me by my fear of what would happen at school when I went back there after New Year's. But I never complained to my father or Aunt Coraline. They would have been only too glad to hear me say that I didn't want to go back. I must somehow stick it until the spring and the end of the first form at least. But I knew that before the spring came the Bully would track me down, and if I met him once again I knew it would be the end of me. I remember in those Christmas holidays that I went walking a lot with Kate over the fields that were dead white with snow. I wished then that we might always do that. I told Kate about my unhappiness at high school and it drew us closer together. If I had told Noreen she would only have called me a silly fool and made me hate her. But Kate was always more sympathetic towards me.

The first morning when I was back at school I found a note in my desk. All it said was this: *I want to see you eating where you should eat today, baby.* At noon I hid myself in the swarm of city students who were going home for lunch and arrived at the mausoleum by a round-about way. I couldn't get over the notion that someone was following me or watching me, which could easily have been true, since he had many friends.

I was just in the middle of eating my lunch. I was sitting on a bench in front of the Hon. Arthur P. Hingham's tomb. I saw the Bully trying to open the great doors to the mausoleum. But he couldn't seem to get them open. At last he did. All I can remember is seeing the advancing edge of the door for I toppled off the bench in a dead faint. By the time I came to it was half-past one so I started to walk home. My head ached violently as if someone had kicked it, which turned out to be the case, there being a red dent just below my left eye that turned blue after a few hours. On the way home that afternoon I had just reached a place in the road where you can see our house when I decided that I could not bear to go to high school any longer. So I went home and I told them that I had been expelled for walking in through the girls' door instead of the boys' door. They never doubted that this was true, so little did they know of high schools and their rules. Noreen doubted me, but by the time she heard about my being expelled it was too late to send me back. Aunt Coraline cried a bit over it all; my father told me the whole thing showed that I really belonged on the farm. Only Kate realized how much school had meant to me and how desperately I had tried to adapt myself to it.

That night as I lay in bed, while outside a cold strong river of wind roared about the house shaking everything and rattling the dishes in the cupboard downstairs, that night I dreamt three dreams. I have never been able to discover what they meant.

First I dreamt that Noreen was the Bully and that I caught her washing off her disguise in the water-trough in the yard. Then I dreamt I saw the Bully make love to Kate and she hugging and kissing him. The last dream I had was the longest of all. I dreamt that just before dawn I crept out of the house and went through the yard. And all the letters Noreen had ever made out of grain there while she was feeding the chickens had all sprouted up into green letters of grass and wheat. Someone touched me on the shoulder and said sadly, *I haven't got a spoon*, but I ran away without answering across the fields into the bush. There was a round pond there surrounded by a grove of young choke-cherry trees. I pushed through these and came to the edge of the pond. There lay the Bully looking almost pitiful, his arms and legs bound with green ropes made out of nettles. He was drowned dead, half in the water and half out of it, but face up. And in the dim light of the dawn I knelt down and kissed him gently on the forehead.

Works by James Reaney

FICTION

The Boy with an R in His Hand. Toronto:
Macmillan, 1965. (children's novel)

AUTOBIOGRAPHY

Fourteen Barrels from Sea to Sea. Erin,
Ont.: Press Porcépic, 1977.

POETRY

The Red Heart. Toronto: McClelland and
Stewart, 1949.
A Suit of Nettles. Toronto: Macmillan,
1958.
Twelve Letters to a Small Town. Toronto:
Ryerson, 1962.
The Dance of Death at London, Ontario.
London, Ont.: Alphabet, 1963.
Poems: James Reaney. Toronto: New Press,
1972.

DRAMA

The Killdeer and Other Plays. Toronto:
Macmillan, 1962.
Colours in the Dark. Vancouver:
Talonbooks, 1969.
Masks of Childhood. Toronto: New Press,
1972.
Listen to the Wind. Vancouver:
Talonbooks, 1972.
Apple Butter and Other Plays for Children.
Vancouver: Talonbooks, 1973.
The Donnellys: Part I, Sticks and Stones.
Erin, Ont.: Press Porcépic, 1975.
All the Bees and All the Keys. Erin, Ont.:
Press Porcépic, 1976.
Baldoon (with C.H. Gervais). Erin, Ont.:
The Porcupine's Quill, 1976.
*The Donnellys: Part II, The St. Nicholas Hotel
Wm. Donnelly Prop.* Erin, Ont.: Press
Porcépic, 1976.
The Donnellys: Part III, Handcuffs. Erin,
Ont.: Press Porcépic, 1977.
*The Dismissal or Twisted Beards and Tangled
Whiskers.* Erin, Ont.: Press Porcépic,
1978.
Geography Match. Vancouver:
Talonbooks, 1978.
Ignoramus. Vancouver: Talonbooks,
1978.
Names and Nicknames. Vancouver:
Talonbooks, 1978.
Wacousta! Toronto: Press Porcépic, 1979.
Stage Voices. Edited by Geraldine
Anthony. Toronto: Doubleday, 1978,
pp. 140-64.
Gyroscope. Toronto: Playwrights Canada,
1980.

Interview with James Reaney

Essays on Canadian Writing, 24-5 (Winter-
Spring, 1982-83), 138-50.

Gabrielle Roy

Gabrielle Roy's first novel, *Bonheur d'occasion* (1941), ushered in a new era of realism in Quebec fiction. Until then novelists had written of rural Quebec with its small towns and farming communities. *Bonheur d'occasion* focused on a working-class family in the St. Henri district of Montreal; Quebec fiction was now confronting the poverty, suffering, and painful isolation of some of its urban people.

Roy was born in St. Boniface, Manitoba in 1909. At that time St. Boniface was linked to Winnipeg by a tram: ''...for the time being few people were tempted to come live in our section; it had its back toward town; its face, as it were, turned toward the fields...and those empty fields near us remained open to our

216

uses." Roy's parents were part of the large Quebec emigration to Western Canada at the end of the nineteenth century. At her birth her father, a colonization agent for the federal government, was sixty, and she was the youngest of eight children. For twelve years she studied in a convent school. When her father died in 1927, she decided to become a teacher and entered the Winnipeg Normal School. For nearly a decade she taught in grade schools before turning to a writing career.

Although Manitoba was her birthplace, Roy regarded Quebec as her spiritual home. "My western heritage is both a blessing and a curse," she asserted, referring to her early geographical separation from the world of Quebec literature. In 1939 she moved to Montreal. "When I landed in Montreal and I discovered St. Henri, as it was then, along the old Lachine Canal, I discovered the people that was my own, and its tragedy, and its sadness, and its gaiety too. Since then, I have tried to give it expression. But I couldn't forget the rest of the country which is also part of my heritage, so I alternate. Sometimes it's Quebec, sometimes it's Manitoba." In all her fiction, whether the setting is Quebec or Manitoba, Roy depicts moments that reveal her characters' humanity in its joy and its sorrow. "Very young I had the ambition to write, in a sense, not *like* Dickens, but to sort of marry, as he has, tears and smiles. Because life is composed of those two things really, tears and smiles. Even today, my main preoccupation perhaps in my writing is to blend as closely as possible those two ingredients that I

find of the greatest importance in life– . . . I am made in such a way that I have no sooner seen the splendor of life . . . than I feel obliged, physically obliged, to look down and also take notice of the sad and of the tragic in life."

Christine, the first-person narrator of *Rue Deschambault* from which "Wilhelm" was taken, is the youngest of eight children and lives with her family on Rue Deschambault in St. Boniface. The eighteen episodes of the book are Christine's reminiscences of her childhood, moments that stand out in her memory– for example, her family's Negro boarder, the Italian neighbors, and, in "Wilhelm," the Dutchman who was her first childish crush. In a prefatory note Roy cautions the reader, "Certain events in this narrative took place in real life; but the characters and almost everything that happens to them are products of the imagination."

It is through Christine's journeys in her memory and her attempts to recapture and understand the past that she comes to realize her calling: "I then saw, not what I should later become, but that I must set forth on my way to becoming it. . . . And so I had the idea of writing. What and why I knew not at all. I would write. It was like a sudden love which, in a moment, binds a heart; it was really a fact as simple, as naïve as love. Having as yet nothing to say . . . I wanted to have something to say." Like Roy herself, Christine pursued a teaching career before turning to a writing career.

In 1952 Roy settled in Quebec City, where she lived until her death in 1983.

Wilhelm

My first suitor came from Holland. He was called Wilhelm and his teeth were too regular; he was much older than I; he had a long, sad face...at least thus it was that others made me see him when they had taught me to consider his defects. As for me, at first I found his face thoughtful rather than long and peaked. I did not yet know that his teeth–so straight and even–were false. I thought I loved Wilhelm. Here was the first man who, through me, could be made happy or unhappy; here was a very serious matter.

I had met him at our friends the O'Neills', who still lived not far from us in their large gabled house on Rue Desmeurons. Wilhelm was their boarder; for life is full of strange things: thus this big, sad man was a chemist in the employ of a small paint factory then operating in our city, and–as I have said–lodged with equally uprooted people, the O'Neills, formerly of County Cork in Ireland. A far journey to have come merely to behave, in the end, like everyone else–earn your living, try to make friends, learn our language, and then, in Wilhelm's case, love someone who was not for him. Do adventures often turn out so tritely? Obviously enough, though, in those days I did not think so.

Evenings at the O'Neills' were musical. Kathleen played "Mother Machree," while her mother, seated on a sofa, wiped her eyes, trying the while to avert our attention, to direct it away from herself, for she did not like people to believe her so deeply stirred by Irish songs. Despite the music, Elizabeth kept right on digging away at her arithmetic; she still was utterly indifferent to men. But Kathleen and I cared a great deal. We

218

feared dreadfully to be left on the shelf; we feared we should fail to be loved and to love with a great and absolutely unique passion.

When Mrs. O'Neill requested it of me–"to relieve the atmosphere," as she put it–I played Paderewski's "Minuet"; then Wilhelm would have us listen to Massenet on a violin of choice quality. Afterward he would show me in an album scenes of his country, as well as his father's house and the home of his uncle, his father's partner. I think he was anxious to convey to me that his family was better off than you might think if you judged by him–I mean by his having had to quit his native land and come live in our small city. Yet he needed have had no fear that I should form an opinion on the basis of silly social appearances; I wanted to judge people in strict accordance with their noble personal qualities. Wilhelm would explain to me how Ruisdael had really most faithfully rendered the full, sad sky of the Low Countries; and he asked me whether I thought I should like Holland enough one day to visit it. Yes, I replied; I should much like to see the canals and the tulip fields.

Then he had had sent to me from Holland a box of chocolates, each one of which was a small vial containing a liqueur.

But one evening he had the ill-starred notion of accompanying me back home, as far as our front door, though it was only two steps away and darkness had not wholly fallen. He was chivalrous: he insisted that a man should not let a woman go home all alone, even if that woman only yesterday had still been playing with hoops or walking on stilts.

Alas! The moment his back was turned, Maman asked me about my young man. "Who is that great beanstalk?"

I told her it was Wilhelm of Holland, and all the rest of it: the box of chocolates, the tulip fields, the stirring sky of Wilhelm's country, the windmills. . . . Now all that was fine and honorable! But why, despite what I thought of appearances, did I believe myself obliged also to speak of the uncle and the father, partners in a small business which... which...made a lot of money?

My mother at once forbade me to return to the O'Neills, so long, said she, as I had not got over the idea of Wilhelm.

But Wilhelm was clever. One or two days each week he finished work early; on those days he waited for me at the convent door. He took over my great bundle of books–Lord, what homework the Sisters piled on us in those days!–my music sheets, my metronome, and he carried all these burdens to the corner of our street. There he would lower upon me his large and sad blue eyes and say to me, "When you are bigger, I'll take you to the opera, to the theatre...."

I still had two years of the convent ahead of me; the opera, the theatre seemed desperately far away. Wilhelm would tell me that he longed to see me in an evening gown; that then he would at last remove from its mothproof bag his dress clothes and that we should go in style to hear symphonic music.

My mother ultimately learned that Wilhelm had the effrontery to carry my books, and it annoyed her very much. She forbade me to see him.

"Still," said I to Maman, "I can hardly prevent his walking next to me along the pavement."

My mother cut through that problem. "If he takes the same sidewalk as you, mind you, cross right over to the other."

Now, she must have sent a message of rebuke to Wilhelm and told him, as she had me, precisely which sidewalk he should take, for I began seeing him only on the opposite side of the street, where he would stolidly await my passage. All the while I was going by, he held his hat in his hand. The other young girls must have been horribly envious of me; they laughed at Wilhelm's baring his head while I was passing. Yet I felt death in my soul at seeing Wilhelm so alone and exposed to ridicule. He was an immigrant, and Papa had told me a hundred times that you could not have too much sympathy, too much consideration for the uprooted, who have surely suffered enough from their expatriation without our adding to it through scorn or disdain. Why then had Papa so completely changed his views, and why was he more set even than Maman against Wilhelm of Holland? True enough, no one at home, since Georgianna's marriage, looked favorably upon love. Perhaps because as a whole we had already had too much to suffer from it. But I—presumably—I had not yet suffered enough at its hands....

And then, as I have said, Wilhelm was clever. Maman had forbidden him to speak to me on the street, but she had forgotten letters. Wilhelm had made great progress in English. He sent me very beautiful epistles which began with: "My own beloved child..." or else "Sweet little maid...." Not to be outdone, I replied: "My own dearest heart...." One day my mother found in my room a scrawl on which I had been practising my handwriting and in which I expressed to Wilhelm a passion that neither time nor cruel obstacles could bend....Had my mother glanced into the volume of Tennyson lying open upon my table, she would have recognized the whole passage in question, but she was far too angry to listen to reason. I was enjoined from writing to Wilhelm, from reading his letters, if, by a miracle, one of them succeeded in penetrating the defenses thrown up by Maman; I was even enjoined from thinking of him. I was allowed only to pray for him, if I insisted upon it.

Until then I had thought that love should be open and clear, cherished by all and making peace between beings. Yet what was happening? Maman was turned into something like a spy, busy with poking about in my wastebasket; and I then thought that she was certainly the last person in the world to understand me! So that was what love accomplished! And where was that fine frankness between Maman and me! Does there always arise a bad period between a mother and her daughter? Is it love that brings it on?...And what, what is love? One's neighbor? Or some person rich, beguiling?

During this interval Wilhelm, unable to do anything else for me, sent me many gifts; and at the time I knew nothing of them, for the moment they arrived, Maman would return them to him: music scores, tulip bulbs from Amsterdam, a small collar of Bruges lace, more liqueur-filled chocolates.

The only means left to us by which to communicate was the telephone. Maman had not thought of that. Obviously she could not think of everything; love is so crafty! Then, too, during her loving days the telephone did not exist, and this, I imagine, was why Maman forgot to ban it for me. Wilhelm often called our number. If it was not I who answered, he hung up gently. And many a time did Maman then protest, "What's going on?...I shall write the company a letter; I'm constantly being bothered for nothing. At the other end I can barely hear a sort of sighing sound." Naturally she could not foresee how far the tenacity of a Wilhelm would extend.

But when it was I who answered, Wilhelm was scarcely better off. There could be between us no real conversation without its exposing us to the discovery of our secret and consequent prohibition of the telephone. Moreover, we neither of us had any taste for ruses; Gervais employed them when he had on the wire the darling of his heart, to whom he spoke as though she were another schoolboy. But Wilhelm and I – without blaming Gervais, for love is love, and when it encounters obstacles, is even more worthy! – we strove to be noble in all things. Thus Wilhelm merely murmured to me, from afar, "Dear heart..." after which he remained silent. And I listened to his silence for a minute or two, blushing to the roots of my hair.

One day, though, he discovered an admirable way to make me understand his heart. As I was saying "Allo!" his voice begged me to hold the wire; then I made out something like the sound of a violin being tuned, then the opening bars of "Thaïs." Wilhelm played me the whole composition over the phone. Kathleen must have been accompanying him. I heard piano chords somewhere in the distance, and – I know not why – this put me out a trifle, perhaps at thinking that Kathleen was in on so lovely a secret. It was the first time, however, that Wilhelm put me out at all.

Our phone was attached to the wall at the end of a dark little hallway. At first no one was surprised at seeing me spend hours there, motionless and in the most complete silence. Only little by little did the people at home begin to notice that at the telephone I uttered no word. And from then on, when I went to listen to "Thaïs" the hall door would open slightly; someone hid there to spy on me, motioning the others to advance one by one and watch me. Gervais was the worst, and it was very mean on his part, for I had respected his secret. He manufactured reasons for making use of the hall; as he went by he tried to hear what I could be listening to. At first, however, I held the receiver firmly glued to my ear. Then I must already have begun to find "Thaïs" very long to hear through. One evening I allowed Gervais to listen for a moment to Wilhelm's music; perhaps I hoped that he would have enough enthusiasm to make me myself admire the composition. But Gervais choked with mirth; later on I saw him playing the fool in front of the others, at the far end of the living room, bowing an imaginary violin. Even Maman laughed a little, although she tried to remain angry. With a long, sad countenance which–I knew not how–he superimposed upon his own features, Gervais was giving a fairly good imitation of Wilhelm in caricature. I was a little tempted to laugh. For it is a fact that there is something quite comic in seeing a sad person play the violin.

When you consider it, it is astonishing that all of them together should not have thought much sooner of parting me from Wilhelm by the means they so successfully employed from that night forward.

All day long, when I went by, someone was whistling the melody of "Thaïs."

My brother grossly exaggerated the Dutchman's slightly solemn gait, his habit of keeping his eyes lifted aloft. They discovered in him the mien of a Protestant minister, dry–said they–and in the process of preparing a sermon. Maman added that the "Netherlander" had a face as thin as a knife blade. This was the way they now referred to him: the "Netherlander" or the "Hollander." My sister Odette–I should say Sister Edouard–who had been informed and was taking a hand in the matter, even though she had renounced the world, my pious Odette herself told me to forget the "foreigner"...that a foreigner is a foreigner....

One evening as I listened to "Thaïs," I thought I must look silly, standing thus stock still, the receiver in my hand. I hung up before the end of the performance.

Thereafter, Wilhelm scarcely crossed my path again.

A year later, perhaps, we learned that he was returning to Holland.

My mother once more became the just and charitable pre-Wilhelm person I had loved so dearly. My father no longer harbored anything against Holland. Maman admitted that Mrs. O'Neill had told her concerning Wilhelm that he was the best man in the world, reliable, a worker, very gentle....And Maman hoped that Wilhelm, in his own country, among his own people, would be loved...as, she said, he deserved to be.

Works by Gabrielle Roy

FICTION

Bonheur d'occasion. Montreal: Editions Pascal, 1945. [*The Tin Flute.* Trans. Hannah Josephson. Toronto: McClelland and Stewart, 1947.]

La Petite Poule d'Eau. Montreal: Beauchemin, 1950. [*Where Nests the Water Hen.* Trans. Harry Binsse. Toronto: McClelland and Stewart, 1951.]

Alexandre Chenevert. Montreal: Beauchemin, 1954. [*The Cashier.* Trans. Harry Binsse. Toronto: McClelland and Stewart, 1955.]

Rue Deschambault. Montreal: Beauchemin, 1955. [*Street of Riches.* Trans. Harry Binsse. Toronto: McClelland and Stewart, 1957.]

La montagne secrète. Montreal: Beauchemin, 1961. [*The Hidden Mountain.* Trans. Harry Binsse. Toronto: McClelland and Stewart, 1962.]

La route d'Altamont. Montreal: Editions HMH, 1966. [*The Road Past Altamont.* Trans. Joyce Marshall. Toronto: McClelland and Stewart, 1967.]

La rivière sans repos. Montreal: Beauchemin, 1970. [*Windflower.* Trans. Joyce Marshall. Toronto: McClelland and Stewart, 1970.]

Cet été qui chantait. Quebec: Editions françaises, 1972. [*Enchanted Summer.* Trans. Joyce Marshall. Toronto: McClelland and Stewart, 1976.]

Un jardin au bout du monde. Montreal: Beauchemin, 1975. [*Garden in the Wind.* Trans. Alan Brown. Toronto: McClelland and Stewart, 1977.]

Ces enfants de ma vie. Montreal: Stanké, 1977. [*Children of My Heart.* Trans. Alan Brown. Toronto: McClelland and Stewart, 1979.]

Ma Vache Bossie. Montreal: Leméac, 1976. (children's book)

Courte-Queue. Montreal: Stanké, 1979. [*Cliptail.* Trans. Alan Brown. Toronto: McClelland and Stewart, 1980.] (children's book)

ESSAYS

Fragiles lumières de la terre. Montreal: Quinze, 1978. [*The Fragile Lights of Earth.* Trans. Alan Brown. Toronto: McClelland and Stewart, 1982.]

Interviews with Gabrielle Roy

Maclean's. April 15, 1947, 23; 51; 54.

Une littérature en ébullition. Edited by Gérard Bessette. Montreal: Editions du Jour, 1968, pp. 303-08.

Conversations with Canadian Novelists. Edited by Donald Cameron. Toronto: Macmillan, 1973. Vol. 1, pp. 128-45.

The Canadian, May 1, 1976, 10; 12-14.

Fredelle Bruser Maynard

Birch Hills, Saskatchewan, a village southeast of Prince Albert, consists of "two streets, a line of grain elevators, and a railway station." Yet *Raisins and Almonds* (1972), Fredelle Bruser Maynard's account of her childhood in Birch Hills, reveals an astonishing richness to the lives of its inhabitants. "Though often lonely I was never, I think, bored," Maynard remarks. "Bounded in a nutshell, I counted myself king of infinite space."

Born in Saskatchewan in 1922, Maynard grew up in a variety of prairie towns. Her family moved to Birch Hills when she was three and left when she was nine. "We passed through many small towns afterwards, but Birch Hills has remained for me always The Town, the essential prairie experience." After attending the University of Manitoba and the University of Toronto, Maynard moved to the United States to obtain her doctorate at Radcliffe; later she taught at such colleges as Radcliffe and Wellesley. Now living in Toronto, she is a free-lance writer, devoting her time to studies of education and child care.

"They are not all happy highways where I went," Maynard notes at the end of *Raisins and Almonds*. "What, then, drives me down them again, after all these years and another life? The effort, I suppose, to understand. Somewhere, in yon far country, lies the answer to the question that confronts me with increasing urgency. Who am I?" Like most autobiographies, *Raisins and Almonds* returns to the author's childhood to comprehend some of the early forces that shape the individual. "We are all marked by the first world that meets our eyes, carrying it with us as a permanent image of the way things are, or should be."

The following selection from *Raisins and Almonds*, "Jewish Christmas," draws attention to the child's unique and lonely position as a Jewish girl in a predominantly Christian community. Like Freidele in this account, Maynard was unique among her childhood classmates and friends, just as her family was unique among the population of Birch Hills. "Strung out along Main Street (one could hardly call it 'downtown') were four false-fronted general stores— .... One Frenchman, one Scot, one Norwegian, and one Jew—my father. I remember them that way because that was their meaning in 1925."

In describing her childhood so movingly, Maynard captures aspects of the world of the prairies and the world of all childhoods. As Margaret Laurence, another child of the prairies, remarks, Maynard "communicates the sadness at the core of laughter.... Her memoirs are so authentically prairie, Depression prairie, but they reach out beyond any place or time."

Jewish
Christmas

Christmas, when I was young, was the season of bitterness. Lights beckoned and tinsel shone, store windows glowed with mysterious promise, but I knew the brilliance was not for me. Being Jewish, I had long grown accustomed to isolation and difference. Difference was in my bones and blood, and in the pattern of my separate life. My parents were conspicuously unlike other children's parents in our predominantly Norwegian community. Where my schoolmates were surrounded by blond giants appropriate to a village called Birch Hills, my family suggested still the Russian plains from which they had emigrated years before. My handsome father was a big man, but big without any suggestion of physical strength or agility; one could not imagine him at the wheel of a tractor. In a town that was all wheat and cattle, he seemed the one man wholly devoted to urban pursuits: he operated a general store. Instead of the native costume–overalls and mackinaws–he wore city suits and pearl-grey spats. In winter he was splendid in a plushy chinchilla coat with velvet collar, his black curly hair an extension of the high Astrakhan hat which he had brought from the Ukraine. I was proud of his good looks, and yet uneasy about their distinctly oriental flavor.

My mother's difference was of another sort. Her beauty was not so much foreign as timeless. My friends had slender young Scandinavian mothers, light of foot and blue of eye; my mother was short and heavyset, but with a face of classic proportions. Years later I found her in the portraits of Ingres and Corot–face a delicate oval, brown velvet eyes, brown silk hair centrally parted and drawn back in a lustrous coil–but in those days I saw only that she too was different. As for my grandparents, they were utterly unlike the benevolent, apple-cheeked characters who presided over happy families in my favorite stories. (Evidently all those happy families were gentile.) My grandmother had no fringed shawl, no steel-rimmed glasses. (She read, if at all, with the help of a magnifying glass from Woolworth's.) Ignorant, apparently, of her natural role as gentle occupant of the rocking chair, she was ignorant too of the world outside her apartment in remote Winnipeg. She had brought Odessa with her, and–on my rare visits–she smiled lovingly, uncomprehendingly, across an ocean of time and space. Even more unreal was my grandfather, a black cap and a long beard bent over the Talmud. I felt for him a kind of amused tenderness, but I was glad that my schoolmates could not see him.

At home we spoke another language–Yiddish or Russian–and ate rich foods whose spicy odors bore no resemblance to the neighbors' cooking. We did not go to church or belong to clubs or, it seemed, take any meaningful part in the life of the town. Our social roots went, not down into the foreign soil on which fate had deposited us, but outwards, in delicate, sensitive connections, to other Jewish families in other lonely prairie towns. Sundays, they congregated around our table, these strangers who were brothers; I saw that they too ate knishes and spoke with faintly foreign voices, but I could not feel for them or for their silent swarthy children the kinship I knew I owed to all those who had been, like us, both chosen and abandoned.

All year I walked in the shadow of difference; but at Christmas above all, I tasted it sour on my tongue. There was no room at the tree. "You have Hanukkah," my father reminded me. "That is *our* holiday." I knew the story, of course–how, over two thousand years ago, my people had triumphed over the enemies of their faith, and how a single jar of holy oil had miraculously burned eight days and nights in the temple of the Lord. I thought of my father lighting each night another candle in the *menorah*, my mother and I beside him as he recited the ancient prayer: "Blessed art Thou, O Lord our God, ruler of the universe, who has sanctified us by thy commandments and commanded us to kindle the light of Hanukkah." Yes, we had our miracle too. But how could it stand against the glamor of Christmas? What was *gelt*, the traditional gift coins, to a sled packed with surprises? What was Judas Maccabaeus the liberator compared with the Christ child in the manger? To my sense of exclusion was added a sense of shame. "You *killed* Christ!" said the boys on the playground. "*You* killed him!" I knew none of the facts behind this awful accusation, but I was afraid to ask. I was even afraid to raise my voice in the chorus of "Come All Ye Faithful" lest I be struck down for my unfaithfulness by my own God, the wrathful Jehovah. With all the passion of my child's heart I longed for a younger, more compassionate deity with flowing robe and silken hair. Reluctant conscript to a doomed army, I longed to change sides. I longed for Christmas.

Although my father was in all things else the soul of indulgence, in this one matter he stood firm as Moses. "You cannot have a tree, *herzele.* You shouldn't even want to sing the carols. You are a Jew." I turned the words over in my mind and on my tongue. What was it, to be a Jew in Birch Hills, Saskatchewan? Though my father spoke of Jewishness as a special distinction, as far as I could see it was an inheritance without a kingdom, a check on a bank that had failed. Being Jewish was mostly not doing things other people did—not eating pork, not going to Sunday school, not entering, even playfully, into childhood romances, because the only boys around were *goyishe* boys. I remember, when I was five or six, falling in love with Edward Prince of Wales. Of the many arguments with which Mama might have dampened my ardor, she chose surely the most extraordinary. "You can't marry him. He isn't Jewish." And of course, finally, definitely, most crushing of all, being Jewish meant not celebrating Christ's birth. My parents allowed me to attend Christmas parties, but they made it clear that I must receive no gifts. How I envied the white and gold Norwegians! Their Lutheran church was not glamorous, but it was less frighteningly strange than the synagogue I had visited in Winnipeg, and in the Lutheran church, each December, joy came upon the midnight clear.

It was the Lutheran church and its annual concert which brought me closest to Christmas. Here there was always a tree, a jolly Santa Claus, and a program of songs and recitations. As the town's most accomplished elocutionist, I was regularly invited to perform. Usually my offering was comic or purely secular—*Santa's Mistake, The Night Before Christmas*, a scene from *A Christmas Carol.* But I had also memorized for such occasions a sweetly pious narrative about the housewife who, blindly absorbed in cleaning her house for the Lord's arrival, turns away a beggar and finds she has rebuffed the Savior himself. Oddly enough, my recital of this vitally un-Jewish material gave my parents no pain. My father, indeed, kept in his safe-deposit box along with other valuables a letter in which the Lutheran minister spoke gratefully of my last Christmas performance. "Through her great gift, your little Freidele has led many to Jesus." Though Papa seemed untroubled by considerations of whether this was a proper role for a Jewish child, reciting *The Visit* made me profoundly uneasy. And I suppose it was this feeling, combined with a natural disinclination to stand unbidden at the feast, which led me, the year I was seven, to rebel.

We were baking in the steamy kitchen, my mother and I–or rather she was baking while I watched, fascinated as always, the miracle of the strudel. First, the warm ball of dough, no larger than my mother's hand. Slap, punch, bang–again and again she lifted the dough and smacked it down on the board. Then came the moment I loved. Over the kitchen table, obliterating its patterned oilcloth, came a damask cloth; and over this in turn a cloud of flour. Beside it stood my mother, her hair bound in muslin, her hands and arms powdered with flour. She paused a moment. Then, like a dancer about to execute a particularly difficult pirouette, she tossed the dough high in the air, catching it with a little stretching motion and tossing again until the ball was ball no longer but an almost transparent rectangle. The strudel was as large as the table-cloth now. *"Unter Freidele's vigele Ligt eyn groys veys tsigele,"* she sang. "Under Freidele's little bed A white goat lays his silken head." *Tsigele iz geforen handlen Rozinkes mit mandlen...."* For some reason that song, with its gay fantastic images of the white goat shopping for raisins and almonds, always made me sad. But then my father swung open the storm door and stood, stamping and jingling his galoshes buckles, on the icy mat.

"Boris, look how you track in the snow!"

Already flakes and stars were turning into muddy puddles. Still booted and icy-cheeked he swept us up–a kiss on the back of Mama's neck, the only spot not dedicated to strudel, and a hug for me.

"You know what? I have just now seen the preacher. Reverend Pederson, he wants you should recite at the Christmas concert."

I bent over the bowl of almonds and snapped the nutcracker.

"I should tell him it's all right, you'll speak a piece?"

No answer.

"Sweetheart–dear one–you'll do it?"

Suddenly the words burst out. "No, Papa! I don't want to!"

My father was astonished. "But why not? What is it with you?"

"I hate those concerts!" All at once my grievances swarmed up in an angry cloud. "I never have any fun! And everybody else gets presents and Santa Claus never calls out 'Freidele Bruser'! They all know I'm Jewish!"

Papa was incredulous. "But, little daughter, always you've had a good time! Presents! What presents? A bag of candy, an orange? Tell me, is there a child in town with such toys as you have? What should you want with Santa Claus?"

It was true. My friends had tin tea sets and dolls with sawdust bodies and crude Celluloid smiles. I had an Eaton Beauty with real hair and delicate jointed body, two French dolls with rosy bisque faces and–new this last Hanukkah–Rachel, my baby doll. She was the marvel of the town: exquisite china head, overlarge and shaped like a real infant's, tiny wrinkled hands, legs convincingly bowed. I had a lace and taffeta doll bassinet, a handmade cradle, a full set of rattan doll furniture, a teddy bear from Germany and real porcelain dishes from England. What *did* I want with Santa Claus? I didn't know. I burst into tears.

Papa was frantic now. What was fame and the applause of the Lutherans compared to his child's tears? Still bundled in his overcoat he knelt on the kitchen floor and hugged me to him, rocking and crooning. "Don't cry, my child, don't cry. You don't want to go, you don't have to. I tell them you have a sore throat, you can't come."

"Boris, wait. Listen to me." For the first time since my outburst, Mama spoke. She laid down the rolling pin, draped the strudel dough delicately over the table, and wiped her hands on her apron. "What kind of a fuss? You go or you don't go, it's not such a big thing. But so close to Christmas you shouldn't let them down. The one time we sit with them in the church and such joy you give them. Freidele, look at me...." I snuffed loudly and obeyed, not without some satisfaction in the thought of the pathetic picture I made. "Go this one time, for my sake. You'll see, it won't be so bad. And if you don't like it–pffff, no more! All right? Now, come help with the raisins."

On the night of the concert we gathered in the kitchen again, this time for the ritual of the bath. Papa set up the big tin tub on chairs next to the black iron stove. Then, while he heated pails of water and sloshed them into the tub, Mama set out my clothes. Everything about this moment contrived to make me feel pampered, special. I was lifted in and out of the steamy water, patted dry with thick towels, powdered from neck to toes with Mama's best scented talcum. Then came my "reciting outfit." My friends in Birch Hills had party dresses mail-ordered from Eaton's–crackly taffeta or shiny rayon satin weighted with lace or flounces, and worn with long white stockings drawn up over long woolen underwear. My dress was Mama's own composition, a poem in palest peach crepe de chine created from remnants of her bridal trousseau. Simple and flounceless, it fell from my shoulders in a myriad of tiny pleats no wider than my thumbnail; on the low-slung sash hung a cluster of silk rosebuds. Regulation drop-seat underwear being unthinkable under such a costume, Mama had devised a snug little apricot chemise which made me, in a world of wool, feel excitingly naked.

When at last I stood on the church dais, the Christmas tree glittering and shimmering behind me, it was with the familiar feeling of strangeness. I looked out over the audience-congregation, grateful for the myopia that made faces indistinguishable, and began:

A letter came on Christmas morn
In which the Lord did say
''Behold my star shines in the east
And I shall come today.
Make bright thy hearth. . . . ''

The words tripped on without thought or effort. I knew by heart every nuance and gesture, down to the modest curtsey and the properly solemn pace with which I returned to my seat. There I huddled into the lining of Papa's coat, hardly hearing the "Beautiful, beautiful!" which accompanied his hug. For this was the dreaded moment. All around me, children twitched and whispered. Santa had come.

"Olaf Swenson!" Olaf tripped over a row of booted feet, leapt down the aisle and embraced an enormous package. "Ellen Njaa! Fern Dahl! Peter Bjorkstrom!" There was a regular procession now, all jubilant. Everywhere in the hall children laughed, shouted, rejoiced with their friends. "What'd you get?" "Look at mine!" In the seat next to me, Gunnar Olsen ripped through layers of tissue: "I got it! I got it!" His little sister wrestled with the contents of a red net stocking. A tin whistle rolled to my feet and I turned away, ignoring her breathless efforts to retrieve it.

And then–suddenly, incredibly, the miracle came. "Freidele Bruser!" For me, too, the star had shone. I looked up at my mother. A mistake surely. But she smiled and urged me to my feet. "Go on, look, he calls you!" It was true, Santa was actually coming to meet me. My gift, I saw, was not wrapped–and it could be no mistake. It was a doll, a doll just like Rachel, but dressed in christening gown and cap. "Oh Mama, look! He's brought me a doll! A twin for Rachel! She's just the right size for Rachel's clothes. I can take them both for walks in the carriage. They can have matching outfits. . . ." I was in an ecstasy of plans.

Mama did not seem to be listening. She lifted the hem of the gown. "How do you like her dress? Look, see the petticoat?"

"They're beautiful!" I hugged the doll rapturously. "Oh, Mama, I *love* her! I'm going to call her Ingrid. Ingrid and Rachel. . . ."

During the long walk home Mama was strangely quiet. Usually I held my parents' hands and swung between them. But now I stepped carefully, clutching Ingrid.

"You had a good time, yes?" Papa's breath frosted the night.

"Mmmmmmm." I rubbed my warm cheek against Ingrid's cold one. "It was just like a real Christmas. I got the best present of anybody. Look, Papa–did you see Ingrid's funny little cross face? It's just like Rachel's. I can't wait to get her home and see them side by side in the crib."

In the front hall, I shook the snow from Ingrid's lace bonnet. "A hot cup cocoa maybe?" Papa was already taking the milk from the icebox. "No, no, I want to get the twins ready for bed!" I broke from my mother's embrace. The stairs seemed longer than usual. In my arms Ingrid was cold and still, a snow princess. I could dress her in Rachel's flannel gown, that would be the thing. . . . The dolls and animals watched glassy-eyed as I knelt by the cradle. It rocked at my touch, oddly light. I flung back the blankets. Empty. Of course.

Sitting on the cold floor, the doll heavy in my lap, I wept for Christmas. Nothing had changed then, after all. For Jews there was no Santa Claus; I understood that. But my parents. . . . *Why* had they dressed Rachel?

From the kitchen below came the mingled aromas of hot chocolate and buttery popcorn. My mother called softly. "Let them call," I said to Ingrid-Rachel. "I don't care!" The face of the Christmas doll was round and blank under her cap; her dress was wet with my tears. Brushing them away, I heard my father enter the room. He made no move to touch me or lift me up. I turned and saw his face tender and sad like that of a Chagall violinist. "Mama worked every night on the clothes," he said. "Yesterday even, knitting booties."

Stiff-fingered, trembling, I plucked at the sleeve of the christening gown. It was indeed a miracle—a wisp of batiste but as richly overlaid with embroidery as a coronation robe. For the first time I examined Rachel's new clothes—the lace insets and lace overlays, the French knots and scalloped edges, the rows of hemstitching through which tiny ribbons ran like fairy silk. The petticoat was tucked and pleated. Even the little diaper showed an edge of hand crochet. There were booties and mittens and a ravishing cap.

"Freidele, dear one, my heart," my father whispered. "We did not think. We could not know. Mama dressed Rachel in the new clothes, you should be happy with the others. We so much love you."

Outside my window, where the Christmas snow lay deep and crisp and even, I heard the shouts of neighbors returning from the concert. "Joy to the world!" they sang,

> *Let earth receive her King!*
> *Let every heart prepare Him room*
> *And heaven and nature sing . . .*

It seemed to me, at that moment, that I too was a part of the song. I wrapped Rachel warmly in her shawl and took my father's hand.

Works by Fredelle Bruser Maynard

AUTOBIOGRAPHY

Raisins and Almonds. Toronto:
  Doubleday, 1972.

PSYCHOLOGY

Guiding Your Child to a More Creative Life.
  Garden City, N.Y.: Doubleday, 1973.

Sinclair Ross

When Sinclair Ross published his first novel, *As for Me and My House*, in New York in 1941, some copies were imported for the Canadian market. Only a few hundred copies in all were sold. Though not originally popular, the book (a diary of a minister's wife living in a small Saskatchewan town during the Depression of the 1930s) has had a tremendous influence on the literature of Canada. "When I first read his extraordinary and moving novel, *As for Me and My House*, at about the age of eighteen," Margaret Laurence has stated, echoing the feelings of many writers, "it had an enormous impact on me, for it seemed the only genuine one I had ever read about my own people, my own place, my own time. It pulled no punches about life in the stultifying atmosphere of small and ingrown towns, and yet it was illuminated with compassion." The novel taught Laurence "that one could write out of the known background of a small prairie town and that everything that happens anywhere also in some ways happens there."

Ross was born in 1908 on a homestead in northern Saskatchewan, nineteen kilometres from Shellbrooke and forty kilometres from Prince Albert. His parents separated when he was a baby. Young Ross remained with his mother, and his older brother and sister lived with their father. As a child, Ross was always interested in writing, though he received no special encouragement from his teachers or even from his mother. On the other hand, his mother urged him to read and she made every effort to insure that he received proper schooling. So determined was she that her son be educated that she let him ride a horse to school, even though it was difficult to spare one from farm duties.

Ross dropped out of school after grade eleven to work in a bank. Apart from wartime service in the Canadian army, he continued his banking career until he retired in 1968.

Before writing *As for Me and My House*, Ross had already written and destroyed two novels, "failures, which publishers write me are interesting and compelling, but of small commercial possibilities." Turning for a while from the long form of the novel, he looked to the short story, remarking, "I am now starting to work on short stories, hoping gradually to build up a better technique without the cramping grind that writing a novel after office hours demands."

"A Day with Pegasus," first published in 1938, focuses on the imaginative universe of nine-year-old Peter Parker. Fettered by the literal minds of his parents; his older brother, Dan; his teacher, Miss Kinley; and his school friends, Peter refuses to accept the boundaries they impose. The birth of a colt leads him to soar "above the limitations of mere time and distance."

A Day
with
Pegasus

"Two white stockings and a star," Mrs. Parker called from the kitchen, and in his bare feet, struggling with suspenders, Peter raced downstairs and across the yard to see.

At the stable door, just for an instant, he hesitated. It was some instinct perhaps of emotional thrift, warning him that so fierce and strange a tingle of expectancy ought to be prolonged a little–some vague apprehension that in Biddy's stall there might be less than he had seen already. Then he advanced slowly–a finger raised to forbid the yellow pup that waited for his word to leap and yelp–on furtive tiptoe past the stalls where Mr. Parker and his grown-up brother Dan stood harnessing their horses for the field. This suddenly was important. In what awaited him there was no place for Dan or his father or the pup. The stable with its gloom and rustling mangerfuls of hay had subdued his excitement to a breathless sense of solemnity–a solemnity that was personal, intimately his own–that he knew the others would misunderstand and mar. He even felt a vague resentment that while he was still sleeping they had been here before him. It was his colt–it should have been his first to see and touch. Five months he had been waiting. "Biddy's colt about the end of May," they had promised him at Christmas, and today now was the twenty-eighth. Marvelling a little at the prophecy he reached the box-stall door. There was a moment's stillness while the pup sat watching with his silly head cocked up as if it were a game. Then the mare whinnied to him and he slipped inside.

It was a small colt–disconcertingly small–even though no smaller

than the other new-born colts that he had seen. It lay, a black, unprepos-
sessing little heap among the straw, its coat still rough and mangy-
looking, its eyes half-closed, its head unsteady. He squatted in front of it,
almost in a conversational attitude, as if he were introducing himself and
awaiting recognition. But the colt, even before the advent of its owner,
showed signs of neither interest nor respect. Even when the owner put
out a finger to touch and verify the star. Even when the finger became
gently importunate in an effort to prod awake some sign of at least
potential speed and grace. The head kept swaying back and forth, the
eyes went shut and open blearily–and nothing more.

Then Biddy came up, and with a no-nonsense push of her nose
toppled him sprawling off his hunkers into the straw. He lay there still a
minute, watching respectfully as she licked the colt between the ears.
Nearly all their horses were Biddy's colts or grand-colts. Big, rangy,
hairy-footed Clydes, and yet with twice the dash and spirit of the horses
that he knew on other farms. Because Biddy had a strain of racing blood.
Even after nearly twenty years of foal-bearing and the plough, she
herself always pranced a little as they led her out of the stable. And every
day of his life young Tim raced the others to the water-trough where,
heels twitching and ears flat to his head, he dared them to approach till
he had drunk his fill. The same with the bay mares Lulu and Marie, who
in town one day last summer had pretended fright at the sight of a truck,
and to the scurrying amazement of all Main Street, taken off a wheel on
the corner of Pandora's Beauty Shop. He remembered gratefully,
encouraging himself with the thought that his colt now, for all its poor
beginnings, was not likely to prove an exception.

Then Dan came in, and eager for an expert's pronouncement, Peter
sprang attentive to his feet. But first, without a word, Dan put his arms
around the colt and lifted it. He steadied the shaky body a minute,
straightened out one of the white-stockinged legs that was buckling at
the knee, and then for a long time–a mercilessly long time–stood
thoughtful and appraising.

It would be final. Dan's opinion. Fearfully, as if in the sober, sun-
tanned features his own destiny were to be read, Peter scanned his face.
"What do you think?" he asked anxiously at last, unable to contain
himself longer. "I mean–will he be all right? Is he as good as her other
colts?"

Dan smiled in answer–the inarticulate smile of a horse-lover, tender,
almost grateful–and pierced with understanding, Peter wheeled and
fled outside.

It was a strange, almost unbearable moment. The horse that for five
months he had lived with, gloried in, and, underneath it all, never quite

expected to come true—it was a reality now—alive, warm and breathing—two white stockings and a star.

He ran; the yellow pup rolled tangling at his feet; and on he ran again. The colt ran with him, more swiftly now than it had ever run before. No earth beneath their feet, they leaped across the garden and around the house—around the house and across the garden—then back to stand a moment eager and irresolute before the stable door.

But this time he stayed outside. His colt, grown fleet of limb, possessed a fire and beauty that enslaved him now, that he could not abandon for the bleary-eyed reality in Biddy's stall. "You'll be late for school," Dan warned him as he led out the horses. "Remember, you've got the calves to feed before you go."

Ordinarily it was a trial, the way Dan disciplined him, the twenty-year-old smugness with which he imposed his own standards of cleanliness and decorum, but this time Peter trotted off for breakfast willingly. Partly because he understood that for a while at least it would be better if he kept away from the box-stall. Partly because in Dan's smile as he appraised the colt there had been a quality of reverence that established between them a kinship stronger than the disparity of eleven years.

He swallowed only a few mouthfuls, slipping most of his breakfast to the pup while Mrs. Parker went on working at the stove. "You're quiet," she noticed presently. "What's wrong? Dan says it's the best colt Biddy's ever had."

"I know—I'm just wondering what's a good name." It would be useless trying to explain. His silence belonged to an emotion that he was sure lay outside her experience. "We've got a King already—and Skinny Saunders called his pony Prince—so he'd think I was copying."

"Bill's a good name," she suggested. "Short and sensible. Or Mike, or Joe. We had a Buster once—before your time."

He asked resignedly, "Is the milk ready for the calves?"

"If you've finished your breakfast." She glanced from his empty plate to the pup, but it was an accomplishment of the pup to swallow instantly, without so much as a smack of his chops, and reassured she went on. "Mind there's no milk spilt this morning, and don't stop in to bother the colt again. You've still got to brush your hair and get into your shoes and stockings."

It was the colt, the colt he had raced with before breakfast across the garden, that made the feeding of the calves this morning such a humiliation. They slobbered milk over his feet, dribbled it down his trousers; one of them got its tongue around the bit of shirt-tail that he hadn't yet tucked in, and annoyed to find no nourishment forthcoming, bunted him elbow-deep into the pail. Mack—Daisy—Dot—as stupid and silly as their names, gurgling and blowing at him till there was no colt left at all—until for beginnings again he had to steal back to the stable and pay another visit to the box-stall.

This time he examined the colt curiously: toy-horse, woolly little tail, trim dainty limbs with both white stockings drawn up neatly to the knees, incredibly small and incredibly perfect hooves. A horse—in astonishing miniature still, but authentically a horse—and this time for just its frail reality he began to feel an enthusiasm that at last made the box-stall too confining, and sent him spinning sky-high to the house to dress for school.

But it was a mile to school, and the reality could not last so far. The white-stockinged legs began to flash more quickly, the long limp neck to arch, the stubby tail to flow. Then suddenly he was mounted, and the still May morning sprang in whistling wind around his ears. Field after field reeled up and fell away. The earth resounded thundering, then dimmed and dropped until it seemed they cleaved their way through flashing light.... Until at last he stood quite still, impaled by the fear and wonder of it, while the sun poured blazing, and the road stretched white and dusty through the fields of early wheat. A long time: reader clutched in one hand, red shining dinner-pail in the other.

He arrived nearly fifteen minutes late. That in itself was always bad enough: forfeit of mid-morning recess, Miss Kinley "picking" on him for the rest of the day; but this time there was the additional penalty of isolation. Penalty because of the sudden ache to tell someone, to share the wonder of his horse. Across the aisle he tried, "It's here, Skinny—it's here—two white stockings—" but instant, like the crack of a sniper's rifle, Miss Kinley's ruler struck the desk. "Indeed, Peter! Fifteen minutes late and wasting time. I'm sure then you will be able to explain the lesson to the rest of us who aren't so clever. Step forward."

An age-long journey. He took a piece of chalk from her outstretched hand, advanced to the blackboard, then stood quite still and blind. It was a matter of papering a room in which there were two doors and three windows, of a careless paper-hanger who spoiled one foot for every ten he used, and paper at fifty-seven cents a roll. "We're waiting," Miss Kinley reminded him, but through the hammer of mortification in his ears her voice came meaningless and faint. Hammer of mortification—of despairing certainty that he would never solve the problem—and at last of galloping hooves.

He couldn't help it. The rhythm persisted, stronger than his will, than his embarrassment, stronger even than the implacability of Miss Kinley's tapping ruler. "We're waiting, Peter," she repeated, but this time he didn't hear at all. Gradually the classroom fell away. The light flashed golden in his eyes again. The fields sped reeling young and green.

The withering voice and stony eyes were all wasted. Back in his seat at last, disgraced, studying the mountains and rivers of South America, he began thinking again of a name for his colt. Last summer on a visit to his uncle's ranch he had met a cowboy with a horse called Tony. A white and sorrel Skewbald: two round patches on his hips that shone when the sun was on them just like copper plates, hot bloodshot eyes and a rakish forelock–but somehow, for his horse, Tony wouldn't do. Too light, too easy. No, he wanted a name to match the look that had come into Dan's eyes when he lifted and held the colt, the little smile of marvelling delight. That was it–he wanted a name to match the miracle.

The same with the cowboy. A big, handsome fellow who had taken time off from roping steers to show Peter the spurs and belt and silver-studded chaps he had won in the big rodeos, who had brought him ten plugs of licorice one Saturday night from town, and a fine red silk bandana. But they had called him Slim, this cowboy, nothing but Slim; and not even to commemorate a hero and a friendship could Peter give a name like *that* to his horse.

Slim, though, must have had another name–a real name–so now that he had his own horse why not set out again to find him? Almost a horse–it wouldn't be long. To his uncle's ranch, then farther west and south. Rodeo to rodeo, round-up to round-up, until word at last must find its way to Slim of this young rider and his white-legged horse. Then on again, all four of them. Unequal, yet in total virtue equalling: himself on the horse that was to be called whatever Slim's name really was, and a great cowboy riding Tony.

They rode a long time. With swaggering sombreros, puff-pommelled saddle, gleaming spurs. Even while the class dismissed for recess, and Miss Kinley came again to learn the cost of papering a room with paper fifty-seven cents a roll. To the wonder and acclaim of crowds, and alone across desert wastelands. Even with the spelling lesson under way, and Skinny whispering across the aisle should "muscle" have one *s* or two?

Until suddenly it was noon around him, with an offer from Skinny before they had even reached their lunch-pails to trade custard pie for gherkins. "That's what keeps you so thin," Peter rebuked him. "Always eating pickles–don't you know they dry up the blood? No–let's sit here on the steps today with the others."

Skinny drove to school, and when the weather was fine they usually sat in his buggy to eat their lunch, just the two of them, working out judicious trades, and for future adjustment keeping strict account of unequal ones. But today, blandly heedless of custom, Peter squeezed his way up to the top step, and left the choice of standing on the bottom one to Skinny. Skinny stood, because on the bottom step one became the irresistible target for everybody's crusts and egg-shells. "Here are the gherkins," Peter offered by way of compensation, holding out his lunch-pail over Rusty Martin's head. "I'm not very hungry so you can keep the pie."

And then, nibbling nervously at a sandwich, he waited. It was wise to wait. Watching the others all intent upon their lunch-pails, he congratulated himself on his foresight and forbearance. Not yet—they were too busy to listen. His announcement would be wasted. Not for at least another five minutes.

For last winter when he told Rusty Martin and the others about the colt they had laughed; and it was to settle that score, not to slight Skinny, that this noon he had chosen the steps for lunch. With the exception of Skinny not one of them had a horse of his own anyway. Not one of their fathers even had a horse that could be compared to Biddy or her colt. They wouldn't laugh now. They wouldn't say it was a funny Christmas present you had to wait five months for. His eyes narrowed as he watched them. It was hard holding back. The blood was pounding in his temples and his stomach felt small and tight. At last, momentously, he began:

"My colt's here, Skinny—the one I told you Biddy's been expecting." It was important to address himself to Skinny, to speak casually, so they would suspect nothing premeditated. Peering into his lunch-pail as if still hungry he went on, "Dan says he's not bad—the best one Biddy's ever had. And he's got a star, and two white stockings."

"A colt that's to be your own?" seven-year-old Willie Thompson squeaked . "Why?"

"Because my father's given him to me, that's why." Peter forgave Willie the absurdity of such a question, because his ear had caught a faint ring of the envy and incredulity he had been hoping for. "Last Christmas he promised. Remember, Skinny! I said all along it was to be May."

"What's two white stockings mean?" Willie squeaked again. "How can a colt—"

"He means white legs," Bud Nicholson broke in, confederate of Rusty in disdain. "I've got a calf with four."

"Me, too," another seven-year-old spoke up. "Three anyway and a foot. I call her Rosie."

Peter flinched. It was the promiscuity that hurt: Biddy's colt in the same breath with a calf called Rosie. To them his announcement could suggest no more than a heap of blear-eyed helplessness not very different from the reality in Biddy's stall before which he even he this morning had stood rather critical and unimpressed; but that, of course, was what he didn't understand. Their indifference as they closed up lunch-pails and flicked away crumbs seemed deliberate, a conspiracy to belittle his colt. He sat still a moment, indignant, tight-lipped; then, determined to exact their respect even at the cost of strict truthfulness:

"My brother says he's got legs to make a runner–and Dan knows horses."

"So brother Dan says," Rusty turned towards him, squinting, "but how do you think a colt out of that old Biddy mare's ever going to make a runner? Too much Clydesdale–you've only got to look at the feet."

"Biddy's not Clydesdale–not *all* Clydesdale. She's got racing blood."

"Maybe," Bud countered, "but the *father* of your colt's a Clydesdale. Pure-bred. I ought to know. Dad's got his papers framed and hanging in the stable. Mother won't have them in the house."

In the past few months faint suspicions of this had already occurred to Peter, but now, roused to defiance of even heredity and its laws, he flared, "I don't care who his father is– he's a runner. Dan says so. You've only got to look at his legs."

"Maybe he's right," Skinny agreed suddenly. "You can't always tell. My mother weighs two hundred and thirty-five and look at me."

"But that's because you're always eating pickles," Rusty snickered. "There's an idea for you, Peter. Feed your nag pickles, and he'll maybe make a runner after all."

It was the insult "nag" that flashed a blaze of red in Peter's eyes, and hurled him both fists doubled square on Rusty's snickering jaw. They struck at each other wildly a few times, then clinched and rolled clattering off the steps among the lunch-pails. The boys made an instant eager ring around them; the girls ran squealing from the other side of the school to watch. Peter regained his feet first, and unethically pounced again before Rusty was off his knees. Rusty jerked up his head, caught Peter in the midriff, and sent him staggering back among the girls. It was a good fight while it lasted. Rusty had a loose tooth and a skinned cheekbone by the time Miss Kinley forced her way between them. Peter's nose was bleeding creditably, and one of his eyes had started to puff.

They washed, shook hands, said they were sorry, and then till classes were resumed at one o'clock worked long division questions on the blackboard. But Peter was too jubilant to mind. The colt, now that he had actually championed it, seemed more real, more dependable. When school called and the little girls tittered at his eye he smiled deeply. His horse was going to be a runner.

For their next period they were to write a composition. "Something that you'll enjoy," Miss Kinley beamed at them over her glasses. "How you spent last Saturday. Just a little story about the little things you did. Watch your spelling and punctuation—and remember the way to start a paragraph."

For a few minutes Peter conscientiously reviewed last Saturday; then he sat idle, wetting his pencil and thinking about the colt. It was useless. He hadn't done anything Saturday but help Dan plant potatoes. Some composition! "We've had enough nonsense from you already, Peter," Miss Kinley warned a second time. "Now hurry. I'm not going to speak to you again."

She sailed on to her desk at the front of the classroom; there was a moment's stillness round him, clear and isolating like a magic crystal globe; and then suddenly he was writing.

As he had never written before. Writing, writing—the words just pouring. "Early in the morning," this Saturday began, "I saddled my horse and rode over to meet Slim. He's a friend of mine. Then we went to the rodeo in town where everybody was waiting to see Slim ride broncos. He had on his leather chaps with the silver studs all over them, and a blue shirt and a yellow handkerchief—"

He wrote and he wrote. Because on the one hand it was impossible not to write at all, because Miss Kinley's threats were never idle; and because on the other it was equally impossible to write about last Saturday in its long-drawn, potato-planting reality. So he transformed it, soared above the limitations of mere time and distance. All the glamor and bravura of the rodeos he had never seen was there, all the fleet-limbed pride and wonder of the horse that still was but a few hours old, all the steadfastness of his vanished comradeship with Slim. Miss Kinley was aghast.

"I'll have to see you at recess," she said tensely; and at recess, white lips and knuckles suppressing tremendous agitation:

"How could you, Peter? Stand up and answer me. How could you? Rodeos—*cowboys*—you surely didn't expect me to believe—"

She was more distressed than angry. It was something she had never encountered before, something that evaded her ordinary, time-tried classifications of good conduct and bad. "You haven't a horse at all. You were at home on Saturday. I drove past your place on my way to town, and you were in the garden with your brother planting potatoes."

"Yes," he nodded quickly, "that was it—Saturday I planted potatoes all day."

"Then why didn't you obey me? Why did you write all this?"

He glanced up and met her eyes, wondering hopelessly how to make her understand. "Because it wasn't worth writing about–because it was just planting potatoes."

"And you think that's excuse enough for all these lies?"

"But they aren't lies, Miss Kinley–not real lies."

She pursed her lips. "You mean you do have a horse–and it did run a race and win a hundred dollars?"

"No–not really–not yet–"

Again she pursed her lips, then turned quickly and spoke over her shoulder. "That's all then, for now. You'd better go outside and play for a few minutes. I'll have to keep you after school to write another composition."

But he couldn't play. He was beginning to feel that perhaps he had written lies, and to wonder what Dan or Slim would say if ever they found out. It was all because of Miss Kinley's strange distress. He had never seen it before, and it made him feel guiltier than if she had remained stern and unmoved as usual. "Just the way you spent the day," she pleaded with him after school–"if it's only six or seven lines–" and in response he wrote penitently:

Saturday morning I had breakfast and fed the calves. Then I cut up potatoes into small pieces for planting with my brother Dan, and then we planted them. It was hot. He plowed furrows and I dropped the potatoes in. Then he plowed them over again with more furrows, but first he helped drop potatoes in too. We had a boiled rooster for dinner, because at this time of the year they're too tough any other way. We planted potatoes in the afternoon too till nearly supper-time and then I had to go for the cows. After supper Dan went to town. He wouldn't take me because he was going to take his girl. My back was stiff, so I went to bed. Dan brought me some gum. He said he bought some candies too, but his girl thought they were for her, so I didn't get them.

"It's very good," Miss Kinley said when he was finished. "Why couldn't you have written it in the first place? There–" With a sharp movement she tore out the two sheets of his scribbler on which he had written his first composition. "Run along now–we'll forget all about it."

He did run–hungry, shame-faced, tired–all his pride in a peerless horse become a humble need to draw comfort from a wobbly-legged one. At top speed every step of the mile. Catercorner over the oat field and garden. Straight past the house and on to the stable. Cuffing the pup away and scattering chickens. Until at the box-stall door he paused again–temples throbbing, eyes for a moment closed.

The box-stall was empty. He stared at it rooted with dread, then slapped down the pup and ran desperate around the stable to the pasture gate. But they were there, both with their ears pricked forward looking at him; and at the sight of the white-stockinged legs again he sprang forward shaking with relief. Biddy was patient. For more than a minute she let him worry and hug the colt, pull at its ears and try to lift its forefeet off the ground. Not till he started searching for teeth did she stretch out and nick him neatly with her own in the behind: a reminder that there were proprieties to be observed towards the newborn of even the equines.

It was getting late now. He flung himself down on the grass to lie watching the colt, but a sudden neigh from Biddy told him that the teams must already be coming in from the field. Supper-time – and he still had to go for the cows. Back at the gate for an instant he took one sandwich for himself from his lunch-pail, tossed out everything else for the pup lest his mother think he needed medicine, then set off slowly towards the far end of the pasture.

Slowly because he was tired now – because he had a black, swollen eye, and knew that at the supper-table there would be interminable questions. First the legitimate and reproachful ones of his mother, then the interfering and sarcastic ones of Dan. Dan was like that of late. Clean hands, good table manners, polite answers – ever since he started going with his girl friend – as if all at once it was his responsibility how the whole family behaved.

Peter wondered a little at this as he started the cows for home: how in the last year Dan could have become such a meddlesome old Miss Kinley, and yet at the same time remain among his horses so infallible and true. Too bad that instead of *riding* horses like Slim he just drove them hitched to a cultivator or plough. Peter himself could now drive six abreast – even climb up in the mangers and put their bridles on. Nothing to it – Dan had wasted himself. The way to a really full and virile life, he decided sagely, was never a girl friend and never a compromise with a plough.

When at last he reached the stable Dan and his father had already gone in for supper. He lingered a few minutes, responsive to the stillness and the nuzzling hunger round him, just as that morning when he tiptoed to Biddy's stall in fearful hope of what awaited him. The same hush, the same solemnity. He looked into the stall again, turned quickly from its emptiness and slipped upstairs to the loft.

To be alone a few minutes longer, to feel his way through and beyond this mystery of beginning – all at once it was important, necessary. A little door in the loft that they used for throwing in feed was open, and he sat down on its sill, his legs dangling out against the stable wall. Before him the prairie spread alight with slanting sun and early grain. For a few miles it fell gently, then with a long slow swell slipped over the horizon. There was a state of mind, a mood, a restfulness, in which one could skim along this curve of prairie floor and, gathering momentum from the downward swing, glide up again and soar away from earth. He succeeded now, borne by a white-limbed steed again. And as they soared the mystery was not solved, but gradually absorbed, a mystery still but intimate, a heartening gleam upon the roof of life to let him see its vault and spaciousness.

"Supper," they called him from the house, "supper—we're waiting—" but he wasn't listening. Biddy had come round the corner of the stable, and slowly, to let the colt keep up with her, was cropping her way towards the well. Trim little white-stockinged legs, toy-horse tail, head up as if in consternation at the windmill and the cock-eared pup. And this time yesterday there had been no colt at all. In a single day he had met the Parkers, seen chickens and cows, smelled grass.

"Supper," they called again, Dan's voice now a boom of warning, but just for a moment longer he sat still. Thinking that beyond a doubt the horses had the best of it, awake the first day, nearly half-grown up as soon as they were born. Legs that could walk—eyes that could see. Able to go into and explore a whole new waiting world....It seemed a pity that a boy was never born that way.

Works by Sinclair Ross

FICTION

As for Me and My House. New York: Reynal and Hitchcock, 1941.

The Well. Toronto: Macmillan, 1958.

The Lamp at Noon and Other Stories. Toronto: McClelland and Stewart, 1968.

Whir of Gold. Toronto: McClelland and Stewart, 1970.

Sawbones Memorial. Toronto: McClelland and Stewart, 1974.

The Race and Other Stories. Ottawa: University of Ottawa Press, 1982.

Interview with Sinclair Ross

Saturday Night, 87 (July, 1972), 33-7.

W.O. Mitchell

Because much of his fiction has a prairie setting, W.O. Mitchell is often regarded as a man of the countryside. He was born in 1914 in Weyburn, Saskatchewan, a town of about five thousand people, yet he lived there only the first twelve years of his life and he was, as he has stated, "not a rural person" thereafter. When his widowed mother discovered that her son was suffering from a tubercular arm, she followed a physician's advice to seek a warm climate; she and her son lived in California and Florida, where Mitchell received his high-school education. In 1931 he entered the pre-medical program at the University of Manitoba, later switching to a major in philosophy. He never completed his undergraduate degree at Manitoba, choosing instead to travel in Europe and then to work for the *Seattle Times* in selling and advertising. Taking a course at the University of Washington in short-story writing taught him "that successful writers write about people and places they know." Later he would elaborate upon this lesson: "Art and the writer's life, the illusion that he builds and the life he lives, pretty well have to parallel or twin. Any writers I know spend a great deal of time consistently and evenly every day, every week, every month, lowering a bucket into themselves and everything that they have been. Whatever art illusion the writer creates, the bubble he blows simply has to grow out of the fact that he inhabits a certain place upon the skin of the earth and a certain point in time."

In 1940 Mitchell enrolled at the University of Alberta to take courses in creative writing and to complete his bachelor's degree. He made Alberta his home, accepting teaching positions in composite schools, settling in High River, and embarking on a writing career. In 1947 he published his first novel, *Who Has Seen the Wind*, the tender evocation of young Brian O'Connal's natural curiosity to understand the world around him.

For Mitchell, the first duty of the writer is to capture life. "There are really two hurdles. One hurdle is to plug into and find and work out of life – and not dish off and contrive and carpenter from the top of your head. The second hurdle is more difficult, and most writers never make it. I call this hurdle, 'Life Ain't Art'– . . . What it means, in effect, is that 'Now, kid, the magician doesn't take a live rabbit by magic out of a hat, and there would be a hell of a lot of blood and guts around if he really did saw that lady in half. Now you have to go to the illusion of life'." To capture life is the first step; to transform life into art is the creative challenge confronting the artist.

The prairie world of *Who Has Seen the Wind* is also the setting for Mitchell's most recent novel, *How I Spent My Summer Holidays* (1981). It is the summer of 1924 and twelve-year-old Hughie and his friends are enjoying life in their small prairie town. "That age and the isolated rural village of my boyhood are long, long gone," the elder Hugh narrates as he looks back on his childhood. "Our town lay in the South Saskatchewan prairies, sixty miles north of the Montana border. The superlative sun that shone down on us was Greek; the grass sea around us was our Aegean. I was born there in 1912, the same year the town was born. By 1924 it had grown to almost five thousand people. If you included the population of the Provincial Mental Hospital."

In this excerpt from the novel, Hughie and his friends carve out a cave in the backyard of Austin Musgrave's house. Later in his reminiscences Hughie will tell of digging a second cave, out in the prairie, that came to be occupied by a dangerous escaped patient from the mental hospital. But the sinister implications of the second cave and its inhabitant are not present in this jubilant recollection of one of the most amusing moments from Hughie's summer holidays.

How I Spent
My Summer
Holidays

That summer of 1924 we dug two caves, or rather, *started* one and finished one. Lobbidy Lon Cavanaugh and the Liar and Angus Hannah and Peter Deane-Cooper and Austin Musgrave and I began one in Austin's back yard. Just Peter Deane-Cooper and I dug the second one in Muhlbiers' sheep pasture between the Mental hole and Brokenshell Grove, our own secret one.

The summer of 1924 was unusually hot and dry with no rain through most of May and June so that we spent a great deal of time swimming out at the Mental hole or the CPR hole in the Little Souris River, or lying under somebody's caragana. The day we began the first cave, we had all been in the shade of Musgraves' hedge, wondering whether we should go out to the Mental hole to swim, or to the building site of the new Co-op Creamery to find tar, or north of town to drown out gophers, or over to the sash-and-door factory for scrap lumber to build stilts or to build kites or to build arrow guns, or to the blacksmith shop for horseshoe nails. Someone said it would be fun to dig a cave which would be lovely cool. Austin said we could do it in his back yard and Lobbidy said he had boards so we ought to build it in his yard so we wouldn't have to haul the boards over to Musgraves' yard, and Musgrave said he couldn't leave because his grampa might wake up from his afternoon nap and go out and get lost and he had promised his mother he wouldn't let that happen again, so we'd better dig the cave in his back yard, and if we pitched in right away we'd have the cave finished before his grampa woke up. We agreed to that.

251

Musgrave's house was four blocks south of our house on Sixth Street; the Liar and Angus Hannah lived closer to me, but I suppose I saw more of Musgrave than I did of them or any other boy in town. This was not my choice. I can still see Musgrave's very freckled face snarling into the sun in birthday-party and school-class photos, though not in my Sunday-school picnic pictures, for the Musgraves were Baptist. We were Presbyterian. Peter Deane-Cooper was Anglican. Lobbidy Lon was Catholic. I think the Liar was Methodist.

Musgrave could make me feel warm and liked. He did this by skilfully creating confidentiality, then bonding me by revealing to me how dirty and mean all the other fellows really were, by telling me what they were saying about me behind my back and what they planned to do to me. He once told me, for instance, that Peter Deane-Cooper had got a four-foot length of half-inch galvanized pipe from behind Nickerson's Plumbing and Heating, and that Peter intended to hide in Hannah's caragana, then stick the pipe into the spokes of my bike's front wheel when I rode by. Musgrave would then fill the sick void within me with protestations of undying friendship and promises that from now on he would never play with anybody but me and that I must play with nobody else but him and that he would help me get even with the others. He would not make all that strong an ally, because he couldn't put anybody down and must have known that, for he never *tried* to put anyone down. Male. He ran. He must have been the fastest runner in town or in Saskatchewan or in Canada or in North America. For his age. Musgrave's totem would have to be the wildebeest. Even more fitting, the coyote.

He had a grampa, his mother's father, a tall, ropy octogenarian with buttermilk-blue eyes and the sad and equine face of William S. Hart. I do not know of any film cowboys who came before William S. Hart; he actually pre-dated the cowboy hat itself, later to be worn by Ken Maynard and Hoot Gibson and Tom Mix. William S. Hart's hat was either Boy Scout or RCMP issue, with leather thongs knotted under his chin. We never were given a close shot of William S. Hart's face next to his horse's; you could not have told it from his horse's. Same with Austin's grampa, if he were near a horse.

Musgrave's after-fours and Saturdays were often ruined by his grampa; Sundays had already been damaged for all of us by adults. Musgrave's grampa was always getting lost. He would get out of the house and the yard and wander down the street in his Boy Scout hat, with his cane and with a lumpy knapsack between his shoulder-blades, and Musgrave would have to go all over town, knocking on strange doors and asking people if they'd seen anything of his grampa who had got lost again. That did not work if the old man had made it out onto the prairie beyond the town limits.

Musgrave's grampa seemed to have led a most interesting life; he said he had been imprisoned in Fort Garry by Louis Riel when the Red River Rebellion started, that he was a close friend of Scott, whom Riel executed in 1869. In the Saskatchewan Rebellion, when Louis came back from Montana to lead the half-breeds again, Musgrave's grampa was the first man out of Colonel Boulton's Rangers to set foot in Batoche after it fell. He sat on the jury that condemned Louis Riel to hang in 1885. By using simple arithmetic and his age, you knew he could have done all these things, and I believed him till Musgrave said his grampa was an historical liar. I still thought he was interesting.

No one was ever able to get behind the old man: he always sat in a corner with the two walls meeting behind his back; this was so in the Musgrave house or anywhere else. Musgrave's mother had to cut her father's hair and shave him because he refused to sit in Leon's barber chair, his back unprotected in the Royal Pool Hall. If he met someone on the street and stopped to talk, he must have felt vulnerable, for he would always circle uneasily until he had a building wall or a hedge or a fence at his back. Sometimes he would have to settle just for a telephone pole.

He had a very sensible reason for this: "They're comin' to get me one day!" It was never quite clear to me *who* was coming to get him one day, though I had my suspicions. Whoever it was pretty nearly had to be a half-breed and a close relative or friend of Louis Riel.

I sincerely believed that someone was after him; nobody would have spent as much time as he did out in the Musgrave privy, if someone weren't coming to get him one day. From the May meadowlark when the sun had got high and strong to fall harvest he spent more time out there, with four walls closing safe around him, than he did in the house. I can hardly recall a visit to Musgraves' that there wasn't blue smoke breathing from the diamond cut-out in their backhouse door. We had inside plumbing.

Another thing about Musgrave's grampa: he had saliva trouble. It was as though his glands manufactured it perpetually so that he had to keep gathering it and gathering it until his mouth had a full cargo of it, then he would shake his head violently from side to side and spit. He did this about every thirty seconds. In the house there were spittoons for him, which Musgrave had to empty every other day. Whenever you saw Austin's grampa going down Sixth Street his expectoration rate was about once to every hundred paces and always on alternating sides. Whoever was coming to get him one day would simply have to follow the saliva trail he left.

The summer of 1924 was a year after Peter Deane-Cooper had migrated to Canada with his family from England. Like me he was an only child. His father was an engineer with the company doing coal strip-mining along the Montana border. All through his first Canadian winter, even in forty-below weather, Peter's mother kept him wearing short English stove-pipe pants, with knee socks that had a length of ribbon hanging down from them just like bookmarkers. Peter had blue knees all that winter.

To make our cave we all carried boards over from Lobbidy's, went home for our own round-nosed shovel or spade or pick or garden fork or bar. Like the gopher and the coyote, the badger and the weasel, we were all digging animals; with the prairie tree situation we pretty well had no choice. Our cave-digging technique never varied: first the sod squares had to be cut out with a spade, then carefully laid aside so that they could be placed back over the cave roof later in exactly the same relationship they'd initially had to each other. After the cave had been dug deep enough, boards would be laid across the excavation, the soil spread out over the boards and tramped down, the sods replaced. The result would be only a slight earth swelling. We hoped. As well we would dig a narrow trench, cover it with short boards, and camouflage the resulting tunnel in the same way we had done the cave itself. Nowhere in *A Thousand Things a Boy Can Do* is this cave-digging method mentioned.

Shovel and spade and fork plunged easily through the eighteen inches of topsoil in Musgraves' back yard, but when we got down to the hardpan the clay was heart- and back-breaking. Rock hard, in this dry year, it loosened under pick and bar in reluctant sugar-lumps. Stinging with sweat, we rested often, reclining at the edge of our shallow excavation.

"If a fellow only had a fresno and a team, he could really scoop her out." That was Lobbidy.

"If a fellow could soak her good," the Liar said, "run her full of water—soften her up..."

"Easy digging then," Angus said.

"Yeah!" I said.

"If a fellow could only blow her out," the Liar said.

"How?" I said.

"Search me," Lobbidy said.

"Stumping-powder—dynamite." That was the Liar again.

"It's our yard."

"Oh yes—indeed—dynamite." Peter always spoke with that polite English accent that English people always have. In southern Saskatchewan they certainly do.

"Whump an' she'd blow our cave for us," the Liar said.

"It's not your yard!"

"She sure would," Lobbidy said.

"Only place I know–where they got dynamite–CPR sheds," the Liar said.

"We can't go swiping dynamite," Angus said.

"I tell you–it's our back yard!"

"I can get you dynamite." Up until Peter said that I had been thinking how stupid Musgrave was to keep right on saying it was his back yard. He ought to know that dynamite simply did not belong in our world, that it was quite *imaginary* dynamite we had been tossing around in conversation. But now I knew that Deane-Cooper meant *real* dynamite, and I felt sick.

"We can't go swiping dynamite." Angus must have felt sick too; he knew just as well as I did that if Peter Deane-Cooper said he could get you dynamite, he not only *could* get you dynamite, you could not *stop* him from getting you dynamite.

"We don't know a thing about handling dynamite," I said.

"I do."

"I think it's a great idea!" The Liar would think that! "Why not?"

"We might wake up Musgrave's grampa." Somehow, even as I said that, I knew there must be a better reason for us not to set off dynamite in Musgraves' back yard.

"Had most of his nap by now–hasn't he?" Peter got up. He said to Austin, "Are you frightened?"

"Uh–no." Musgrave was lying. "Won't it be dangerous?"

"No."

"Why won't it be?" I said.

"In the first place–our cave location. There's nothing dangerously near it at all. Over sixty yards from the back porch." That was true. Our cave site was about halfway between the Musgrave house and the Musgrave backhouse, beyond which there was open prairie. To the right and a good hundred feet away was a pile of wood chunks, perhaps four cords of them. Not stacked. Just in a heap. Almost the same distance on the other side were two clothes-line poles. "In the second place," Peter was saying, "I'm very good with dynamite. I helped my father–in the old country."

"We can't go swiping dynamite," Angus said.

"My father has a whole case of sixty percent in the garage. You– Lobbidy–have them do the hole."

"I'll come with you," the Liar said, the skunk!

"What hole?" Lobbidy said.

"For the dynamite–with the bar–straight down about four foot, I should say."

"I'll come with you."

"Whole damn case?" Lobbidy said.

"Dead centre–the hole." Peter and the Liar were already heading for the Deane-Cooper garage.

"Is he bringing back a whole case?" Angus's face was worried.

"Damn the Liar!" Lobbidy said.

I agreed with him. If the Liar hadn't been so enthusiastic about the dynamite, maybe Peter wouldn't have insisted we blow our cave.

"Anything happens it's his fault just as much as Peter's." Musgrave always knew whose fault everything was.

We never called Russell Matheson the Liar to his face. He lied a great deal. There was nothing *useful* about his lies; he was a pure liar. Strangler Lewis, he said, was his uncle. On his mother's side. The Minister of Agriculture, Federal, was his uncle too. Also by marriage. Another uncle had invented the Eskimo pie. He had an older sister, much older, who had grown up and left the Matheson family to be a missionary in India. Her name was Vera and she seemed quite important to the Liar, for the way he always said her name made me think of Rogers' Golden Corn Syrup pouring. Vera was brilliant. Vera possessed a brain three times larger than your average human brain, and indeed scientists in Germany had already made arrangements to get her brain for study purposes. After she died. I never ever saw the Liar's sister, Vera, but if she ever came home on sabbatical from the mission fields of India, I knew I'd sure as hell recognize her even at a long distance, with that great big, puffed-up head three times larger than normal.

I preferred the Liar to Musgrave; if the Liar said something mean about you, it didn't damage you, because everybody knew that nine times out of ten he was lying. He always smelled like sheep because he had eczema and the ointment for it must have had a lanolin base. The very fact that he never said his eczema ointment was made out of sheep would lead a person to believe that was a true explanation of why he always smelled like a sheep.

With the Liar it was hard to tell whether he even had an older sister named Vera.

The hole went down rather slowly until Peter and the Liar returned with the dynamite. Three sticks. Peter just tossed them on the ground and took over authority. He did twice his share of punching down the dynamite hole, stopping only to estimate how much further we had left to go down. When it suited him, he dropped two of the sticks down, one on top of the other. There was no tenderness in the way he handled that dynamite. Besides the three sticks he had brought back a length of fuse and a copper tube, which he explained was a detonator; then he crimped it with his teeth. He used a spike to work a hole in the third stick of dynamite to receive the cap and fuse. He sure as hell told the truth when he said he was very good with dynamite.

We watched him shove loose clay in around the sticks, then tamp it firm with the bar. With his jack-knife he split the free end of the fuse protruding from the ground. He took a match from his pocket.

"Hold on a minute!" Musgrave said. "Where do we–what do we–how long do we…"

"Once it's going there should be three minutes. Plenty of time to take cover."

"What cover!" I said.

"Round the corner of the house, I suggest. You may go there now if you wish. I shall come when the fuse is ignited. They're rather difficult to start, you know–it might take several matches."

We all stayed. The fuse took only three matches. Then we ran and we threw ourselves round the corner of the Musgrave house and looked back. Peter had not run with us; he was still coming. He did it by strolling–with his hands in those sissy-looking English pants of his.

The way it told you how in *A Thousand Things a Boy Can Do*, I had begun to count to myself so that I would have a rough notion of when the three minutes would be up. I had reached fifty-and-nine when we heard the Musgrave screen door slap the afternoon stillness.

Lobbidy said, "Judas priest!"

Angus said, "He's headed for the backhouse!"

"He's got his knapsack and his Boy Scout hat and his cane on," I said. "Maybe he's just going out to get lost!"

Musgrave started round the corner of the house, but Lobbidy grabbed him back. "Let him keep going, Musgrave! Let him keep going so's he'll get into the clear!"

"He's my grampa!"

"I shall get him!"

"There ain't even one minute left!" Lobbidy said. That stopped Peter.

I had no way of telling if Lobbidy was right, for I had stopped counting as soon as the Musgrave screen door had slapped.

"He's stopped!" Angus yelled.

He had–right between the clothes-line poles and the woodpile, on our side of the project, which meant he was no more than twelve feet from the sputtering fuse. I don't think he stopped because of our digging, but to gather spit. He shook his head and spit.

Peter launched himself round the corner of the house, and belly to the ground he ran up behind Austin's grampa. *Behind* that old man. Musgrave's grampa heard the running footsteps coming from *behind* him. They *had* finally come to get him!

He did not even look back to see who it was. After all these years I suppose he still had a pretty clear idea of who it would be. With Peter close behind him, he set a new octogenarian thirty-yard-dash record, and not the one for level ground, either: both of them hurdled the pile of sods, into and then across, then up and out of our excavation, then on to the privy. The old man jumped to safety inside and pulled the door shut. Without missing a stride, Peter pounded past and out to the prairie beyond. Out there he was still running with his head back, chin out, arms pumping, knees high, when the three sticks of sixty-percent dynamite let go.

The first effect was not sound at all. Initially the Musgrave yard was taken by one giant and subterranean hiccup; an earth fountain spouted; the four cords of wood took flight; the two clothes-line posts javelined into the air, their wires still stretched between them in an incredible aerial cat's-cradle. And the privy. And Musgrave's grampa. They leapt. Straight up. I think the bottom of the backhouse must have lifted six feet from ground level.

The privy was the first thing to return to earth, and when it fell its descent obeyed Newton's Law of Falling Backhouses, which says: "A falling privy shall always come to rest upon the door side." The corollary: "A loved one trapped within cannot be taken out on the vertical, only through the hole and upon the horizontal."

After the lambasting explosion we looked at each other wildly; we swallowed to unbung our ears, heard the lovely Japanese chiming of glass shards dropping from every Musgrave house window, the thud of wood chunks returning to earth. I saw Musgrave lick with the tip of his tongue at a twin blood yarn unravelling from his nostrils. No one said anything; we simply moved as a confused body in the direction of the backhouse. And Musgrave's grampa.

We had to go out and around the great, shallow saucer the dynamite had blown in Musgraves' back yard, and I remember thinking, "They're never going to ever fill that in." How could they? To get the thousands of cubic feet of dirt to fill that crater, they would have to dig another hole to get an equal quantity of dirt to fill in the new hole. And another–and another–

It was not all that deep, possibly four feet at the centre, but it was wide; if we had completed the project it would have taken all the lumber from a grain elevator to roof it in. I'm certain it would have been the biggest cave dug in southern Saskatchewan that summer.

It took all of us to upright the privy and Musgrave's grampa. When we opened the door to let the poor old man out, he was not grateful. He swung at us with his cane a couple of times before he would let Musgrave and Lobiddy help him to the house and into his room off the kitchen. Seated there on a Winnipeg couch, he stared straight ahead as Musgrave removed his Boy Scout hat, slipped off his knapsack, then with an arm around the old man's shoulders eased him down on the pillow. He motioned us out of the room.

We were all whipped, of course; it was difficult to keep a thing like that quiet. As well, each of us was quarantined in his own yard. Until then the maximum punishment had been one week. Peter and the Liar and Lobbidy Lon and Angus and I received two-week sentences. Austin got three. Since it was summer holidays the punishment was much more severe than during a school term, when classes would have been a daily reprieve from nine to four. Actually I served a week, Peter the same time. Lobbidy did only four days, unless they trapped him in his grandmother's yard in Havre down in Montana, where he always spent his vacations. Musgrave had to finish the whole sentence, of course.

Works by W.O. Mitchell

FICTION

Who Has Seen the Wind. Toronto: Macmillan, 1947.
Jake and the Kid. Toronto: Macmillan, 1961.
The Kite. Toronto: Macmillan, 1962.
The Vanishing Point. Toronto: Macmillan, 1973.
How I Spent My Summer Holidays. Toronto: Macmillan, 1981.

DRAMA

The Black Bonspiel of Wullie MacCrimmon. Calgary: Frontiers Unlimited, 1965.
The Devil's Instrument. Toronto: Simon and Pierre, 1973.
Dramatic W.O. Mitchell. Toronto: Macmillan, 1982.

Interviews with W.O. Mitchell

Canadian Literature, 14 (Autumn, 1962), 53-6.
Conversations with Canadian Novelists. Edited by Donald Cameron. Toronto: Macmillan, 1973. Vol. 2, pp. 48-63.
Essays on Canadian Writing, 20 (Winter, 1980-81), 149-59.

Jack Hodgins

In "The Concert Stages of Europe," Barclay Philip Desmond is a red-blooded, thirteen-year-old from a logging and farming settlement on Vancouver Island. His artistic temperament makes him shy; his six-foot, two-inch frame makes him awkward. He "trips over his own bike in front of your house, falls up your bottom step, blushes red with embarrassment when you open the door, and tells you he wants your money for a talent contest so he can become a Great Artist."

Like Barclay, Jack Hodgins was born (1938) in the Comox Valley on Vancouver Island, the son of a logger and the grandson of pioneer farmers. He grew up in Merville, a small rural community of loggers and farmers between Courtenay and Campbell River. From an early age he wanted to be a writer: "My mother contributed a very strong sense that you could do whatever you wanted—if you wanted it badly enough. The fact that I wanted to be something ludicrous and impossible like a writer didn't seem to faze her. Her stock answer whenever I ran out of reading matter was, 'Well, go write your own.' I did. I thought it was sort of a sarcastic, flippant remark, but she meant it, I'm sure. And that might be what motivates my whole life. I'm trying to write the books that nobody else has written for me to read."

In his four books, *Spit Delaney's Island* (1976), *The Invention of the World* (1977), *The Resurrection of Joseph Bourne* (1979), and *The Barclay Family Theatre* (1981), Hodgins captures the unique world of Vancouver Island with comedy and pathos. Vancouver Island is the edge of the world, a frontier society, constantly aware that the rest of the country is to one side of it.

For Hodgins, the essence of fiction is to capture the reality of the characters, to make the reader "believe that the person who is talking to him is real." Though critics have tried to define his fiction with various labels, "realistic" remains the most appropriate. "Reality to me," Hodgins confesses, "isn't the same thing as it is to some of the other people. . . . Each of us sees the world according to his own particular vision. What I write is to me 'realistic,' though not everyone thinks I'm describing 'reality.' I'm often considered weird or almost surrealistic, though I never write about anything that I don't want people to believe quite literally."

Though Hodgins is not inclined to incorporate autobiography into his fiction, *The Barclay Family Theatre* does borrow and then embellish some episodes from his own upbringing, and the opening chapter, "The Concert Stages of Europe," involves an incident that actually happened to him as a boy. "I'm one of those people," Hodgins admits, "who like being put in the spotlight but are also absolutely terrified by it. After I'd been taking piano lessons for several years, I learned about an amateur show on a Vancouver radio station. If you got past the audition, you had to go around collecting votes from people, which cost a dollar each. The grand prize was a trip to Hawaii." He joined in wholeheartedly: "Part of me was shrivelling every time I knocked on a door; the other part was really looking forward to the contest on the radio. There were about thirteen contenders. The show was held in a movie theatre, and there was even a clapping machine. I played the piano on the radio and came in fourth. I was also in plays. I was the lead, Prince So-True, in *Princess Chrysanthemum*, the high-school operetta. I always hated the part I was playing and wondered, 'What am I doing here? They're all going to walk out or laugh at me'."

Like Hodgins himself, Barclay grew up to be a novelist.

The Concert Stages of Europe

Now I know Cornelia Horncastle would say I'm blaming the wrong person. I know that. I know too that she would say thirty years is a long time to hold a grudge, and that if I needed someone to blame for the fact that I made a fool of myself in front of the whole district and ruined my life in the process, then I ought to look around for the person who gave me my high-flown ideas in the first place. But she would be wrong; because there is no doubt I'd have led a different sort of life if it weren't for her, if it weren't for that piano keyboard her parents presented her with on her eleventh birthday. And everything–everything would have been different if that piano keyboard hadn't been the kind made out of stiff paper that you unfolded and laid out across the kitchen table in order to do your practising.

I don't suppose there would have been all that much harm in her having the silly thing, if only my mother hadn't got wind of it. What a fantastic idea, she said. You could learn to play without even making a sound! You could practise your scales without having to hear that awful racket when you hit a wrong note! A genius must have thought of it, she said. Certainly someone who'd read his Keats: *Heard melodies are sweet, but those unheard are sweeter*. "And don't laugh," she said, "because Cornelia Horncastle is learning to play the piano and her mother doesn't even have to miss an episode of *Ma Perkins* while she does it."

That girl, people had told her, would be giving concerts in Europe some day, command performances before royalty, and her parents hadn't even had to fork out the price of a piano. It was obvious proof, if you needed it, that a person didn't have to be rich to get somewhere in this world.

In fact, Cornelia's parents hadn't needed to put out even the small amount that paper keyboard would have cost. A piano teacher named Mrs. Humphries had moved onto the old Dendoff place and, discovering that almost no one in the district owned a piano, gave the keyboard to the Horncastles along with a year's free lessons. It was her idea, apparently, that when everyone heard how quickly Cornelia was learning they'd be lining up to send her their children for lessons. She wanted to make the point that having no piano needn't stop anyone from becoming a pianist. No doubt she had a vision of paper keyboards in every house in Waterville, of children everywhere thumping their scales out on the kitchen table without offending anyone's ears, of a whole generation turning silently into Paderewskis without ever having played a note.

They would, I suppose, have to play a real piano when they went to her house for lessons once a week, but I was never able to find out for myself, because all that talk of Cornelia's marvellous career on the concert stages of Europe did not prompt my parents to buy one of those fake keyboards or sign me up for lessons with Mrs. Humphries. My mother was born a Barclay, which meant she had a few ideas of her own, and Cornelia's glorious future prompted her to go one better. We would buy a *real* piano, she announced. And I would be sent to a teacher we could trust, not to that newcomer. If those concert stages of Europe were ever going to hear the talent of someone from the stump ranches of Waterville, it wouldn't be Cornelia Horncastle, it would be Barclay Desmond. Me.

My father nearly choked on his coffee. "But Clay's a boy!"

"So what?" my mother said. *All* those famous players used to be boys. What did he think Chopin was? Or Tchaikovsky?

My father was so embarrassed that his throat began to turn a dark pink. Some things were too unnatural even to think about.

But eventually she won him over. "Think how terrible you'd feel," she said, "if he ended up in the bush, like you. If Mozart's father had worked for the Comox Logging Company and thought piano-playing was for sissies, where would the world be today?"

My father had no answer to that. He'd known since before his marriage that though my mother would put up with being married to a logger, expecting every day to be made a widow, she wouldn't tolerate for one minute the notion that a child of hers would follow him up into those hills. The children of Lenora Barclay would enter the professions.

She was right, he had to agree; working in the woods was the last thing in the world he wanted for his sons. He'd rather they take up ditch-digging or begging than have to work for that miserable logging company,...or get their skulls cracked open like Stanley Kirck. It was a rotten way to make a living, and if he'd only had a decent education he could have made something of himself.

Of course, I knew he was saying all this just for my mother's benefit. He didn't really believe it for a minute. My father loved his work. I could tell by the way he was always talking about Ab Jennings and Shorty Cresswell, the men he worked with. I could tell by the excitement that mounted in him every year as the time grew near for the annual festival of loggers' sports where he usually won the bucking contest. It was obvious, I thought, that the man really wanted nothing more in this world than that one of his sons should follow in his footsteps. And much as I disliked the idea, I was sure that I was the one he'd set his hopes on. Kenny was good in school. Laurel was a girl. I was the obvious choice. I even decided that what he'd pegged me for was high-rigger. I was going to be one of those men who risked their necks climbing hundreds of feet up the bare lonely spar tree to hang the rigging from the top. Of course I would fall and kill myself the first time I tried it, I knew that, but there was no way I could convey my hesitation to my father since he would never openly admit that this was really his goal for me.

And playing the piano on the concert stages of Europe was every bit as unattractive. "Why not Kenny?" I said, when the piano had arrived, by barge, from Vancouver.

"He's too busy already with his school work," my mother said. Kenny was hoping for a scholarship, which meant he got out of just about everything unpleasant.

"What about Laurel?"

"With her short fat fingers?"

In the meantime, she said, though she was no piano-player herself (a great sigh here for what might have been), she had no trouble at all identifying which of those ivory keys was the all-important Middle C and would show it to me, to memorize, so that I wouldn't look like a total know-nothing when I showed up tomorrow for my first lesson. She'd had one piano lesson herself as a girl, she told me, and had learned all about Mister Middle C, but she'd never had a second lesson because her time was needed by her father, outside, helping with the chores. Seven daughters altogether, no sons, and she was the one who was the most often expected to fill the role of a boy. The rest of them had found the time to learn chords and chromatic scales and all those magic things she'd heard them practising while she was scrubbing out the dairy and cutting the runners off strawberry plants. They'd all become regular show-offs in one way or another, learning other instruments as well, putting on their own concerts and playing in dance bands and earning a reputation all over the district as entertaining livewires–The Barclay Sisters. And no one ever guessed that all the while she was dreaming about herself at that keyboard, tinkling away, playing beautiful music before huge audiences in elegant theatres.

"Then it isn't me that should be taking lessons," I said. "It's you."

"Don't be silly." But she walked to the new piano and pressed down one key, a black one, and looked as if I'd tempted her there for a minute. "It's too late now," she said. And then she sealed my fate: "But I just know that you're going to be a great pianist."

When my mother "just knew" something, that was as good as guaranteeing it already completed. It was her way of controlling the future and, incidentally, the rest of us. By "just knowing" things, she went through life commanding the future to fit into certain patterns she desired while we scurried around making sure that it worked out that way so she'd never have to be disappointed. She'd had one great disappointment as a girl–we were never quite sure what it was, since it was only alluded to in whispers with far-off looks–and it was important that it never happen again. I was trapped.

People were always asking what you were going to be when you grew up. As if your wishes counted. In the first six years of my life the country had convinced me it wanted me to grow up and get killed fighting Germans and Japanese. I'd seen the coils of barbed wire along the beach and knew they were there just to slow down the enemy while I went looking for my gun. The teachers at school obviously wanted me to grow up and become a teacher just like them, because as far as I could see nothing they ever taught me could be of any use or interest to a single adult in the world except someone getting paid to teach it to someone else. My mother was counting on my becoming a pianist with a swallow-tail coat and standing ovations. And my father, despite all his noises to the contrary, badly wanted me to climb into the crummy every morning with him and ride out those gravelly roads into mountains and risk my life destroying forests.

I did not want to be a logger. I did not want to be a teacher. I did not want to be a soldier. And I certainly did not want to be a pianist. If anyone had ever asked me what I did want to be when I grew up, in a way that meant they expected the truth, I'd have said quite simply that what I wanted was to be a Finn.

Our new neighbors, the Korhonens, were Finns. And being a Finn, I'd been told, meant something very specific. A Finn would give you the shirt off his back, a Finn was as honest as the day is long, a Finn could drink anybody under the table and beat up half a dozen Germans and Irishmen without trying, a Finn was not afraid of work, a Finn kept a house so clean you could eat off the floors. I knew all these things before ever meeting our neighbors, but as soon as I had met them I was able to add a couple more generalizations of my own to the catalogue: Finnish girls were blonde and beautiful and flirtatious, and Finnish boys were strong, brave, and incredibly intelligent. These conclusions were reached immediately after meeting Lilja Korhonen, whose turned-up nose and blue eyes fascinated me from the beginning, and Larry Korhonen, who was already a teenager and told me for starters that he was actually Superman, having learned to fly after long hours of practice off their barn roof. Mr. And Mrs. Korhonen, of course, fitted exactly all the things my parents had told me about Finns in general. And so I decided my ambition in life was to be just like them.

I walked over to their house every Saturday afternoon and pretended to read their colored funnies. I got in on the weekly steam-bath with Larry and his father in the sauna down by the barn. Mr. Korhonen, a patient man whose eyes sparkled at my eager attempts, taught me to count to ten—*yksi, kaksi, kolme, nelja, viisi, kuusi, seitseman, kahdeksan, yhdeksan, kymmenen.* I helped Mrs. Korhonen scrub her linoleum floors and put down newspapers so no one could walk on them, then I gorged myself on cinnamon cookies and *kala loota* and coffee sucked through a sugar cube. If there was something to be caught from just being around them, I wanted to catch it. And since being a Finn seemed to be a full-time occupation, I didn't have much patience with my parents, who behaved as if there were other things you had to prepare yourself for.

The first piano teacher they sent me to was Aunt Jessie, who lived in a narrow, cramped house up a gravel road that led to the mountains. She'd learned to play as a girl in Toronto, but she had no pretensions about being a real teacher, she was only doing this as a favor to my parents so they wouldn't have to send me to that Mrs. Humphries, an outsider. But one of the problems was that Aunt Jessie—who was no aunt of mine at all, simply one of those family friends who somehow get saddled with an honorary family title—was exceptionally beautiful. She was so attractive, in fact, that even at the age of ten I had difficulty keeping my eyes or my mind on my lessons. She exuded a dreamy sort of delicate femininity; her soft, intimate voice made the hair on the back of my neck stand on end. Besides that, her own playing was so much more pleasant to listen to than my own stumbling clangs and clunks that she would often begin to show me how to do something and become so carried away with the sound of her own music that she just kept right on playing through the rest of my half-hour. It was a simple matter to persuade her to dismiss me early every week so that I'd have a little time to play in the creek that ran past the back of her house, poling a homemade raft up and down the length of her property while her daughters paid me nickels and candies for a ride. At the end of a year my parents suspected I wasn't progressing as fast as I should. They found out why on the day I fell in the creek and nearly drowned, had to be revived by a distraught Aunt Jessie, and was driven home soaked and shivering in the back seat of her old Hudson.

Mr. Korhonen and my father were huddled over the taken-apart cream separator on the verandah when Aunt Jessie brought me up to the door. My father, when he saw me, had that peculiar look on his face that was halfway between amusement and concern, but Mr. Korhonen laughed openly. "That boy lookit like a drowny rat."

I felt like a drowned rat too, but I joined his laughter. I was sure this would be the end of my piano career, and could hardly wait to see my mother roll her eyes to the ceiling, throw out her arms, and say, "I give up."

She did nothing of the sort. She tightened her lips and told Aunt Jessie how disappointed she was. "No wonder the boy still stumbles around on that keyboard like a blindfolded rabbit; he's not going to learn the piano while he's out risking his life on the *river*!"

When I came downstairs in dry clothes Aunt Jessie had gone, no doubt wishing she'd left me to drown in the creek, and my parents and the Korhonens were all in the kitchen drinking coffee. The Korhonens sat at either side of the table, smoking hand-rolled cigarettes and squinting at me through the smoke. Mrs. Korhonen could blow beautiful white streams down her nostrils. They'd left their gumboots on the piece of newspaper just inside the door, of course, and wore the same kind of grey work-socks on their feet that my father always wore on his. My father was leaning against the wall with both arms folded across his chest inside his wide elastic braces, as he sometimes did, swishing his mug gently as if he were trying to bring something up from the bottom. My mother, however, was unable to alight anywhere. She slammed wood down into the firebox of the stove, she rattled dishes in the sink water, she slammed cupboard doors, she went around the room with the coffee pot, refilling mugs, and all the while she sang the song of her betrayal, cursing her own stupidity for sending me to a friend instead of to a professional teacher, and suddenly in a flash of inspiration dumping all the blame on my father: "If you hadn't made me feel it was somehow pointless I wouldn't have felt guilty about spending more money!"

From behind the drifting shreds of smoke Mr. Korhonen grinned at me. Sucked laughter between his teeth. "Yust *teenk*, boy, looks like-it you're saved!"

Mrs. Korhonen stabbed out her cigarette in an ashtray, picked a piece of tobacco off her tongue, and composed her face into the most serious and ladylike expression she could muster. "Yeh! Better he learn to drive the tractor." And swung me a conspirator's grin.

"Not on your life," my mother said. Driving a machine may have been a good enough ambition for some people, she believed, but the Barclays had been in this country for four generations and she knew there were a few things higher. "What we'll do is send him to a real teacher. Mrs. Greensborough."

Mrs. Greensborough was well known for putting on a public recital in town once a year, climaxing the program with her own rendition of Grieg's Piano Concerto–so beautiful that all went home, it was said, with tears in their eyes. The problem with Mrs. Greensborough had nothing to do with her teaching. She was, as far as I could see, an excellent piano teacher. And besides, there was something rather exciting about playing on her piano, which was surrounded and nearly buried by a thousand tropical plants and dozens of cages full of squawking birds. Every week's lesson was rather like putting on a concert in the midst of the Amazon jungle. There was even a monkey that swung through the branches and sat on the top of the piano with the metronome between its paws. And Mrs. Greensborough was at the same time warm and demanding, complimentary and hard to please–though given a little, like Aunt Jessie, to taking off on long passages of her own playing, as if she'd forgotten I was there.

It took a good hour's hard bicycling on uphill gravel roads before I could present myself for the lesson–past a dairy farm, a pig farm, a turkey farm, a dump, and a good long stretch of bush–then more washboard road through heavy timber where driveways disappeared into the trees and one dog after another lay in wait for its weekly battle with my right foot. Two spaniels, one Irish setter, and a bulldog. But it wasn't a spaniel or a setter or even a bulldog that met me on the driveway of the Greensboroughs' chicken farm, it was a huge German shepherd that came barking down the slope the second I had got the gate shut, and stuck its nose into my crotch. And kept it there, growling menacingly, the whole time it took me to back him up to the door of the house. There was no doubt in my mind that I would come home from piano lesson one Saturday minus a few parts. Once I had got to the house, I tried to get inside quickly and shut the door in his face, leaving him out there in the din of cackling hens; but he always got his nose between the door and the jamb, growled horribly and pushed himself inside so that he could lie on the floor at my feet and watch me hungrily the whole time I sat at the kitchen table waiting for Ginny Stamp to finish off her lesson and get out of there. By the time my turn came around my nerves were too frayed for me to get much benefit out of the lesson.

Still, somehow I learned. That Mrs. Greensborough was a marvellous teacher, my mother said. The woman really knew her stuff. And I was such a fast-learning student that it took less than two years for my mother to begin thinking it was time the world heard from me.

"Richy Ryder," she said, "is coming to town."

"What?"

"Richy Ryder, CJMT. *The Talent Show.*"

I'd heard the program. Every Saturday night Richy Ryder was in a different town somewhere in the province, hosting his one-hour talent contest from the stage of a local theatre and giving away free trips to Hawaii.

Something rolled over in my stomach.

"And here's the application form right here," she said, whipping two sheets of paper out of her purse to slap down on the table.

"No thank you," I said. If she thought I was going in it, she was crazy.

"Don't be silly. What harm is there in trying?" My mother always answered objections with great cheerfulness, as if they were hardly worth considering.

"I'll make a fool of myself."

"You play beautifully," she said. "It's amazing how far you've come in only two years. And besides, even if you don't win, the experience would be good for you."

"You have to go door-to-door ahead of time, begging for pledges, for money."

"Not begging," she said. She plunged her hands into the sink, peeling carrots so fast I couldn't see the blade of the vegetable peeler. "Just giving people a chance to vote for you. A dollar a vote." The carrot dropped, skinned naked, another one was picked up. She looked out the window now toward the barn and, still smiling, delivered the argument that never failed. "I just know you'd win it if you went in, I can feel it in my bones."

"Not this time!" I shouted, nearly turning myself inside out with the terror. "Not this time, I just can't do it."

Yet somehow I found myself riding my bicycle up and down all the roads around Waterville, knocking at people's doors, explaining the contest, and asking for their money and their votes. I don't know why I did it. Perhaps I was doing it for the same reason I was tripping over everything, knocking things off tables, slamming my shoulder into doorjambs; I just couldn't help it, everything had gone out of control. I'd wakened one morning that year and found myself six feet two inches tall and as narrow as a fence stake. My feet were so far away they seemed to have nothing to do with me. My hands flopped around on the ends of those lanky arms like fish, something alive. My legs had grown so fast the bones in my knees parted and I had to wear elastic bandages to keep from falling apart. When I turned a corner on my bicycle, one knee would bump the handlebar, throwing me into the ditch. I was the same person as before, apparently, saddled with this new body I didn't know what to do with. Everything had gone out of control. I seemed to have nothing to do with the direction of my own life. It was perfectly logical that I should end up playing the piano on the radio, selling myself to the countryside for a chance to fly off to Hawaii and lie on the sand under the whispering palms.

There were actually two prizes offered. The all-expense, ten-day trip to Hawaii would go to the person who brought in the most votes for himself, a dollar a vote. But lest someone accuse the radio station of getting its values confused, there was also a prize for the person judged by a panel of experts to have the most talent. This prize, which was donated by Nelson's Hardware, was a leatherette footstool.

"It's not the prize that's important," people told me. "It's the chance to be heard by all those people."

I preferred not to think of all those people. It seemed to me that if I were cut out to be a concert pianist it would be my teacher and not my parents encouraging me in this thing. Mrs. Greensborough, once she'd forked over her two dollars for two votes, said nothing at all. No doubt she was hoping I'd keep her name out of it.

But it had taken no imagination on my part to figure out that if I were to win the only prize worth trying for, the important thing was not to spend long hours at the keyboard, practising, but to get out on the road hammering at doors, on the telephone calling relatives, down at the General Store approaching strangers who stopped for gas. Daily piano practice shrank to one or two quick run-throughs of "The Robin's Return," school homework shrank to nothing at all, and home chores just got ignored. My brother and sister filled in for me, once in a while, so the chickens wouldn't starve to death and the woodbox would never be entirely empty, but they did it gracelessly. It was amazing, they said, how much time a great pianist had to spend out on the road, meeting his public. Becoming famous, they said, was more work than it was worth.

And becoming famous, I discovered, was what people assumed I was after. "You'll go places," they told me. "You'll put this place on the old map." I was a perfect combination of my father's down-to-earth get-up-and-go and my mother's finer sensitivity, they said. How wonderful to see a young person with such high ambition!

"I always knew this old place wouldn't be good enough to hold you," my grandmother said as she fished out a five-dollar bill from her purse. But my mother's sisters, who appeared from all parts of the old farm-house in order to contribute a single collective vote, had some reservations to express. Eleanor, the youngest, said she doubted I'd be able to carry it off, I'd probably freeze when I was faced with a microphone, I'd forget what a piano was for. Christina announced she was betting I'd faint, or have to run out to the bathroom right in the middle of my piece. And Mabel, red-headed Mabel who'd played accordion once in an amateur show, said she remembered a boy who made such a fool of himself in one of these things that he went home and blew off his head. "Don't be so morbid," my grandmother said. "The boy probably had no talent. Clay here is destined for higher things."

From behind her my grandfather winked. He seldom had a chance to contribute more than that to a conversation. He waited until we were alone to stuff a five-dollar bill in my pocket and squeeze my arm.

I preferred my grandmother's opinion of me to the aunts'. I began to feed people lies so they'd think that about me–that I was destined for dizzying heights. I wanted to be a great pianist, I said, and if I won that trip to Hawaii I'd trade it in for the money so that I could go off and study at the Toronto Conservatory. I'd heard of the Toronto Conservatory only because it was printed in big black letters on the front cover of all those yellow books of finger exercises I was expected to practise.

I don't know why people gave me their money. Pity, perhaps. Maybe it was impossible to say no to a six-foot-two-inch thirteen-year-old who trips over his own bike in front of your house, falls up your bottom step, blushes red with embarrassment when you open the door, and tells you he wants your money for a talent contest so he can become a Great Artist. At any rate, by the day of the contest I'd collected enough money to put me in the third spot. I would have to rely on pledges from the studio audience and phone-in pledges from the radio audience to rocket me up to first place. The person in second place when I walked into that theatre to take my seat down front with the rest of the contestants was Cornelia Horncastle.

I don't know how she managed it so secretly. I don't know where she found the people to give her money, living in the same community as I did, unless all those people who gave me their dollar bills when I knocked on their doors had just given her two the day before. Maybe she'd gone into town, canvassing street after street, something my parents wouldn't let me do on the grounds that town people already had enough strangers banging on their doors every day. Once I'd got outside the vague boundaries of Waterville I was to approach only friends or relatives or people who worked in the woods with my dad, or stores that had–as my mother put it–done a good business out of us over the years. Cornelia Horncastle, in order to get herself secretly into that second place, must have gone wild in town. Either that or discovered a rich relative.

She sat at the other end of the front row of contestants, frowning over the sheets of music in her hands. A short nod and a quick smile were all she gave me. Like the other contestants, I was kept busy licking my dry lips, rubbing my sweaty palms together, wondering if I should whip out to the bathroom one last time, and rubbernecking to get a look at people as they filled up the theatre behind us. Mrs. Greensborough, wearing dark glasses and a big floppy hat, was jammed into the far corner at the rear, studying her program. Mr. and Mrs. Korhonen and Lilja came partway down the aisle and found seats near the middle. Mr. Korhonen winked at me. Larry, who was not quite the hero he had once been, despite the fact that he'd recently beat up one of the teachers and set fire to the bus shelter, came in with my brother Kenny–both of them looking uncomfortable–and slid into a back seat. My parents came all the way down front, so they could look back up the slope and pick out the seats they wanted. My mother smiled as she always did in public, as if she expected the most delightful surprise at any moment. They took seats near the front. Laurel was with them, reading a book.

My mother's sisters–with husbands, boyfriends, a few of my cousins–filled up the entire middle section of the back row. Eleanor, who was just a few years older than myself, crossed her eyes and stuck out her tongue when she saw that I'd turned to look. Mabel pulled in her chin and held up her hands, which she caused to tremble and shake. Time to be nervous, she was suggesting, in case I forgot. Bella, Christina, Gladdy, Frieda–all sat puffed up like members of a royal family, or the owners of this theatre, looking down over the crowd as if they believed every one of these people had come here expressly to watch their nephew and for no other reason. "Look, it's the Barclay girls," I heard someone behind me say. And someone else: "Oh, *them*." The owner of the first voice giggled. "It's a wonder they aren't all entered in this thing, you know how they like to perform." A snort. "They *are* performing, just watch them." I could tell by the muffled "Shhh" and the rustling of clothing that one of them was nudging the other and pointing at me, at the back of my neck. "One of them's son." When I turned again, Eleanor stood up in the aisle by her seat, did a few steps of a tap dance, and quickly sat down. In case I was tempted to take myself seriously.

When my mother caught my eye, she mouthed a silent message: stop gawking at the audience, I was letting people see how unusual all this was to me, instead of taking it in my stride like a born performer. She indicated with her head that I should notice the stage.

As if I hadn't already absorbed every detail. It was exactly as she must have hoped. A great black concert grand with the lid lifted sat out near the front of the stage, against a painted backdrop of palm trees along a sandy beach, and–in great scrawled letters–the words "Richy Ryder's CJMT Talent Festival." A long blackboard leaned against one end of the proscenium arch, with all the contestants' names on it and the rank order of each. Someone named Brenda Roper was in first place. On the opposite side of the stage, a microphone seemed to have grown up out of a heap of pineapples. I felt sick.

Eventually Richy Ryder came out of whatever backstage room he'd been hiding in and passed down the row of contestants, identifying us and telling us to get up onto the stage when our turns came without breaking our necks on those steps. "You won't be nervous, when you get up there," he said. "I'll make you feel at ease." He was looking off somewhere else as he said it, and I could see his jaw muscles straining to hold back a yawn. And he wasn't fooling me with his "you won't be nervous" either, because I knew without a doubt that the minute I got up on that stage I would throw up all over the piano.

Under the spotlight, Richy Ryder acted like a different person. He did not look the least bit like yawning while he told the audience the best way of holding their hands to get the most out of applause, cautioned them against whistling or yelling obscenities, painted a glorious picture of the life ahead for the talented winner of this contest, complimented the audience on the number of happy, shiny faces he could see out there in the seats, and told them how lucky they were to have this opportunity of showing off the fine young talent of the valley to all the rest of the province. I slid down in my seat, sure that I would rather die than go through with this thing.

The first contestant was a fourteen-year-old girl dressed up like a gypsy, singing something in a foreign language. According to the blackboard she was way down in ninth place, so I didn't pay much attention until her voice cracked open in the middle of a high note and she clutched at her throat with both hands, a look of incredulous surprise on her face. She stopped right there, face a brilliant red, and after giving the audience a quick curtsey hurried off the stage. A great beginning, I thought. If people were going to fall to pieces like that through the whole show no one would even notice my upchucking on the Heintzman. I had a vision of myself dry-heaving the whole way through "The Robin's Return."

Number two stepped up to the microphone and answered all of Richy Ryder's questions as if they were some kind of test he had to pass in order to be allowed to perform. Yes sir, his name was Roger Casey, he said with a face drawn long and narrow with seriousness, and in case that wasn't enough he added that his father was born in Digby, Nova Scotia, and his mother was born Esther Romaine in a little house just a couple blocks up the street from the theatre, close to the Native Sons' Hall, and had gone to school with the mayor though she'd dropped out of Grade Eight to get a job at the Safeway cutting meat. And yes sir, he was going to play the saxophone because he'd taken lessons for four years from Mr. D. P. Rowbottom on Seventh Street though he'd actually started out on the trumpet until he decided he didn't like it all that much. He came right out to the edge of the stage, toes sticking over, leaned back like a rooster about to crow, and blasted out "Softly As in a Morning Sunrise" so loud and hard that I thought his bulging eyes would pop right out of his head and his straining lungs would blast holes through that red-and-white shirt. Everyone moved forward, tense and straining, waiting for something terrible to happen—for him to fall off the stage or explode or go sailing off into the air from the force of his own fantastic intensity—but he stopped suddenly and everyone fell back exhausted and sweaty to clap for him.

The third contestant was less reassuring. A kid with talent. A smart-aleck ten-year-old with red hair, who told the audience he was going into show business when he grew up, started out playing "Swanee River" on his banjo, switched in the middle of a bar to a mouth organ, tapdanced across the stage to play a few bars on the piano, and finished off on a trombone he'd had stashed away behind the palm tree. He bowed, grinned, flung himself around the stage as if he'd spent his whole life on it, and looked as if he'd do his whole act again quite happily if the audience wanted him to. By the time the tremendous applause had died down my jaw was aching from the way I'd been grinding my teeth the whole time he was up there. The audience would not have gone quite so wild over him, I thought, if he hadn't been wearing a hearing aid and a leg brace.

Then it was my turn. A strange calm fell over me when my name was called, the kind of calm that I imagine comes over a person about to be executed when his mind finally buckles under the horror it has been faced with, something too terrible to believe in. I wondered for a moment if I had died. But no, my body at least hadn't died, for it transported me unbidden across the front of the audience, up the staircase (with only a slight stumble on the second step, hardly noticeable), and across the great wide stage of the theatre to stand facing Richy Ryder's enormous expanse of white smiling teeth, beside the microphone.

"And you are Barclay Philip Desmond," he said.

"Yes," I said.

And again "yes," because I realized that not only had my voice come out as thin and high as the squeal of a dry buzz-saw, but the microphone was at least a foot too low. I had to bend my knees to speak into it.

"You don't live in town, do you?" he said. He had no intention of adjusting that microphone. "You come from a place called . . . Waterville. A logging and farming settlement?"

"Yes," I said.

And again "yes" because while he was speaking my legs had straightened up, I'd returned to my full height and had to duck again for the microphone.

He was speaking to me but his eyes, I could see, were busy keeping all that audience gathered together, while his voice and his mind were obviously concentrated on the thousands of invisible people who were crouched inside that microphone, listening, the thousands of people who—I imagined now—were pulled up close to their sets all over the province, wondering if I was actually a pair of twins or if my high voice had some peculiar way of echoing itself, a few tones lower.

"Does living in the country like that mean you have to milk the cows every morning before you go to school?"

"Yes."

And again "yes."

I could see Mrs. Greensborough cowering in the back corner. I promise not to mention you, I thought. And the Korhonens, grinning. I had clearly passed over into another world they couldn't believe in.

"If you've got a lot of farm chores to do, when do you find the time to practise the piano?"

He had me this time. A "yes" wouldn't be good enough. "Right after school," I said, and ducked to repeat. "Right after school. As soon as I get home. For an hour."

"And I just bet," he said, throwing the audience an enormous wink, "that like every other red-blooded country kid you hate every minute of it. You'd rather be outside playing baseball."

The audience laughed. I could see my mother straining forward; she still had the all-purpose waiting-for-the-surprise smile on her lips but her eyes were frowning at the master of ceremonies. She did not approve of the comment. And behind that face she was no doubt thinking to herself "I just know he's going to win" over and over so hard that she was getting pains in the back of her neck. Beside her, my father had a tight grin on his face. He was chuckling to himself, and sliding a look around the room to see how the others were taking this.

Up at the back, most of my aunts–and their husbands, their boyfriends–had tilted their chins down to their chests, offering me only the tops of their heads. Eleanor, however, had both hands behind her neck. She was laughing harder than anyone else.

Apparently I was not expected to respond to the last comment, for he had another question as soon as the laughter had died. "How old are you, son?"

"Thirteen."

For once I remembered to duck the first time.

"Thirteen. Does your wife like the idea of your going on the radio like this?"

Again the audience laughed. My face burned. I felt tears in my eyes. I had no control over my face. I tried to laugh like everyone else but realized I probably looked like an idiot. Instead, I frowned and looked embarrassed and kicked at one shoe with the toe of the other.

"Just a joke," he said, "just a joke." The jerk knew he'd gone too far. "And now seriously, one last question before I turn you loose on those ivories over there."

My heart had started to thump so noisily I could hardly hear him. My hands, I realized, had gone numb. There was no feeling at all in my fingers. How was I ever going to play the piano?

"What are you going to be when you grow up?"

The thumping stopped. My heart stopped. A strange, cold silence settled over the world. I was going to die right in front of all those people. What I was going to be was a corpse, dead of humiliation, killed in a trap I hadn't seen being set. What must have been only a few seconds crawled by while something crashed around in my head, trying to get out. I sensed the audience, hoping for some help from them. My mother had settled back in her seat and for the first time that surprise-me smile had gone. Rather, she looked confident, sure of what I was about to say.

And suddenly, I was aware of familiar faces all over that theatre. Neighbors. Friends of the family. My aunts. People who had heard me answer that question at their doors, people who thought they knew what I wanted.

There was nothing left of Mrs. Greensborough but the top of her big hat. My father, too, was looking down at the floor between his feet. I saw myself falling from that spar tree, high in the mountains.

"Going to be?" I said, turning so fast that I bumped the microphone with my hand, which turned out after all not to be numb.

I ducked.

"Nothing," I said. "I don't know. Maybe…maybe nothing at all."

I don't know who it was that snorted when I screwed up the stool, sat down, and stood up to screw it down again. I don't know how well I played, I wasn't listening. I don't know how loud the audience clapped, I was in a hurry to get back to my seat. I don't know what the other contestants did, I wasn't paying any attention, except when Cornelia Horncastle got up on the stage, told the whole world she was going to be a professional pianist, and sat down to rattle off Rachmaninoff's Rhapsody on a Theme of Paganini as if she'd been playing for fifty years. As far as I know it may have been the first time she'd ever heard herself play it. She had a faint look of surprise on her face the whole time, as if she couldn't quite get over the way the keys went down when you touched them.

As soon as Cornelia came down off the stage, smiling modestly, and got back into her seat, Richy Ryder announced a fifteen-minute intermission while the talent judges made their decision and the studio audience went out into the lobby to pledge their money and their votes. Now that the talent had been displayed, people could spend their money according to what they'd heard rather than according to who happened to come knocking on their door. Most of the contestants got up to stretch their legs but I figured I'd stood up once too often that night and stayed in my seat. The lower exit was not far away; I contemplated using it; I could hitch-hike home and be in bed before any of the others got out of there.

I was stopped, though, by my father, who sat down in the seat next to mine and put a greasy carton of popcorn in my lap.

"Well," he said, "that's that."

His neck was flushed. This must have been a terrible evening for him. He had a carton of popcorn himself and tipped it up to gather a huge mouthful. I had never before in my life, I realized, seen my father eat popcorn. It must have been worse for him than I thought.

Not one of the aunts was anywhere in sight. I could see my mother standing in the far aisle, talking to Mrs. Korhonen. Still smiling. She would never let herself fall apart in public, no matter what happened. My insides ached with the knowledge of what it must have been like right then to be her. I felt as if I had just betrayed her in front of the whole world. Betrayed everyone.

"Let's go home," I said.

"Not yet. Wait a while. Might as well see this thing to the end."

True, I thought. Wring every last drop of torture out of it.

He looked hard at me a moment, as if he were trying to guess what was going on in my head. And he did, he always knew. "My old man wanted me to be a doctor," he said. "My mother wanted me to be a florist. She liked flowers. She thought if I was a florist I'd be able to send her a bouquet every week. But what does any of that matter now?"

Being part of a family was too complicated. And right then I decided I'd be a loner. No family for me. Nobody whose hearts could be broken every time I opened my mouth. Nobody *expecting* anything of me. Nobody to get me all tangled up in knots trying to guess who means what and what is it that's really going on inside anyone else. No temptations to presume I knew what someone else was thinking or feeling or hoping for.

When the lights had flickered and dimmed, and people had gone back to their seats, a young man with a beard came out onto the stage and changed the numbers behind the contestants' names. I'd dropped to fifth place, and Cornelia Horncastle had moved up to first. She had also, Richy Ryder announced, been awarded the judges' footstool for talent. The winner of the holiday in sunny Hawaii would not be announced until the next week, he said, when the radio audience had enough time to mail in their votes.

"All that," my mother said when she came down the aisle with her coat on, "is the end of a long and tiring day." I could find no disappointment showing in her eyes, or in the set of her mouth. Just relief. The same kind of relief that I felt myself. "You did a good job," she said, "and thank goodness it's over."

As soon as we got in the house I shut myself in the bedroom and announced I was never coming out. Lying on my bed, I tried to read my comic books but my mind passed from face to face all through the community, imagining everyone having a good laugh at the way my puffed-up ambition had got its reward. My face burned. Relatives, the aunts, would be ashamed of me. Eleanor would never let me forget. Mabel would remind me of the boy who'd done the only honorable thing, blown off his head. Why wasn't I doing the same? I lay awake the whole night, torturing myself with these thoughts. But when morning came and the hunger pains tempted me out of the bedroom as far as the breakfast table, I decided the whole wretched experience had brought one benefit with it: freedom from ambition. I wouldn't worry any more about becoming a high-rigger for my father. I was free at last to concentrate on pursuing the only goal that ever really mattered to me: becoming a Finn.

Of course I failed at that too. But then neither did Cornelia Horncastle become a great pianist on the concert stages of Europe. In fact, I understand that once she got back from her holiday on the beaches of Hawaii she announced to her parents that she was never going to touch a piano again as long as she lived, ivory, or cardboard, or any other kind. She had already, she said, accomplished all she'd ever wanted from it. And as far as I know, she's kept her word to this day.

Works by Jack Hodgins

FICTION

Spit Delaney's Island. Toronto: Macmillan,
    1976.
The Invention of the World. Toronto:
    Macmillan, 1977.
The Resurrection of Joseph Bourne. Toronto:
    Macmillan, 1979.
The Barclay Family Theatre. Toronto:
    Macmillan, 1981.

Interviews with Jack Hodgins

Canadian Fiction Magazine, 32/33, (1979),
    33-63.
For Openers. Edited by Alan Twigg.
    Madeira Park, B.C.: Harbour, 1981,
    pp. 185-95.

Guy Vanderhaeghe

Guy Vanderhaeghe is one of the most important new voices in Canadian fiction of the 1980s. He was born in 1951 and raised in Esterhazy, a small town in southeast Saskatchewan, where "the prairie verges on parkland, breaking into rolling swells of land." He moved to Saskatoon to attend the University of Saskatchewan, where he obtained his bachelor's and master's degrees in history. He also pursued graduate studies in education at the University of Regina. Having worked as a teacher, an archivist, and a researcher, he now devotes his time chiefly to writing.

Under the influence of such prairie novelists as Sinclair Ross, Margaret Laurence, and Robert Kroetsch, Vanderhaeghe began writing short stories in the late 1970s. His first book is a collection of twelve short stories titled *Man Descending* (1982). The book follows in a roughly chronological pattern, from childhood to old age, the pain and disillusionment of various male protagonists as they struggle against their feelings of fear and loneliness. In his fiction, Vanderhaeghe captures the alienation of modern living, and the undying hope for some method of overcoming it.

In "What I Learned from Caesar" the son of George Vander Elst reflects on his father and the effects of the Depression on him. A proud and courageous man, George Vander Elst wanted to leave a record of himself; he wanted a life far grander than was possible in the economic situation on the prairies. He wanted to be "a success."

"There's no such thing as a success," Vanderhaeghe has commented. "The world around us wants to believe in success stories. But no one is really a success. You can only believe in success if you believe in the glamor of the lives which society claims to be successful." This kind of belief contributes much to George Vander Elst's breakdown. It also prevents his young son from realizing that his embarrassment at his father's financial ruin is a reflection of his own weakness, not a consequence of his father's plight.

Though the similarity between the names Vanderhaeghe and Vander Elst may invite speculation about a possible autobiographical dimension to the story, Vanderhaeghe cautions that he is not an autobiographical writer. "I think writers write out of memory. By that I don't mean that they're autobiographical writers. I'm not one myself either. But often writers, I think, are in the process of re-ordering their past. And if they've grown up on a farm, that's their past. And when you go to work on it imaginatively, you work with the external features of it, whether it's the clump of poplars behind the barn you remember or the way the dusty street looked at nine o'clock on a Saturday evening."

What I Learned from Caesar

The oldest story is the story of flight, the search for greener pastures. But the pastures we flee, no matter how brown and blighted–these travel with us; they can't be escaped.

My father was an immigrant. You would think this no penalty in a nation of immigrants, but even his carefully nurtured, precisely colloquial English didn't spare him much pain. Nor did his marriage to a woman of British stock (as we called it then, before the vicious-sounding acronym Wasp came into use). That marriage should have paid him a dividend of respectability, but it only served to make her suspect in marrying him.

My father was a lonely man, a stranger who made matters worse by pretending he wasn't. It's true that he was familiar enough with his adopted terrain, more familiar than most because he was a salesman. Yet he was never really *of* it, no matter how much he might wish otherwise. I only began to understand what had happened to him when I, in my turn, left for greener pastures, heading east. I didn't go so far, not nearly so far as he had. But I also learned that there is a price to be paid. Mine was a trivial one, a feeling of mild unease. At odd moments I betrayed myself and my beginnings; I knew that I lacked the genuine ring of a local. And I had never even left my own country.

Occasionally I return to the small Saskatchewan town near the Manitoba border where I grew up. To the unpractised eye of an easterner the countryside around that town might appear undifferentiated and monotonous, part and parcel of that great swath of prairie that vacationers drive through, pitying its inhabitants and deploring its restrooms, intent only on leaving it all behind as quickly as possible. But it is just here that the prairie verges on parkland, breaking into rolling swells of land, and here, too, that it becomes a little greener and easier on the eye. There is still more sky than any country is entitled to, and it teases the traveller into believing he can never escape it or find shelter under it. But if your attention wanders from that hypnotic expanse of blue and the high clouds drifting in it, the land becomes more comfortable as prospects shorten, and the mind rests easier on attenuated distances. There is cropland: fields of rye, oats, barley, and wheat; flat, glassy sloughs shining like mirrors in the sun; a solitary clump of trembling poplar; a bluff that gently climbs to nudge the sky.

When I was a boy it was a good deal bleaker. The topsoil had blown off the fields and into the ditches to form black dunes; the crops were withered and burnt; there were no sloughs because they had all dried up. The whole place had a thirsty look. That was during the thirties when we were dealt a doubly cruel hand of drought and economic depression. It was not a time or place that was kindly to my father. He had come out of the urban sprawl of industrial Belgium some twenty-odd years before, and it was only then, I think, that he was beginning to come to terms with a land that must have seemed forbidding after his own tiny country, so well tamed and marked by man. And then this land played him the trick of becoming something more than forbidding; it became fierce, and fierce in every way.

It was in the summer of 1931, the summer that I thought was merely marking time before I would pass into high school, that he lost his territory. For as long as I could remember I had been a salesman's son, and then it ended. The company he worked for began to feel the pinch of the Depression and moved to merge its territories. He was let go. So one morning he unexpectedly pulled up at the front door and began to haul his sample cases out of the Ford.

"It's finished," he said to my mother as he flung the cases on to the lawn. "I got the boot. I offered to stay on—strictly commission. He wouldn't hear of it. Said he couldn't see fit to starve two men where there was only a living for one. I'd have starved that other bastard out by the time I was through with him." He paused, took off his fedora and nervously ran his index finger around the sweat-band. Clearing his throat, he said, "His parting words were, 'Good luck, Dutchie!' I should have spit in his eye. Jesus H. Christ himself wouldn't dare call me Dutchie. The bastard."

Offence compounded offence. He thought he was indistinguishable, that the accent wasn't there. Maybe his first successes as a salesman owed something to his naivety. Maybe in good times, when there was more than enough to go around, people applauded his performance by buying from him. He was a counterfeit North American who paid them the most obvious of compliments, imitation. Yet hard times make people less generous. Jobs were scarce, business was poor. In a climate like that, perceptions change, and perhaps he ceased to be merely amusing and became, instead, a dangerous parody. Maybe that district manager, faced with a choice, could only think of George Vander Elst as Dutchie. Then again, it might have been that my father just wasn't a good enough salesman. Who can judge at this distance?

But for the first time my father felt as if he had been exposed. He had never allowed himself to remember that he was a foreigner, or if he had, he persuaded himself he had been wanted. After all, he was a northern European, a Belgian. They had been on the preferred list.

He had left all that behind him. I don't even know the name of the town or the city where he was born or grew up. He always avoided my questions about his early life as if they dealt with a distasteful and criminal past that was best forgotten. Never, not even once, did I hear him speak Flemish. There were never any of the lapses you might expect. No pet names in his native language for my mother or myself; no words of endearment which would have had the comfort of childhood use. Not even when driven to one of his frequent rages did he curse in the mother tongue. If he ever prayed, I'm sure it was in English. If a man forgets the cradle language in the transports of prayer, love, and rage—well, it's forgotten.

The language he did speak was, in a sense, letter-perfect, fluent, glib. It was the language of wheeler-dealers, and of the heady twenties, of salesmen, high-rollers, and persuaders. He spoke of people as live-wires, go-getters, self-made men. Hyphenated words to describe the hyphenated life of the seller, a life of fits and starts, comings and goings. My father often proudly spoke of himself as a self-made man, but this description was not the most accurate. He was a remade man. The only two pictures of him which I have in my possession are proof of this.

The first is a sepia-toned photograph taken, as nearly as I can guess, just prior to his departure from Belgium. In this picture he is wearing an ill-fitting suit, round-toed, clumsy boots, and a cloth cap. The second was taken by a street photographer in Winnipeg. My father is walking down the street, a snap-brim fedora slanting rakishly over one eye. His suit is what must have been considered stylish then—a three-piece pin-stripe— and he is carrying an overcoat casually over one arm. He is exactly what he admired most, a "snappy dresser," or, since he always had trouble with his p's, a "snabby dresser." The clothes, though they mark a great change, aren't really that important. Something else tells the story.

In the first photograph my father stands rigidly with his arms folded across his chest, unsmiling. Yet I can see that he is a young man who is hesitant and afraid; not of the camera, but of what this picture-taking means. There is a reason why he is having his photograph taken. He must leave something of himself behind with his family so he will not be forgotten, and carry something away with him so that he can remember. That is what makes this picture touching; it is a portrait of a solitary, an exile.

In the second picture his face is blunter, fleshier: nothing surprising in that, he is older. But suddenly you realize he is posing for the camera– not in the formal, European manner of the first photograph but in a manner far more unnatural. You see, he is pretending to be entirely natural and unguarded; yet he betrays himself. The slight smile, the squared shoulder, the overcoat draped over the arm, all are calculated bits of a composition. He has seen the camera from a block away. My father wanted to be caught in exactly this negligent, unassuming pose, sure that it would capture for all time his prosperity, his success, his adaptability. Like most men, he wanted to leave a record. And this was it. And if he had coached himself in such small matters, what would he ever leave to chance?

That was why he was so ashamed when he came home that summer. There was the particular shame of having lost his job, a harder thing for a man then than it might be today. There was the shame of knowing that sooner or later we would have to go on relief, because being a lavish spender he had no savings. But there was also the shame of a man who suddenly discovers that all his lies were transparent, and everything he thought so safely hidden had always been in plain view. He had been living one of those dreams. The kind of dream in which you are walking down the street, meeting friends and neighbors, smiling and nodding, and when you arrive at home and pass a mirror you see for the first time you are stark naked. He was sure that behind his back he had always been Dutchie. For a man with so much pride a crueller epithet would have been kinder; to be hated gives a man some kind of status. It was the condescension implicit in that diminutive, its mock playfulness, that made him appear so undignified in his own eyes.

And for the first time in my life I was ashamed of him. He didn't have the grace to bear an injustice, imagined or otherwise, quietly. At first he merely brooded, and then like some man with a repulsive sore, he sought pity by showing it. I'm sure he knew that he could only offend, but he was under a compulsion to justify himself. He began with my mother by explaining, where there was no need for explanation, that he had had his job taken from him for no good reason. However, there proved to be little satisfaction in preaching to the converted, so he carried his tale to everyone he knew. At first his references to his plight were tentative and oblique. The responses were polite but equally tentative and equally oblique. This wasn't what he had hoped for. He believed that the sympathy didn't measure up to the occasion. So his story was told and retold, and each time it was enlarged and embellished until the injustice was magnified beyond comprehension. He made a damn fool of himself. This was the first sign, although my mother and I chose not to recognize it.

In time everyone learned my father had lost his job for no good reason. And it wasn't long before the kids of the fathers he had told his story to were following me down the street chanting, "No good reason. No good reason." That's how I learned my family was a topical joke that the town was enjoying with zest. I suppose my father found out too, because it was about that time he stopped going out of the house. He couldn't fight back and neither could I. You never can.

After a while I didn't leave the house unless I had to. I spent my days sitting in our screened verandah reading old copies of *Saturday Evening Post* and *Maclean's*. I was content to do anything that helped me forget the heat and the monotony, the shame and the fear, of that longest of summers. I was thirteen then and in a hurry to grow up, to press time into yielding the bounty I was sure it had in keeping for me. So I was killing time minute by minute with those magazines. I was to enter high school that fall and that seemed a prelude to adulthood and independence. My father's misfortunes couldn't fool me into believing that maturity didn't mean the strength to plunder at will. So when I found an old Latin grammar of my mother's I began to read that too. After all, Latin was the arcane language of the professions, of lawyers and doctors, those divinities owed immediate and unquestioning respect. I decided I would become either one, because respect could never be stolen from them as it had been from my father.

That August was the hottest I can remember. The dry heat made my nose bleed at night, and I often woke to find my pillow stiff with blood. The leaves of the elm tree in the front yard hung straight down on their stems; flies buzzed heavily, their bodies tip-tapping lazily against the screens, and people passing the house moved so languidly they seemed to be walking in water. My father, who had always been careful about his appearance, began to come down for breakfast barefoot, wearing only a vest undershirt and an old pair of pants. He rarely spoke, but carefully picked his way through his meal as if it were a dangerous obstacle course, only pausing to rub his nose thoughtfully. I noticed that he had begun to smell.

One morning he looked up at me, laid his fork carefully down beside his plate and said, "I'll summons him."

"Who?"

"Who do you think?" he said scornfully. "The bastard who fired me. He had no business calling me Dutchie. That's slander."

"You can't summons him."

"I can," he said emphatically. "I'm a citizen. I've got rights. I'll go to law. He spoiled my good name."

"That's not slander."

"It is."

"No it isn't."

"I'll sue the bastard," he said vaguely, looking around to appeal to my mother, who had left the room. He got up from the table and went to the doorway. "Edith," he called, "tell your son I've got the right to summons that bastard."

Her voice came back faint and timid, "I don't know, George."

He looked back at me. "You're in the same boat, sonny. And taking sides with them don't save you. When we drown we all drown together."

"I'm not taking sides," I said indignantly. "Nobody's taking sides. It's facts. Can't you see,. . . ." but I didn't get a chance to finish. He left, walked out on me. I could hear his steps on the stairway, tired, heavy steps. There was so much I wanted to say. I wanted to make it plain that being on his side meant saving him from making a fool of himself again. I wanted him to know he could never win that way. I wanted him to win, not lose. He was my father. But he went up those steps, one at a time, and I heard his foot fall distinctly, every time. Beaten before he started, he crawled back into bed. My mother went up to him several times that day, to see if he was sick, to attempt to gouge him out of that room, but she couldn't. It was only later that afternoon, when I was reading in the verandah, that he suddenly appeared again, wearing only a pair of undershorts. His body shone dully with sweat, his skin looked grey and soiled.

"They're watching us," he said, staring past me at an empty car parked in the bright street.

Frightened, I closed my book and asked who was watching us.

"The relief people," he said tiredly. "They think I've got money hidden somewhere. They're watching me, trying to catch me with it.

The joke's on them. I got no money.'' He made a quick, furtive gesture that drew attention to his almost-naked body, as if it were proof of his poverty.

"Nobody is watching us. That car's empty."

"Don't take sides with them," he said, staring through the screen. I thought someone from one of the houses across the street might see him like that, practically naked.

"The neighbors'll see," I said, turning my head to avoid looking at him.

"See what?" he asked, surprised.

"You standing like that. Naked almost."

"There's nothing they can do. A man's home is his castle. That's what the English say, isn't it?"

And he went away laughing.

Going down the hallway, drawing close to his door that always stood ajar, what did I hope? To see him dressed, his trousers rolled up to mid-calf to avoid smudging his cuffs, whistling under his breath, shining his shoes? Everything as it was before? Yes. I hoped that. If I had been younger then and still believed that frogs were turned into princes with a kiss, I might even have believed it could happen. But I didn't believe, I only hoped. Every time I approached his door (and that was many times a day, too many), I felt the queasy excitement of hope.

It was always the same. I would look in and see him lying on the tufted pink bedspread, naked or nearly so, gasping for breath in the heat. And I always thought of a whale stranded on a beach because he was such a big man. He claimed he slept all day because of the heat, but he only pretended to. He could feel me watching him and his eyes would open. He would tell me to go away, or bring him a glass of water; or, because his paranoia was growing more marked, asked me to see if they were still in the street. I would go to the window and tell him, yes, they were. Nothing else satisfied him. If I said they weren't, his jaw would shift from side to side unsteadily and his eyes would prick with tears. Then he imagined more subtle and intricate conspiracies.

I would ask him how he felt.

"Hot," he'd say, "I'm always hot. Can't hardly breathe. Damn country," and turn on his side away from me.

My mother was worried about money. There was none left. She asked me what to do. She believed women shouldn't make decisions.

"You'll have to go to the town office and apply for relief," I told her.

"No, no," she'd say, shaking her head. "I couldn't go behind his back.

I couldn't do that. He'll go himself when he feels better. He'll snap out of it. It takes a little time."

In the evening my father would finally dress and come downstairs and eat something. When it got dark he'd go out into the yard and sit on the swing he'd hung from a limb of our Manitoba maple years before, when I was a little boy. My mother and I would sit and watch him from the verandah. I felt obligated to sit with her. Every night as he settled himself onto the swing she would say the same thing. "He's too big. It'll never hold him. He'll break his back." But the swing held him up and the darkness hid him from the eyes of his enemies, and I like to think that made him happy, for a time.

He'd light a cigarette before he began to swing, and then we'd watch its glowing tip move back and forth in the darkness like a beacon. He'd flick it away when it was smoked, burning a red arc in the night, showering sparks briefly, like a comet. And then he'd light another and another, and we'd watch them glow and swing in the night.

My mother would lean over to me and say confidentially, "He's thinking it all out. It'll come to him, what to do."

I never knew whether she was trying to reassure me or herself. At last my mother would get to her feet and call to him, telling him she was going up to bed. He never answered. I waited a little longer, believing that watching him I kept him safe in the night. But I always gave up before he did and went to bed too.

The second week of September I returned to school. Small differences are keenly felt. For the first time there was no new sweater, or unsharpened pencils, or new fountain pen whose nib hadn't spread under my heavy writing hand. The school was the same school I had gone to for eight years, but that day I climbed the stairs to the second floor that housed the high school. Up there the wind moaned more persistently than I remembered it had below, and intermittently it threw handfuls of dirt and dust from the schoolyard against the windows with a gritty rattle.

Our teacher, Mrs. MacDonald, introduced herself to us, though she needed no introduction since everyone knew who she was–she had taught there for over ten years. We were given our texts and it cheered me a little to see I would have no trouble with Latin after my summer's work. Then we were given a form on which we wrote a lot of useless information. When I came to the space which asked for Racial Origin I paused, and then, out of loyalty to my father, numbly wrote in "Canadian."

After that we were told we could leave. I put my texts away in a locker for the first time—we had had none in public school—but somehow it felt strange going home from school empty-handed. So I stopped at the library door and went in. There was no school librarian and only a few shelves of books, seldom touched. The room smelled of dry paper and heat. I wandered around aimlessly, taking books down, opening them, and putting them back. That is, until I happened on Caesar's *The Gallic Wars*. It was a small, thick book that nestled comfortably in the hand. I opened it and saw that the left-hand pages were printed in Latin and the right-hand pages were a corresponding English translation. I carried it away with me, dreaming of more than proficiency in Latin.

When I got home my mother was standing on the front step, peering anxiously up and down the street.

"Have you seen your father?" she asked.

"No," I said. "Why?"

She began to cry. "I told him all the money was gone. I asked him if I could apply for relief. He said he'd go himself and have it out with them. Stand on his rights. He took everything with him. His citizenship papers, baptismal certificate, old passport, bank book, everything. I said, 'Everyone knows you. There's no need.' But he said he needed proof. Of what? He'll cause a scandal. He's been gone for an hour."

We went into the house and sat in the living-room. "I'm a foolish woman," she said. She got up and hugged me awkwardly. "He'll be all right."

We sat a long time listening for his footsteps. At last we heard someone come up the walk. My mother got up and said, "There he is." But there was a knock at the door.

I heard them talking at the door. The man said, "Edith, you better come with me. George is in some trouble."

My mother asked what trouble.

"You just better come. He gave the town clerk a poke. The constable and doctor have him now. The doctor wants to talk to you about signing some papers."

"I'm not signing any papers," my mother said.

"You'd better come, Edith."

She came into the living-room and said to me, "I'm going to get your father."

I didn't believe her for a minute. She put her coat on and went out.

She didn't bring him home. They took him to an asylum. It was a shameful word then, asylum. But I see it in a different light now. It seems the proper word now, suggesting as it does a refuge, a place to hide.

I'm not sure why all this happened to him. Perhaps there is no reason anyone can put their finger on, although I have my ideas.

But I needed a reason then. I needed a reason that would lend him a little dignity, or rather, lend me a little dignity; for I was ashamed of him out of my own weakness. I needed him to be strong, or at least tragic. I didn't know that most people are neither.

When you clutch at straws, anything will do. I read my answer out of Caesar's *The Gallic Wars*, the fat little book I had carried home. In the beginning of Book I he writes, "Of all people the Belgae are the most courageous. . . ." I read on, sharing Caesar's admiration for a people who would not submit but chose to fight and see glory in their wounds. I misread it all, and bent it until I was satisfied. I reasoned the way I had to, for my sake, for my father's. What was he but a man dishonored by faceless foes? His instincts could not help but prevail, and like his ancestors, in the end, on that one day, what could he do but make the shadows real, and fight to be free of them?

Work by Guy Vanderhaeghe

Man Descending. Toronto: Macmillan, 1982.

Interview with Guy Vanderhaeghe

NeWest Review, 8 (September, 1982), 8-10.

Sheila Watson

Sheila Watson, the second of four children, was born in 1909 in New Westminster, British Columbia. Her father was Superintendent of the Provincial Mental Hospital in New Westminster, and the family lived in one wing of the asylum until his death in 1922. Higher up the hill beyond the asylum was a cemetery, and below the asylum flowed the Fraser River.

A graduate of the University of British Columbia, Watson taught in elementary and high schools on the British Columbia mainland and on Vancouver Island before embarking on part-time graduate studies in English at the University of Toronto after the Second World War.

In 1951 Watson began a two-year residence in Calgary, where she wrote much of her novel *The Double Hook* (1959), now regarded as the beginning of modern Canadian fiction. In the same decade she completed her graduate studies at the University of Toronto and began her doctoral dissertation. In 1961 she joined the Department of English at the University of Alberta, where she played a major role in the development of the department and in the creation of its graduate program. In 1970, in co-operation with colleagues, she was a founder and editor of the *White Pelican*, an avant-garde journal of literature and the visual arts.

The poet T.S. Eliot once commented that modern writers find themselves compelled to employ myth in their own work as "a way of controlling, of ordering, of giving a shape and a significance to the immense panorama of futility and anarchy which is contemporary society." Watson's fiction uses myth to organize and structure the contemporary, to distance such material, and to endow seemingly homely actions or gestures with the significance and clarity usually associated with myth.

Watson's story "Antigone," published in 1959, relies on elements from the Greek tale of King Oedipus, in which his daughter Antigone plays a major role. In the ancient myth, two sons of Oedipus, formerly king of Thebes, killed each other in battle after one brother had led a foreign army against the kingdom. The new king, Oedipus' brother Creon, decreed that as punishment for his crime against Thebes, the invading brother must be refused the honor of burial. Anyone who disobeyed this edict would be executed.

Though Oedipus' two daughters, Antigone and Ismene, found Creon's law offensive, only Antigone was moved to action. She disobeyed her uncle's decree, setting above it the higher laws of heaven that demand burial for the dead. She performed the symbolic act of sprinkling dust on the corpse. This civil disobedience prompted Creon to banish Antigone to a cave to die of starvation. Such stern justice, permitting no mercy or moderation, came to have tragic consequences not only for Antigone but also for those around her.

In her story, Watson has taken the Antigone plot as a point of departure; material from Watson's childhood stands beside evocative allusions to the classical world. The Greek names and the subtle echoes of the older story serve to distance the more contemporary details about the Provincial Mental Health Hospital in New Westminster. The narrator talks about the asylum as if it were a kingdom and about the patients as if they were figures from myth; he himself is the son of the kingdom's ruler, looking back on his upbringing and on his friendship with his two cousins, Antigone and Ismene. Watson's Antigone, no longer a princess burying her dead brother, is a child disobeying her uncle's inflexible rules by burying a bird in six inches of asylum lawn.

Antigone

My father ruled a kingdom on the right bank of the river. He ruled it with a firm hand and a stout heart though he was often more troubled than Moses, who was simply trying to bring a stubborn and moody people under God's yoke. My father ruled men who thought they were gods or the instruments of gods or, at very least, god-afflicted and god-pursued. He ruled Atlas who held up the sky, and Hermes who went on endless messages, and Helen who'd been hatched from an egg, and Pan the gardener, and Kallisto the bear, and too many others to mention by name. Yet my father had no thunderbolt, no trident, no helmet of darkness. His subjects were delivered bound into his hands. He merely watched over them as the hundred-handed ones watched over the dethroned Titans so that they wouldn't bother Hellas again.

Despite the care which my father took to maintain an atmosphere of sober common sense in his whole establishment, there were occasional outbursts of self-indulgence which he could not control. For instance, I have seen Helen walking naked down the narrow cement path under the chestnut trees for no better reason, I suppose, than that the day was hot and the white flowers themselves lay naked and expectant in the sunlight. And I have seen Atlas forget the sky while he sat eating the dirt which held him up. These were things which I was not supposed to see.

If my father had been as sensible through and through as he was thought to be, he would have packed me off to boarding school when I was old enough to be disciplined by men. Instead he kept me at home with my two cousins who, except for the accident of birth, might as well have been my sisters. Today I imagine people concerned with our welfare would take such an environment into account. At the time I speak of most people thought us fortunate—especially the girls, whose father's affairs had come to an unhappy issue. I don't like to revive old scandal and I wouldn't except to deny it; but it takes only a few impertinent newcomers in any community to force open cupboards which have been decently sealed by time. However, my father was so busy setting his kingdom to rights that he let weeds grow up in his own garden.

As I said, if my father had had all his wits about him he would have sent me to boarding school—and Antigone and Ismene too. I might have fallen in love with the headmaster's daughter and Antigone might have learned that no human being can be right always. She might have found out besides that from the seeds of eternal justice grow madder flowers than any which Pan grew in the gardens of my father's kingdom.

Between the kingdom which my father ruled and the wilderness flows a river. It is this river which I am crossing now. Antigone is with me.

How often can we cross the same river, Antigone asks.

Her persistence annoys me. Besides, Heraklitos made nonsense of her question years ago. He saw a river too—the Inachos, the Kephissos, the Lethaios. The name doesn't matter. He said: See how quickly the water flows. However agile a man is, however nimbly he swims, or runs, or flies, the water slips away before him. See, even as he sets down his foot the water is displaced by the steam which crowds along in the shadow of its flight.

But after all, Antigone says, one must admit that it is the same kind of water. The oolichans run in it as they ran last year and the year before. The gulls cry above the same banks. Boats drift towards the Delta and circle back against the current to gather up the catch.

At any rate, I tell her, we're standing on a new bridge. We are standing so high that the smell of mud and river weeds passes under us out to the straits. The unbroken curve of the bridge protects the eye from details of river life. The bridge is foolproof as a clinic's passport to happiness.

The old bridge still spans the river, but the cat-walk with its cracks and knot-holes, with its gap between planking and hand-rail has been torn down. The centre arch still grinds open to let boats up and down the river, but a child can no longer be walked on it or swung out on it beyond the water-gauge at the very centre of the flood.

I've known men who scorned any kind of bridge, Antigone says. Men have walked into the water, she says, or, impatient, have jumped from the bridge into the river below.

But these, I say, didn't really want to cross the river. They went Persephone's way, cradled in the current's arms, down the long halls under the pink feet of the gulls, under the booms and tow-lines, under the soft bellies of the fish.

Antigone looks at me.

There's no coming back, she says, if one goes far enough.

I know she's going to speak of her own misery and I won't listen. Only a god has the right to say: Look what I suffer. Only a god should say: What more ought I to have done for you that I have not done?

Once in winter, she says, a man walked over the river.

Taking advantage of nature, I remind her, since the river had never frozen before.

Yet he escaped from the penitentiary, she says. He escaped from the guards walking round the walls or standing with their guns in the sentry-boxes at the four corners of the enclosure. He escaped.

Not without risk, I say. He had to test the strength of the ice himself. Yet safer perhaps than if he had crossed by the old bridge where he might have slipped through a knot-hole or tumbled out through the railing.

He did escape, she persists, and lived forever on the far side of the river in the Alaska tea and bulrushes. For where, she asks, can a man go farther than to the outermost edge of the world?

The habitable world, as I've said, is on the right bank of the river. Here is the market with its market stalls—the coops of hens, the long-tongued geese, the haltered calf, the bearded goat, the shoving pigs, and the empty bodies of cows and sheep and rabbits hanging on iron hooks. My father's kingdom provides asylum in the suburbs. Near it are the convent, the churches, and the penitentiary. Above these on the hill the cemetery looks down on the people and on the river itself.

It is a world spread flat, tipped up into the sky so that men and women bend forward, walking as men walk when they board a ship at high tide. This is the world I feel with my feet. It is the world I see with my eyes.

I remember standing once with Antigone and Ismene in the square just outside the gates of my father's kingdom. Here from a bust set high on a cairn the stone eyes of Simon Fraser look from his stone face over the river that he found.

It is the head that counts, Ismene said.

It's no better than an urn, Antigone said, one of the urns we see when we climb to the cemetery above.

And all I could think was that I didn't want an urn, only a flat green grave with a chain about it.

A chain won't keep out the dogs, Antigone said.

But his soul could swing on it, Ismene said, like a bird blown on a branch in the wind.

And I remember Antigone's saying: The cat drags its belly on the ground and the rat sharpens its tooth in the ivy.

I should have loved Ismene, but I didn't. It was Antigone I loved. I should have loved Ismene because, although she walked the flat world with us, she managed somehow to see it round.

The earth is an oblate spheroid, she'd say. And I knew that she saw it there before her comprehensible and whole like a tangerine spiked through and held in place while it rotated on the axis of one of Nurse's steel sock needles. The earth was a tangerine and she saw the skin peeled off and the world parcelled out into neat segments, each segment sweet and fragrant in its own skin.

It's the head that counts, she said.

In her own head she made diagrams to live by, cut and fashioned after the eternal patterns spied out by Plato as he rummaged about in the sewing basket of the gods.

I should have loved Ismene. She would live now in some pre-fabricated and perfect chrysolite by some paradigm which made love round and whole. She would simply live and leave destruction in the purgatorial ditches outside her own walled paradise.

Antigone is different. She sees the world flat as I do and feels it tip beneath her feet. She has walked in the market and seen the living animals penned and the dead hanging stiff on their hooks. Yet she defies what she sees with a defiance which is almost denial. Like Atlas she tries to keep the vaulted sky from crushing the flat earth. Like Hermes she brings a message that there is life if one can escape to it in the brush and bulrushes in some dim Hades beyond the river. It is defiance not belief and I tell her that this time we walk the bridge to a walled cave where we can deny death no longer.

Yet she asks her question still. And standing there I tell her that Heraklitos has made nonsense of her question. I should have loved Ismene for she would have taught me what Plato meant when he said in all earnest that the union of the soul with the body is in no way better than dissolution. I expect that she understood things which Antigone is too proud to see.

I turn away from her and flatten my elbows on the high wall of the bridge. I look back at my father's kingdom. I see the terraces rolling down from the red-brick buildings with their barred windows. I remember hands shaking the bars and hear fingers tearing up paper and stuffing it through meshes. Diktynna, mother of nets and high leaping fear. O Artemis, mistress of wild beasts and wild men.

The inmates are beginning to come out on the screened verandas. They pace up and down in straight lines or stand silent like figures which appear at the same time each day from some depths inside a clock.

On the upper terrace Pan the gardener is shifting sprinklers with a hooked stick. His face is shadowed by the brim of his hat. He moves as economically as an animal between the beds of lobelia and geranium. It is high noon.

Antigone has cut out a piece of sod and has scooped out a grave. The body lies in a coffin in the shade of the magnolia tree. Antigone and I are standing. Ismene is sitting between two low angled branches of the monkey puzzle tree. Her lap is filled with daisies. She slits the stem of one daisy and pulls the stem of another through it. She is making a chain for her neck and a crown for her hair.

Antigone reaches for a branch of the magnolia. It is almost beyond her grip. The buds flame above her. She stands on a small fire of daisies which smoulder in the roots of the grass.

I see the magnolia buds. They brood above me, whiteness feathered on whiteness. I see Antigone's face turned to the light. I hear the living birds call to the sun. I speak private poetry to myself: Between four trumpeting angels at the four corners of the earth a bride stands before the altar in a gown as white as snow.

Yet I must have been speaking aloud because Antigone challenges me: You're mistaken. It's the winds the angels hold, the four winds of the earth. After the just are taken to paradise the winds will destroy the earth. It's a funeral, she says, not a wedding.

She looks towards the building.

Someone is coming down the path from the matron's house, she says.

I notice that she has pulled one of the magnolia blossoms from the branch. I take it from her. It is streaked with brown where her hands have bruised it. The sparrow which she has decided to bury lies on its back. Its feet are clenched tight against the feathers of its breast. I put the flower in the box with it.

Someone is coming down the path. She is wearing a blue cotton dress. Her cropped head is bent. She walks slowly carrying something in a napkin.

It's Kallisto the bear, I say. Let's hurry. What will my father say if he sees us talking to one of his patients?

If we live here with him, Antigone says, what can he expect? If he spends his life trying to tame people he can't complain if you behave as if they were tame. What would your father think, she says, if he saw us digging in the Institution lawn?

Pan comes closer. I glower at him. There's no use speaking to him. He's deaf and dumb.

Listen, I say to Antigone, my father's not unreasonable. Kallisto thinks she's a bear and he thinks he's a bear tamer, that's all. As for the lawn, I say quoting my father without conviction, a man must have order among his own if he is to keep order in the state.

Kallisto has come up to us. She is smiling and laughing to herself. She gives me her bundle.

Fish, she says.

I open the napkin.

Pink fish sandwiches, I say.

For the party, she says.

But it isn't a party, Antigone says. It's a funeral.

For the funeral breakfast, I say.

Ismene is twisting two chains of daisies into a rope. Pan has stopped pulling the sprinkler about. He is standing beside Ismene resting himself on his hooked stick. Kallisto squats down beside her. Ismene turns away, preoccupied, but she can't turn far because of Pan's legs.

> *Father said we never should*
> *Play with madmen in the wood.*

I look at Antigone.

It's my funeral, she says.

I go over to Ismene and gather up a handful of loose daisies from her lap. The sun reaches through the shadow of the magnolia tree.

It's my funeral, Antigone says. She moves possessively toward the body.

An ant is crawling into the bundle of sandwiches which I've put on the ground. A file of ants is marching on the sparrow's box.

I go over and drop daisies on the bird's stiff body. My voice speaks ritual words: Deliver me, O Lord, from everlasting death on this dreadful day. I tremble and am afraid.

The voice of a people comforts me. I look at Antigone. I look her in the eye.

It had better be a proper funeral then, I say.

Kallisto is crouched forward on her hands. Tears are running down her cheeks and she is licking them away with her tongue.

My voice rises again: I said in the midst of my days, I shall not see–

Antigone just stands there. She looks frightened, but her eyes defy me with their assertion.

It's my funeral, she says. It's my bird. I was the one who wanted to bury it.

She is looking for a reason. She will say something which sounds eternally right.

Things have to be buried, she says. They can't be left lying around anyhow for people to see.

Birds shouldn't die, I tell her. They have wings. Cats and rats haven't wings.

Stop crying, she says to Kallisto. It's only a bird.

It has a bride's flower in its hand, Kallisto says.

We shall rise again, I mutter, but we shall not all be changed.

Antigone does not seem to hear me.

Behold, I say in a voice she must hear, in a moment, in the twinkling of an eye, the trumpet shall sound.

Ismene turns to Kallisto and throws the daisy chain about her neck.

Shall a virgin forget her adorning or a bride the ornament of her breast?

Kallisto is lifting her arms towards the tree.

The bridegroom has come, she says, white as a fall of snow. He stands above me in a great ring of fire.

Antigone looks at me now.

Let's cover the bird up, she says. Your father will punish us all for making a disturbance.

He has on his garment, Kallisto says, and on his thigh is written King of Kings.

I look at the tree. If I could see with Kallisto's eyes I wouldn't be afraid of death, or punishment, or the penitentiary guards. I wouldn't be afraid of my father's belt or his honing strap or his bedroom slipper. I wouldn't be afraid of falling into the river through a knot-hole in the bridge.

But, as I look, I see the buds falling like burning lamps and I hear the sparrow twittering in its box: Woe, woe, woe because of the three trumpets which are yet to sound.

Kallisto is on her knees. She is growling like a bear. She lumbers over to the sandwiches and mauls them with her paw.

Ismene stands alone for Pan the gardener has gone.

Antigone is fitting a turf in place above the coffin. I go over and press the edge of the turf with my feet. Ismene has caught me by the hand.

Go away, Antigone says.

I see my father coming down the path. He has an attendant with him. In front of them walks Pan holding the sprinkler hook like a spear.

What are you doing here? my father asks.

Burying a bird, Antigone says.

Here? my father asks again.

Where else could I bury it? Antigone says.

My father looks at her.

This ground is public property, he says. No single person has any right to an inch of it.

I've taken six inches, Antigone says. Will you dig the bird up again?

Some of his subjects my father restrained since they were moved to throw themselves from high places or to tear one another to bits from jealousy or rage. Others who disturbed the public peace he taught to walk in the airing courts or to work in the kitchen or in the garden.

If men live at all, my father said, it is because discipline saves their life for them.

From Antigone he simply turned away.

Works by Sheila Watson

FICTION

The Double Hook. Toronto: McClelland and Stewart, 1959.
Four Stories. Toronto: Coach House, 1979.

CRITICISM

Sheila Watson: A Collection. Open Letter, series three, number one (Winter, 1974-75).

Acknowledgments

I am deeply grateful to many of my friends whose explorations with me of these stories led to deeper insights and sharper questions: to Ed DeVos, Valerie Lester, Pam Matz, Sharon Lamb, Brent Bambury, Gordon Bailey, Bernard Aboba, Andrew Terris, Jeremy Vincent and David Wingrove. Germaine Warkentin and the late Alden Nowlan kindly pointed me in the direction of further reading and lent their moral support. Most especially am I indebted to Gail Taylor and Robert Kilkenny for their subtle reading of literature and for their consistently helpful observations and recommendations, and to Professors Lawrence Kohlberg, Carol Gilligan and Robert Kegan of the Harvard Graduate School of Education for encouraging me and giving me the opportunity to be a teaching assistant in their courses on adolescent development. My former Canadian literature students at Saint John High School, Saint John, New Brunswick, are owed a special thanks. It was with them that much of our text was initially tried out.

A. GARROD

IN THE VILLAGE: Reprinted by permission of Farrar, Straus and Giroux, Inc. From QUESTIONS OF TRAVEL by Elizabeth Bishop. Copyright © 1953, 1965 by Elizabeth Bishop.

THERE WAS AN OLD WOMAN FROM WEXFORD: From VARIOUS PERSONS NAMED KEVIN O'BRIEN by Alden Nowlan. © 1973 by Clarke, Irwin & Company Limited. Used by permission.

THE PLAY: From THE MOUNTAIN AND THE VALLEY by Ernest Buckler. Used by permission of The Canadian Publishers, McClelland and Stewart Limited, Toronto.

THE BOAT: From THE LOST SALT GIFT OF BLOOD by Alistair MacLeod. Used by permission of The Canadian Publishers, McClelland and Stewart Limited, Toronto.

Selection from A SEASON IN THE LIFE OF EMMANUEL. Reprinted by permission of Farrar, Straus and Giroux, Inc. Selection from A SEASON IN THE LIFE OF EMMANUEL by Marie-Claire Blais. Copyright © 1966 by Marie-Claire Blais.

THE NUN WHO RETURNED TO IRELAND: By Roch Carrier, translated by Sheila Fischman, from THE HOCKEY SWEATER AND OTHER STORIES (Toronto: House of Anansi Press, 1979).

THE SUMMER MY GRANDMOTHER WAS SUPPOSED TO DIE: From THE STREET by Mordecai Richler. Used by permission of The Canadian Publishers, McClelland and Stewart Limited, Toronto.

Questions for Discussion and Writing

OVERVIEW

The twenty-one stories in this anthology offer interpretations of childhood and adolescence as experienced by boys and girls, young men and young women, in different regions of Canada. They deal with the vital processes of growth and the central themes of youth: separation and attachment, sibling and parental relationships, loyalty and loss, empathy and egoism, the need for intimacy coupled with the striving for autonomy, and, finally, the search for identity.

In exploring these issues, the questions are intended to be suggestive rather than comprehensive. Whether the questions are dealt with systematically or selectively will depend on the extent to which any one story or issue captures the readers' interest. In general, the discussion questions tend to invite, first, an exploration of the readers' imaginative engagement with the story. The aim here is to anchor the readers' thoughts or the classroom discussion in the significant details of the story to verify that key events and relationships are understood. Second, where appropriate, some questions draw attention to matters of form, style, and language, in the hope that with an understanding of the connections among these elements and the author's intention, the story's impact will be enriched.

In the writing questions, some focus on particular aspects of a story, others prompt comparisons and contrasts in theme and techniques among two or more stories, and still others use the story as a springboard for the readers' exploration of issues important to their own lives. Throughout, the questions are informed by a developmental focus which invites readers to think about how people of different ages construct their own versions of reality, how they form relationships, make judgments, and interpret the world around them.

The assumption in this anthology is that reading about the childhood of others and coming to understand our own past enables us to see the continuity of our growth and thus grapple more adequately with the immediate present. The hope is that, guided by the questions, the readers' engagement with these stories will induce a flash of illumination that urges self-discovery.

In the Village

FOR DISCUSSION

1. In this story, basic facts are presented in fragments. Attempt to piece together information about what is wrong with the mother; where she has been for the past two years; what happened to her husband; why she finally leaves the village.

2. What sound does the story begin with? End with? Why do you think the child responds the way she does to each sound?

3. What is the impression you get of village life in this story? Describe what you think are the advantages and disadvantages of this girl growing up in that village.

4. The little girl spends a lot of time in the blacksmith shop. Explain what you think the blacksmith and his work represent to her.

5. Why does she want to hide the labels on the packages she carries addressed to the sanatorium?

6. Childlike, the little girl confuses *mourning* and *morning*. What other parts of the story strike you as particularly characteristic of a small child's perspective?

7. Consider some of the reasons that the author may have had for including the fire in the story.

FOR WRITING

1. Because of her mother's condition, the child's situation is potentially very stressful. Yet Bishop includes scenes that suggest the child is actually quite secure in her sense of self. Discuss some of these scenes, explaining how they create this effect.

2. Discuss attitudes toward emotional illness in this story. How do you think they compare with attitudes today?

There Was an Old Woman from Wexford

FOR DISCUSSION

1. Part of a writer's challenge is to create a world–a time and place–that appears real, even if foreign, to the reader. How would you describe the world of this story? What details does the author include to establish this world?

2. We are told that as Kevin grew older, he became increasingly more ashamed of his grandmother. What are some of her outlandish habits and behaviors that particularly embarrassed him? How common is it for children to be embarrassed by adults?

3. How do you think Kevin felt toward his grandmother on the night she was dying? How does he feel about her now?

4. What do you think Kevin means when he says at the end that it mattered "ever afterwards that his grandmother, an old peasant woman, had sat up all through the last night of her life, singing songs to entertain herself and Death"?

5. The author has included extensive quotations of lyrics in the story. What is the range and tone of these lyrics? Why are there so many of them? Do you learn anything about the grandmother or about the boy's experience from hearing a song's exact words that you wouldn't have known if the lyrics were summarized or put into indirect speech?

6. Nowlan's keen eye for detail is evident in his descriptions of how young Kevin perceives his grandmother and his father. Of the grandmother, he writes, "And what she smelled of was burning wool and ginger cloves and a liniment called Oil of Wintergreen." Of the father, "Shoeless, grey wool socks darned with yarn of another color, Levis pulled on over long-sleeved flannel underwear, the underwear partially unbuttoned because of the heat, thick curly grey hair on his chest, a vest, and suspenders that bore the word 'Police' on their clasps."

How do the details in these passages make the characters seem more real?

7. Beginning consecutive sentences in a similar way is often considered bad writing, as is the use of choppy, apparently disconnected sentences. Yet on p. 36, Nowlan does both. Discuss possible reasons for writing this way.

FOR WRITING

1. Traditional wisdom has it that adolescents often get on better with their grandparents than with their parents, partly because the parents are perceived as authority figures whereas the grandparents are not. Discuss what your relationship with one of your grandparents means or meant to you. Try to include anecdotes that illuminate the kind of relationship it is or was. Try also to make use of vivid details and comparisons the way Nowlan does in his story.

2. Write a story in which the protagonist is about the age of Kevin (seven or eight). Explore the child's reaction to a major family event—

an event seen solely from the child's perspective (for example, a wedding, a separation, a loss, a disgrace, an inheritance, or a triumph). Whatever event you choose, try to capture as accurately as you can, from memory, observation, imagination, or a combination of these three, exactly what the child thinks and feels. The child's perspective will be different from an adult's, and you will need to be very specific in your details in order to convey the child's response. Before you begin to write, decide which narrative point of view will be best suited to your purposes. You might take the first-person perspective as used here, or the third, as used in a story like "A Day with Pegasus."

3. Like Mordecai Richler's story, "The Summer My Grandmother Was Supposed to Die," this story explores a boy's reaction to his grandmother's dying. Contrast the reactions of the two boys. In what ways might the difference in setting (urban Montreal, rural Nova Scotia) affect their reactions?

The Play

FOR DISCUSSION

1. The narrator complains that the other children in the dramatic presentation said their pieces "doggedly" and that when they came back to the dressing room "their excitement was only because it was over, not because for a minute they had made themselves into something else." What does this observation tell about how David views his own dramatic role?

2. How does Buckler emphasize David's nervousness before the concert begins and just before he is to go onstage?

3. The climax of the story occurs when David kisses Effie in the middle of the Christmas play. This event is preceded by David's getting caught up in the glamor and magic of the moment. Had David simply kissed Effie on stage as a joke or as a simple affectionate gesture, would he have felt the same kind and degree of shame? What is the essential difference?

4. Buckler explores David's emotional reaction to his humiliation in the "treacherous" play in some depth. What are the particular targets of David's anger? What purpose is served by his saying all the "oaths" and "words of sex" he knows? What does David's reaction tell about his emotional make-up and character? Discuss whether his reaction is consistent with how an eleven-year-old would behave in these circumstances.

5. Do you think you would react to David or understand him any differently if the story were told by him as a first-person narrator—in the manner of "The Concert Stages of Europe"?

6. Discuss the effects of some of the comparisons in the story (for example, about the tableau, "It was as if some beautiful flower that grew only in warm climates had suddenly sprung up in their own fields.")

7. In what way does David seem to his mother, Martha, to be unlike her other children? Discuss how other members of the family see David.

8. What illumination comes to David in this story?

9. In the later part of *The Mountain and the Valley*, David grows up to be a talented, though deeply isolated, writer. What signs do you see in "The Play" that might lead a reader to expect such a development?

FOR WRITING

1. Write about a time or an event in your life when your self-esteem depended on the successful outcome of your performance (for example, a sporting event, a debate, a date, a musical or play).

   Why did the event mean so much to you? What was at stake for you? How did things turn out? How did you feel about the outcome? How do you feel about it now? In your writing, try to make the reader experience the emotions you went through. Try using some extended comparisons, as Buckler does.

2. "A shine like that went out over everything now." Did you ever have an experience like this? Use the quotation as your opening sentence and go on from there.

3. Both David in "The Play" and Barclay in "The Concert Stages of Europe" performed in front of home-town audiences, and both were devastated by the experience. With references to the preparations, the performances, and the consequences, write an essay discussing what meaning these experiences had for David and Barclay.

The Boat

FOR DISCUSSION

1. The opening paragraphs of this story are set in the present and lead into the reminiscence that forms the body of the story. What purpose is served by these introductory paragraphs? How would you define the narrator's state of mind represented here? What inferences can be drawn about the origins of the narrator's emotional condition?

2. The mother is portrayed as having a deep antipathy for reading books. From what you know of her character, what do you suppose underlies her feelings in this? What is it about reading that might threaten her world? Is it books she fears, or the children's relationship and identification with a father symbolized by books?

3. What evidence is there that the father "had never been intended for a fisherman either physically or mentally"?

4. The narrator's situation in his family has some striking features: he was the youngest of six children, the only boy, and born when his father was at the comparatively advanced age of fifty-six. What role, if any, do you think these factors have in explaining the family dynamics, the pressures placed on the boy, and the way he reacts to his parents' hopes for him?

5. What cause-and-effect relationship do you see between the sisters' reading of books and their escape from village life: did they read books in order to escape the boredom of village life or did the boredom of village life lead them to seek escape in books?

6. How did the mother interpret her daughters' leaving that caused her to reject them for it? In what way was their relationship with their father different so that they continued a warm relationship with him?

7. "So I told him one night very resolutely and very powerfully that I would remain with him as long as he lived and we would fish the sea together. And he made no protest but only smiled through the cigarette smoke that wreathed his bed and replied, 'I hope you will remember what you've said.'" How does the father's final statement, "I hope you will remember what you've said," offer an element of foreboding about what is to become of him in the end? Do you believe the father's death was an accident or of his own choosing, as a way of releasing his son from his promise?

8. In the end the narrator does leave home, but this does not end his deep personal conflict. Discuss.

FOR WRITING

1. "And it is not an easy thing to know that your mother looks upon the sea with love and on you with bitterness because the one has been so constant and the other so untrue." Throughout the story the sea has a central presence and plays a central role. Write an essay that examines the importance of the sea in the lives of the villagers. Pay some attention to the shifting attitudes toward the sea that the narrator expresses as he describes his growing up.

2. Recall Dickens' novel *David Copperfield*. Why does the narrator of "The Boat" regard this book as his friend when he is young? Compare in some detail the world of this Cape Breton family and the world of the Peggotys in *David Copperfield*.

3. Both "What I Learned from Caesar" and "The Boat" are poignant first-person narratives about a son's relationship with his father. Compare the sympathy and understanding that the two narrators, when young, had for their fathers.

A Season in the Life of Emmanuel

FOR DISCUSSION

1. Suggest words that fit the tone of this story. How would you describe the author's attitude toward her subject? What are some of the details that Blais includes to convey the sort of world that Emmanuel has been born into?

2. Why do you think the author never identifies Emmanuel's mother and father by name, yet repeatedly calls the grandmother by her name, Antoinette?

3. Why does the author spend so much time describing the grandmother's feet in the opening paragraph? Why does she use the words "authority" and "patience"?

4. In her description of the grandchildren tumbling up to Grand-mère for handouts (p. 81), Blais creates a vivid sense of movement and confusion. Examine the passage to determine how she achieves this effect.

5. Jean-Le Maigre becomes the centre of attention in the last pages of this chapter. What does the author accomplish by emphasizing his presence?

6. Although the chapter underscores the dreariness and defeat of extreme poverty, it is not all bleak. What examples of humor, hope, endurance, and vitality are included?

7. For the most part, Blais adopts the position of the third-person narrator. Yet she attempts in various places to present the scene from the point of view of either the baby or the grandmother. Identify some of these places and explain how you can tell whose perspective is at work.

FOR WRITING

1. In preparation for writing, reread the parts where Blais attempts to capture a world seen by the eyes and mind of a child. Now write about an early experience in your life (up to the age of seven or eight), drawing upon your memory or reconstructing that experience through the use of your imagination and your understanding of how very young children interpret reality. If you use dialogue in your story, try to sound like a young child.

2. The mother in "The Boat" and the father in this story are both hostile to books and education. Write a brief comment in which you speculate about their reasons for this hostility.

The Nun Who Returned to Ireland

FOR DISCUSSION

1. What are the people of this village like? What does the reference to Monsieur Cassidy tell about the way they think? What is the nun's relationship to the village?

2. Like many of Carrier's stories, this one conveys the innocent voice and vision of a young child, and yet the reader can also hear the voice of the older narrator looking back at his younger self. Which

moments in this story remind the reader that an adult, not the young child himself, is recounting the events?

3. Discuss what the narrator recognizes now about his village that he would not have noticed as a child.

4. The boy's questions to the nun seem motivated by genuine curiosity, yet they elicit perhaps an unexpected emotional reaction from her. As she replies to the boy, what emotions do you think she is feeling? How do you interpret her numerous references to God's plan for her?

5. When the men find Sister Brigitte, why do you think she answers them in English?

6. What do you think the author intends the reader's reaction to be to the image of the barefoot, storm-driven nun in the last two sentences?

FOR WRITING

1. Write about an incident involving a teacher you knew in your early years of school. Try to write from a child's perspective, as Carrier does in his story.

2. The little girl in "In the Village" and Freidele in "Jewish Christmas" are about the same age as the boy in this story. And the Nova Scotia, Saskatchewan, and Quebec villages are all about the same size. What other similarities among the stories do you perceive?

The Summer My Grandmother Was Supposed to Die

FOR DISCUSSION

1. The story describes the love and dedication of the narrator's mother in caring for her aged mother. Yet, at one point, she says, "It's not my mother anymore in the back room, Doctor. It's an animal. I want her

to die." The doctor replies, "Hush. You don't mean it. You're tired." Is the doctor right, or do you think in some sense she does mean it?

2. Why are the offhand and sometimes sensational remarks of the boy's street pals included in this story?

3. What is the attitude of the boy's father toward the grandmother's condition? Indicate how Richler conveys this in the story.

4. Describe the boy's attitude toward his dying grandmother.

5. Discuss reasons why the boy's dead grandfather is mentioned so often.

6. How would you characterize the tone of this piece of writing—nostalgic? bitter? sentimental? satiric? Explain.

7. In this story, Richler overlaps the perspectives of child and adult. Discuss instances in which you are particularly aware of the adult narrator speaking through the child.

FOR WRITING

1. One school of thought has it that children should not be screened and protected from realities of life such as the suffering of a dying grandmother, that they should be treated as equal participants in the family, and that it is even healthy for them, for example, to attend a funeral. Others believe that those realities will strike soon enough, in adolescence, and that children should be protected from them for as long as possible. What is your point of view? What are some of your reasons?

2. In both "There Was an Old Woman from Wexford" and this story we are presented with the effect on a young boy of his grandmother's dying. Compare the situations of the two boys, one in urban Jewish Montreal, the other in rural Nova Scotia.

The Accident

FOR DISCUSSION

1. Why do you think that the summer in this story was a particularly "difficult and edgy summer" for Martha?

2. The narrator asks, "Did I make Hilary too in part as I struggled to make myself?" What does she mean?

3. What details does Marshall use to create the impression that in this story the children and the adults live in separate worlds? Discuss whether such a situation is common in many families.

4. What evidence of class snobbery do you find in the story? What are some ways to teach children to respect the rights and values of others?

5. As the three girls come upon the disturbing scene of the accident, the narrator describes her new and sudden awareness of her sister Laura. What is the connection between the accident and this moment of illumination? It is at this point that the narrator "saw all sorts of other things, whether or not I put them in words." What do you think she means?

6. What does the narrator mean when she says that "success in childhood...depends in large part on one's gifts as a mimic"? Do you agree?

7. Does the fact that the story is told from the eldest child's point of view make a difference? Discuss how the perspectives of the younger siblings would differ from Martha's. Might they too feel competitive but not threatened like the eldest? How might that make a difference in their behavior?

FOR WRITING

1. Even though the narrator was already nine at the time of the story, she says that she is not certain of the details of the accident. She wonders "whether it really happened as I seem to remember it." Consider your own memory of some childhood event. How clear is it in your mind now? Would others in your family remember it differently? Why?

2. In very different contexts and with children of varying ages, both "The Accident" and "The Play" explore sibling love, alliances, and tension. Compare and contrast the nature of the love, alliances, and tension in the children of these families.

In Youth Is Pleasure

FOR DISCUSSION

1. The interweaving references to time and place in this story make a close reading essential. For your own clarity, establish a chronology including the following information: age of Linnet Muir; residences; other family members; approximate year of her return to Montreal. Why do you consider the author creates such a labyrinth of time and place instead of simply presenting Linnet's story in a linear and causal structure?

2. Linnet claims to feel "abrupt unconcern" and "simple indifference" toward her mother. Discuss why she feels this way. How does she feel about her father?

3. What is she "shedding" when she leaves New York? If she likes New York and Americans so much, what impels her to return to Montreal?

4. Find evidence to suggest that Linnet sees her return to Montreal as a liberation from bondage.

5. What does she mean when she says she arranged the meetings with her father's old friends to "obtain special information about despair"? Why does she decide to believe that he died of homesickness for England?

6. Compare the Montreal Linnet remembers from her childhood with the Montreal she experiences when she returns. Why are they so different?

7. The interrelated themes of exile, dispossession, and reconciliation of past and present identities are prominent in this story. Discuss how Linnet develops and changes from the time of her arrival in Montreal to the end of the story, referring to these themes.

8. What does the author mean by the story title?

FOR WRITING

1. For some people, childhood is experienced as a period of unbounded and delightful freedom—a time when responsibilities have yet to be taken on. Others, however, view it as a period of constriction and deference to authority figures. Linnet, for example, talks of "the prison of childhood." Based on your own experience, how do you view childhood?

2. Some people claim that moving to another country or even to another province enables you to see your mother country or province more objectively because it frees you from the restrictions and

"baggage" of your past. Others disagree. Explain your point of view on this subject.

3. How do you think Linnet as the adult narrator looks upon her younger self?

The Ottawa Valley

FOR DISCUSSION

1. In the last paragraph, the narrator explains her intention in this story. What do you understand that purpose to have been? Why should she wish to be "rid" of her mother? Why does she feel that she did not fulfill her intention successfully? Does this failure to describe and be "rid" of her mother have implications for people about their ability to see their parents accurately and finally to be "rid" of them? Discuss.

2. Why does the narrator say that if she had been making "a proper story out of this" she would have ended it with "my mother not answering and going ahead of me across the pasture"? Discuss how your reaction to the story might be different if it had ended this way.

3. The narrator compares her story to a series of brownish snapshots with fancy borders. In what ways is this an appropriate metaphor?

4. The theme of the story centres around the nature of the relationship between the author and her mother. In what ways do you think the story attempts to illuminate more universal aspects of mother-daughter relationships? Why are relationships between mothers and daughters or fathers and sons so important in the development from child to mature adult? In your opinion, what would help to make such relationships positive and satisfying for both child and parent?

5. What does the narrator mean when she says of her mother, "Luck was not without its shadow, in her universe"?

6. Referring to Aunt Dodie, the narrator states, "The tragedy of her life was that she had been jilted." Yet Aunt Dodie gives a different impression, "Lots of girls would've cried, but me, I laughed." The mother, on the other hand, says, "When I went home two years after that, I used to wake up and hear her crying in the night. Night after night." In what ways do these passages illustrate the manner in which Aunt Dodie managed to cope with her feelings about this event in her life? In what ways are psychological defences like Aunt Dodie's useful in coping with pain and stress, and in what ways troublesome?

7. With reference to Aunt Lena's violence toward her children, the narrator says that within a few minutes Aunt Lena's children would have forgotten the beating, whereas if the same thing were to happen to her "such a humiliation could last for weeks, or forever." What personal character trait is the narrator revealing by this remark? Where else in the story do you find this same trait?

8. What do you learn about the mother and Aunt Dodie from the trick they played on Allen Durrand and from their reactions as adults when retelling the incident?

9. The episode of the sewn-up fly and that of Uncle James singing to his family as he drives to town are separated by a short sequence in which Parkinson's disease is described. What impact does this short sequence have on the reader in this context?

FOR WRITING

1. Although this piece is written from the perspective of a pre-teenage girl, the narrator is obviously not this age. Examine, with close reference to the text, how the author overlaps adult impressions with childhood ones, explaining why you think certain insights and particular choices of language seem to belong to one age rather than to another. What do you consider the purpose of interweaving two perspectives within this story?

2. Discuss emotional similarities and dissimilarities that you see between Vanessa in "A Bird in the House" and the narrator in "The Ottawa Valley."

A Bird in the House

FOR DISCUSSION

1. Why does Vanessa refuse to go to the parade? Do you think her father understands her reasons for not going? Explain.

2. Who seems to dominate the MacLeod family? Support your view with details from the story.

3. At one point Vanessa says, "in some families *please* is described as the magic word. In our house, however, it was *sorry*." What do you think this suggests about the way members of this family interact?

4. Look closely at the incident of the bird. Discuss how Laurence's choice of words conveys Vanessa's reactions so vividly. Find other passages in the story where the author uses vivid language to describe Vanessa's emotions or behavior.

5. Why is Vanessa fascinated by Noreen's religious beliefs? Why does she later reject them?

6. Vanessa never says why she attacks Noreen after the funeral. Why do you think she does?

7. It seems in this story that the cold judgmental eye of the grandmother is omnipresent even though she is rarely involved in the action. How does Laurence create this impression?

8. Later on, at seventeen, Vanessa discovers the letter and the snapshot in her father's old desk. What does Vanessa mean when she says she hopes that the French girl in the picture "had meant some momentary and unexpected freedom"?

9. As the story develops, Vanessa comes to see her mother and her father each in a new light. There is a significant change in her relationship with her mother. Why does it occur? In what way does her perspective on her father change toward the end of the story?

FOR WRITING

Write about a time in your life when you realized that your understanding and sympathy were vital to somebody important to you. Describe that time, being sure to include how you felt as well as how you acted.

A Cap for Steve

FOR DISCUSSION

1. At two key points in the story—after the loss of the cap and after the return home with the twenty dollars—Steve's parents react in different ways to his situation. How does each react at these two points?

What do you learn about their understanding of Steve from their reactions?

2. After reading this exchange between Dave and Mr. Hudson, consider the questions that follow.

> "But that's not right. It's not justice," Dave protested. "Not when it's my boy's cap."
>
> "I know it isn't right. But that's what they do."

Why does Dave think that what the policeman would do is not right? What is your view of a lawyer like Mr. Hudson who chooses to follow the rule of "that's what they do" rather than what is right and just? What is your opinion of Dave for going along with Mr. Hudson's solution?

3. "It's unfair," says Dave, shortly after leaving Mr. Hudson's house with the twenty dollars. What does he mean? What do you think would have been the fairest way to resolve the problem of the cap? Discuss your reasons.

4. In most of the stories in this anthology, a major revelation occurs to the young person. In this story, however, the major illumination comes to the father. At the end, how does Dave see his son and their relationship differently? Why does Dave finally feel "humble, then strangely exalted"? Do you think there is also a change in the way Steve understands his father and their relationship?

5. At first it appears that the Hudsons have triumphed in the matter of the cap. Yet as the story comes to an end, the reader can see that there is more than one way to look at victory in a situation like this. Discuss.

6. The Hudson boy buys the cap, whereas Steve is given it. Does this difference make the cap more or less valuable to either boy? What is it that makes something valuable?

7. Callaghan obviously does not wish the reader to like Mr. Hudson. By referring to specific details, point out how Callaghan predisposes the reader against him.

8. Read the opening paragraph. How does it prepare the reader for developments in the story?

FOR WRITING

1. Imagine that you are Steve, that you are seventeen, and for an English homework assignment have decided to retell the incident of the cap. Write that account, making it clear how you as a seventeen-year-old now understand and assess your parents' and Mr. Hudson's earlier attitudes and behavior. If you prefer, use the third-person perspective as Callaghan does.

2. To the twelve-year-old Steve, the cap that Eddie Condon gave him was beyond price. Perhaps in your childhood or early adolescence there has been some possession that meant a very great deal to you, even if no one else quite appreciated just how special it was. Write about it, trying to suggest to the reader just how invaluable it was. What is your feeling now toward the object? You may wish to include a personal or family anecdote in your account.

Lady Oracle

FOR DISCUSSION

1. What do the two dreams at the beginning of the chapter tell about Joan's attitude toward her mother?

2. Of her father, Joan says, "...he treated me more like a colleague than a daughter, more like an accomplice." Of her mother, she says, "Our relationship was professionalized early. She was to be the manager, the creator, the agent; I was to be the product." What evidence is there in the story that Joan is treated as an accomplice by her father and a product by her mother?

3. In your opinion, what features of the family situation might have led Joan to overeat? You may wish to consider possible connections between overeating, rebellion, and power.

4. What tactics does the mother employ in her effort to win the war over the "disputed territory" of Joan's overweight body? How well-

judged and insightful do you find the mother's tactics? What do you think the mother should have said or done to have had a chance of winning the battle over Joan's size?

5. What insights about her mother have come to the narrator as an adult? What is your evidence? Many adults come to some form of resolution and acceptance of an unhappy childhood or adolescence. Discuss whether the adult Joan has achieved this.

6. This excerpt is presented entirely from Joan's perspective; except in dialogue we never hear her mother's or father's side. Discuss how her mother or her father might have recounted the events.

7. There are three extended passages of dialogue in the story (pp. 195-6, pp. 197-9, p. 200). Why do you think Atwood uses dialogue for these particular scenes?

8. Show how Atwood's choice of words creates humor in the story.

FOR WRITING

1. Choose an episode from your life that involved a disagreement (for example, over a TV channel, use of the car) and write about it. Try to present it primarily through dialogue, as Atwood presents the scene between the father and Mr. Currie.

2. James Reaney's "The Bully" and this selection from *Lady Oracle* explore the capacity for insensitivity to the suffering of others. What do you learn about the nature of cruelty in these stories? Compare causes and reactions in the two.

The Bully

FOR DISCUSSION

1. The setting of this story is rural Ontario. Using details from the story, describe what life in this area was like at that time.

2. Surely the narrator must have known the bully's name. Why do you think he never mentions it in the story?

3. Why do you think the bully went on tormenting him? Could the boy have behaved in some way to make the bully stop? If so, what should he have done?

4. The bully was not the narrator's only problem that year. What were some of the others?

5. What parts of the story strike you as humorous?

6. The narrator seems to link Noreen's insensitivity with "strength" and Kate's kind-heartedness with "weakness." Discuss whether these equations are necessarily fair–in the story and in real life.

7. The narrator says that he has never been able to discover the meaning of his three dreams. Discuss some possible interpretations of them.

8. Explain why the story is called "The Bully" even though the bully himself does not come in until halfway through the story.

9. When a character is unwarrantedly cruel, then it is perhaps a natural reaction on the part of the reader to wish that the character receive his or her just deserts. How satisfactory do you find the conclusion of this story?

FOR WRITING

1. Write about an episode in your childhood or adolescence in which you now wish you had acted differently. Describe the episode, how you felt at the time and how you feel now. If possible, bring in some humorous touches the way Reaney does.

2. "The narrator is not so much interested in capturing the experience of being bullied as it felt at the time as he is in reconstructing events from an adult perspective so that the humor of the situation is played up." Discuss the validity of this statement, referring to the story to show why you agree or disagree.

3. The protagonist of Mavis Gallant's "In Youth Is Pleasure" rejoices in escaping the "prison of childhood." In "The Bully," by contrast, the boy hates the thought of growing up. How do you account for these two very different reactions to the experience of childhood and the anticipation of adulthood?

Wilhelm

FOR DISCUSSION

1. Why do you think the narrator chooses this particular incident from her adolescence to remember and relive?

2. What is the attitude of the narrator's parents to Wilhelm? What do you think are some reasons for their attitude?

3. In writing about her parents' attitude to Wilhelm, the narrator offers a clear portrait of them. How would you characterize her mother and father? How would you describe the family as a whole?

4. How would you characterize what the adolescent girl felt for Wilhelm? Now that she is an adult, what change do you see in her feelings?

5. The narrator asks herself, "But why, despite what I thought of appearances, did I believe myself obliged also to speak of the uncle and the father, partners in a small business which…which…made a lot of money?" What do you think the answer is?

6. How would you describe the tone of "Wilhelm"–sentimental? nostalgic? bitter? humorous? Support your choice with references to the text.

FOR WRITING

1. As early as the first paragraph, the narrator prepares the reader for a love story that is unlikely to have a happy ending. How does she accomplish this?

2. Select a person or a situation from your past that you now see in a different light. Tell what your view was then and what it is now. If you go about this exercise in story form, try to use some foreshadowing in the opening paragraph, as Roy does in the first paragraph of "Wilhelm."

Jewish Christmas

FOR DISCUSSION

1. "Difference was in my bones and my blood, and in the pattern of my separate life," writes the narrator early in her reminiscence. What details of her parents' and grandparents' physical appearance add to Freidele's feeling of being different from the people she later calls the "white and gold Norwegians"? In what way is the pattern in her life separate from that of the other children in the community?

2. Of her grandfather, the narrator writes, "I felt for him a kind of amused tenderness, but I was glad that my schoolmates could not see him." What does this division in her feelings suggest? Discuss whether it is usual for a child to have divided feelings about a close relative.

3. Though Freidele's father speaks of being Jewish as a "special distinction," Freidele feels it is a distinction she would just as soon not have. Why is she less proud of their heritage than her father? Discuss whether it is fair for the parents to force their beliefs and identity on the child.

4. Why does Freidele's father want her to make the presentation at the annual Lutheran Church concert?

5. Freidele complains, "Santa Claus never calls out 'Freidele Bruser'!" But then she asks herself, "What *did* I want with Santa Claus?" and bursts into tears. How do you explain this behavior?

6. How well do you think Freidele's parents handle the situation of the Christmas present for their daughter? Discuss whether she comes to understand their intentions.

7. The narrator uses figures of speech such as "All year I walked in the shadow of difference," and "but at Christmas above all, I tasted it

sour on the tongue," and "then, like a dancer about to execute a particularly difficult pirouette, she tossed the dough high in the air." What effect does language like this achieve?

FOR WRITING

1. This reminiscence explores the pain of exclusion. Write about a time in your past when you were excluded from something that you very much wanted to be a part of. How did it feel then? How do you feel about it now? (If you prefer, write about a similar situation that happened to someone else.) You might want to experiment with contrast of the sort that Maynard uses at the beginning of her account.

2. How easy is it for each of the protagonists in "What I Learned from Caesar" and "Jewish Christmas" to appreciate their fathers' different cultural or religious backgrounds? Do you think age and sex play a significant role in their different levels of appreciation?

A Day with Pegasus

FOR DISCUSSION

1. The title of the story, with its allusion to the winged horse from Greek mythology, hints at a central opposition: the world of dreams and fantasy and the real world of mundane demands and hard facts. Look for scenes in the story that show the real world dragging Peter back down to earth, and consider how Ross makes the contrast so clear.

2. The author vividly suggests the thrill and sense of wonder that Peter experiences at the stable door and in the box-stall with his newborn colt. What are some of the words that he uses to achieve these effects?

3. Discuss the relationships between Peter and Dan and Peter and Slim. What do you learn about Peter through his feelings about Dan and Slim?

4. Look closely at Peter's conversation with the boys in the playground at lunchtime. Why does he put off telling about the colt? How do you account for the differing reactions of the other boys to his news? Why does Peter get into a fight? Do you think that standing up for the colt in this way was worth it?

5. Miss Kinley accuses Peter of telling lies in his composition. Do you agree with her opinion? Do you think that what Peter wrote is the same as lying? How do you rate Miss Kinley as a teacher? Give your reasons.

6. In this story the author adopts a third-person omniscient viewpoint. Do you think you would have reacted to the story in any way differently if Peter himself had narrated the entire story? What are the gains and losses of the method the author adopts?

7. What does Peter mean at the end of the story when he thinks, "beyond doubt the horses had the best of it, awake the first day, nearly half-grown up as soon as they were born..."?

FOR WRITING

1. In this story we are given an overwhelming impression that no one quite understands the profound thrill that Peter experiences at the birth of his colt. Try writing about an experience that you once had that you felt no one else understood. Perhaps it so totally captured your imagination that it was hard to focus on the real world. What was there about the experience that so impressed you? Has your perspective on it changed? How do you look back on it now—with fondness? regret? amusement? guilt?

2. One might argue that Miss Kinley treated Peter quite unfairly, although no doubt she did not see it that way. Write about a time in your life when you thought you were treated unfairly. What emotions did you feel at the time? What do you think the other person felt? If your attitude toward the unfair person has changed over the years, how would you explain the change? Consider whether, if the same situation were to repeat itself today, you would feel and react differently, and in what way.

How I Spent My Summer Holidays

FOR DISCUSSION

1. With close attention to detail, Mitchell boldly sketches the narrator's friends, Musgrave and the Liar. What are your impressions of these boys? What details are most striking in suggesting their personalities?

2. The story is told from the perspective of a twelve-year-old boy. Discuss how the author achieves this perspective, referring to specific details in the story.

3. The explosion as the boys originally experienced it was probably very frightening, yet its presentation here is humorous. How does Mitchell's writing make this incident seem humorous rather than frightening?

4. The episode where the boys decide to use dynamite is told mainly through dialogue. What would be lost if this sequence were depicted entirely through narration?

5. Although this story is written from the boy's perspective, the writer is obviously not his age. Show how the author overlaps adult impressions with childhood ones, explaining which insights and choices of language seem to belong to one age rather than to the other. What might be the purpose of including more than one angle of age perception within this story?

1. Looking back at your earlier years, you will probably come across at least one experience that appears less frightening now than it did then–perhaps it even appears humorous to you now. Before you write about it, reread Mitchell's description of the explosion, noting the figures of speech and specific details that he uses. Then try to go about your description in the same way.

2. Compare and contrast the portraits of the grandfather in *How I Spent My Summer Holidays* and the grandmothers in "The Summer My Grandmother Was Supposed to Die" and "There Was An Old Woman from Wexford."

The Concert Stages of Europe

FOR DISCUSSION

1. What is Mrs. Desmond's opinion of the community she is living in? Find instances that show the contrast between Waterville's values and quality of life and Mrs. Desmond's aspirations for her son.

2. Why does Barclay's mother say she wants him to become a pianist? What do you think is her real reason? What kinds of problems can occur in a family when people mask their true motivations?

3. Find other places in the story where Barclay realizes that people do not always say what they mean. In your own experience, what can cause people to behave this way?

4. What does Barclay mean when he says he wants to be a Finn?

5. Why does Barclay end up entering the contest after all, despite his strong aversion to selling himself?

6. Why is the last question that Richy Ryder asks Barclay particularly humiliating to him?

7. After the concert, Barclay's father speaks to him. "My old man wanted me to be a doctor," he said. "My mother wanted me to be a florist. She liked flowers. She thought if I was a florist I'd be able to send her a bouquet every week. But what does any of that matter now?" What do you think his reasons for saying this are?

8. What does Barclay mean at the end when he says, "I decided the whole wretched experience had brought one benefit with it: freedom from ambition"?

9. What incidents in the story do you think are funny? What situations suggest that the now-grown Barclay is looking back on his younger self with humor?

FOR WRITING

1. Describe a time when you or someone else were embarrassed in front of an audience. Try to use the easygoing, humorous tone that Hodgins uses.

2. Compare the opening of this story to the opening of "A Cap for Steve." What are some changes that would occur if the narrators were reversed: a first-person narrator for Callaghan's story and a third-person narrator for Hodgins'?

What I Learned from Caesar

FOR DISCUSSION

1. Where do your sympathies lie in this story? What particular events make you feel the way you do?

2. As the father is "let go" by his company, the boss says, "Good luck, Dutchie." What does the son mean when he remarks later that "a crueller epithet would have been kinder"?

3. With close reference to the text, explain what the narrator means by calling his father a "remade man" rather than a "self-made man." How do the two photographs support this distinction?

4. What role does the narrator's mother play in the story?

5. Trace the major steps in the decline of the father from the time he loses his job until he is committed to the asylum.

6. Discuss what the word "asylum" means to the narrator as a boy and as an adult. How do you account for the shift in attitude?

7. Explain the title of the story.

8. As the narrator reflects on his father's breakdown he says, "I'm not sure why all of this happened to him. Perhaps there is no reason anyone can put their finger on, although I have my reasons. But I needed a reason then." Why do you think he needed a reason then? How do you interpret the phrase "although I have my reasons"? Why does it seem apparently less important *now* to the adult narrator to have a reason?

FOR WRITING

1. The narrator says about his father, "I only began to understand what had happened to him when I, in my turn, left for greener pastures, heading east. I didn't go so far, not nearly so far as he had. But I also learned that there is a price to be paid. Mine was a trivial one, a feeling of mild unease. At odd moments I betrayed myself and my beginnings; I knew that I lacked the genuine ring of a local. And I had never even left my own country." What does he seem to be suggesting about human beings in general here? Write about a time in your life when you had a sense of being out of place.

2. For those people who have never been out of work, the agonizing experience of losing a job and having little hope of gaining a new one is hard to imagine. What do you learn from this story about the impact job loss can have on a person and on a family?

Antigone

FOR DISCUSSION

1. Watson uses elements of myth to distance the events from a particular time or setting. Yet it is possible to find details in this story that do suggest place and era. What words or phrases seem to you to indicate the modern period? What details hint at a Canadian landscape?

2. In the fifth paragraph the narrator moves from looking back on the past to the actual past world of his childhood, which forms the major section of the story. How would the omission of the first five paragraphs affect the reader's understanding?

3. "Today I imagine people concerned with our welfare would take such an environment into account," the narrator says at the beginning of his reminiscence. Describe the kind of environment he is talking about. What might be some of the positive and negative effects of an environment like this one?

4. Though it is difficult to know the exact ages of Antigone, Ismene, and the narrator, roughly how old do you think they are? What details in the text offer you some clues to their ages?

5. The narrator says that Ismene sees the world as an "oblate spheroid," whereas he, like Antigone, sees the world "flat." Try to explicate these world views as they are explored in the story. Since the narrator's view is in sympathy with Antigone's, why then does he repeatedly say he "should have loved Ismene"?

6. Find evidence in the story that the children are exceedingly conscious of rules and regulations. Why does Antigone disobey?

7. What difference does it make to Antigone's uncle whether she buries the bird or not?

8. The story ends with the line, "From Antigone he simply turned away." Who seems to have won in this contest of wills?

9. Antigone's question, "How often can we cross the same river?" echoes the supposed remark of the ancient Greek philosopher Heraklitos, "You can never step twice in the same river." What do you suppose his remark means? Why does Antigone allude to it?

FOR WRITING

1. The story is called "Antigone," yet the narrator is Antigone's cousin. Discuss whether Antigone or her cousin is the more central figure.

2. Write a story in a realistic framework using symbols and characters based on mythology. You may use classical mythology, science fiction, or modern mythology.